PORTLAND

New View of the Rosy City

Other GrassRoutes Titles:

San Francisco: New View of Yerba Buena
Oakland: The Soul of the City Next Door
Olympia: The Sound of the City Next Door
GrassRoutes Kids **Bay Area**

A Few Upcoming Titles:

Circle Guide Series
California Wine Country

Backroutes Series
The Sierra Nevadas
The Cascades

GrassRoutes Kids
Oregon Coast and Valleys

New View Series
Seattle
Chicago
Vancouver

City Next Door Series
Baltimore
Detroit
Brooklyn

GrassRoutes Travel™

PORTLAND

New View of the Rosy City

Serena Bartlett and Diana Morgan
Illustrated by Daniel Ling

NOTE TO THE READER

GRASSROUTES, GRASSROUTES TRAVEL and the GRASSROUTES TRAVEL logo are trademarks of GrassRoutes Travel. Product or corporate names referred to in this publication may be trademarks or registered trademarks, and are used only for identification and explanation without intent to infringe.

GrassRoutes Travel™ guidebooks provide independent advice. GrassRoutes accepts no advertising, nor do we accept payment in exchange for listings or endorsements for any place or business. GrassRoutes writers do not accept discounts or payments in exchange for positive coverage of any sort.

We try to assure accurate and up-to-date information, but cannot accept any responsibility for loss, injury or inconvenience sustained by any person using this book.

Bulk discounts are available.

For each book purchased online we'll plant a Yew Tree for both the ecosystem and cancer research.

Tell us about your discoveries, and check out what's new at GrassRoutes Travel:
www.grassroutestravel.com
info@grassroutestravel.com

GrassRoutes Travel Press, Oakland 94609

LIBRARY OF CONGRESS CATALOGING-IN-PUBLICATION DATA

Bartlett, Serena.
Portland : new view of the rosy city / by Serena Bartlett and Diana Morgan ; illustrated by Daniel Ling. -- 1st ed.
p. cm.
Includes index.
LCCN 2007934507
ISBN-13: 978-0-9791462-1-3
ISBN-10: 0-9791462-1-6

1. Portland (Or.)--Guidebooks. 2. Portland (Or.)--Description and travel. 3. Ecotourism--Guidebooks. I. Morgan, Diana, 1983- II. Title.

F884.P83B37 2007 917.95'490444
QBI07-600226

Printed on 100% post-consumer recycled paper in Canada.

Dedicated to

All those who boldly explore as part of the collective pursuit of world peace

"Certainly, travel is more than the seeing of sights; it is a change that goes on, deep and permanent, in the ideas of living."

-Miriam Beard

Table of Contents

Acknowledgements

We'd both like to thank our talented contributors: Nicky Kriara Peterson, Raina Rose McClellan, Emily Crabtree, William Schwartz, Sara Miller, Perrin Randelette, Emily Picha, Kelly Schierholz, and Jon Ostar and our editors: Brenda Mallory, Margo Ketchum, Joel Bartlett, and Leanna McClellan.

Serena would like to thank:

Writers and travelers before me, and the people who have listened to their inner voice to speak up in a world of contradictions. Thanks to my friends and family for their encouragement and support, spending time with me across this globe, laughing with me and always inspiring me to live out my dreams. Thanks to my incomparable and wise mother, my loving and encouraging Aunt Barbara, and my talented and utopian father.

Diana would like to thank:

My family whose love and relentless support has offered me a safe and empowering starting point for exploration. These strong and generous individuals are an ever-present and ever-forgiving part of me and I am thankful to them all. The many friends, leaders, teachers, and heroes from different stages of my life are irreplaceable and have encouraged me to live with intention and heaps of giddy laughter. I am grateful to every person I have met, have yet to meet, and may never know, persisting towards happiness with the unrepentant belief in its power to create a healthier world and more peaceful collective humanity.

Introduction

The GrassRoutes Story

Like cracking open a dusty geode, travel has revealed to me the many facets of the world. The crystals I found brought me the clarity to compare my known world with that of the previously unexplored. I was able to connect truly with the rich diversity that abounds. No other activity has had quite the same impact, offering a unique experience where both commonalities and differences in the quilt of humanity were vibrantly displayed. Inspirations occurred while traveling around the globe and around the corner. The cities I have called home have given me plenty of refreshing surprises. Whether boarding a plane for another continent or walking a few blocks to a nearby neighborhood, no matter what my pocketbook dictated, I always managed to find new cultural gems.

As I walked the gangway on each return flight, I noticed that culture shock was as potent going home as when I had discovered new countries and traditions. Each time my reality was challenged with new ways of thinking and acting, I found I was less attached to one specific culture. After each journey I found I had new interests, different ways of dealing with difficult situations, and an altogether new perspective. The most important souvenir I brought home wasn't tangible—it was a more open mind.

As the pages of my passport filled up with stamps, I had greater insight into each culture that could never have come from pictures or words. I also had plenty of stories to share. A minor bike accident I had in a Kyoto suburb brought a fleet of firemen to my rescue. A similar situation in Denmark roused little notice by other biking commuters but meant a gratis cup of black coffee as I waited for the city bike to be repaired. (Copenhagen is equipped with its own fleet of public bikes for anyone and everyone's use.) In London, a city stigmatized by many Americans as having the worst food, I have enjoyed some of the finest international cuisines. The more I traveled, the more stereotypes were turned on their head. In short, travel has taught me that no generalization really holds up.

I became a detective of sorts, unearthing cultures. Out of earshot from town squares or famous landmarks, I became familiar with local traditions. When I returned home I kept up the habit, discovering a wealth of intrigue in my own country. As a cultural tourist I discovered unique adventures right around the block. I have since made it my mission to seek out the non-traditional attractions and cities.

The people who hovered around the cathedrals and museums were of greater interest to me than the cold monuments. The living, breathing collection of foods and voices, footsteps on the roads and walkways—those were the things that attracted me. I witnessed the world around me blinking like a disco ball, with authenticity being overtaken by all things virtual, but I trusted another kind of travel. Wherever I was, the locals gave me the chance to have unique experiences rather than manufactured ones. By focusing on human interaction, serendipity soon replaced artificial stimulation.

GrassRoutes Travel was born out of my growing collection of ideas, inspirations, and frustrations. I remembered the grim fact that Americans (United Statesians, actually) have the fewest passports per capita. I made up my mind to promote world citizenship, but search as I might, I found no vehicle that expressed my ideas about travel. The Dalai Lama's wise words turned like a prayer wheel in my head: "If you have some [distress] you should examine whether there is anything you can do about it. If you can, there is no need to worry; if you cannot do anything, then there is also no need to worry." Doing something about it turned into GrassRoutes Travel.

The concept evolved from a bundle of notes collected on the road. Since I had never seen cities as separate boroughs, but as one entity, I didn't want my guides to divide chapters by neighborhoods. Most cities weren't so expansive that they warranted being divided by neighborhood. Also, chowing down on some messy barbeque didn't equate with a three star meal of braised rabbit, so I chose not to organize the guides simply by activity. I thought of the times I had woken up really early, the times I wanted to have a casual night out, or when I needed to get my creative juices flowing. GrassRoutes Travel had to be designed around these states of being: the mood of the traveler and the timing. To find a smash hit burrito at 1 a.m., just turn to the **Stay Up Late** chapter.

But organization wasn't the only thing I wanted to help evolve travel guides. GrassRoutes Travel is true to its name by including local businesses and their corresponding contributions to the greater good of the community. Restaurants that serve sustainably grown produce share the pages with shops that showcase works by local artists. Wildlife preserves are in the mix with co-operative bakeries and amusements that use energy saving techniques. Some of the best travel experiences I have had have been through meeting the locals in volunteer situations, so an entire chapter focuses on easy ways for visitors and residents alike to interact while giving back. Being conscientious about society and environment is a recipe for peace. Greet the world with an open mind: this is a message I hope to convey.

I was not born with a silver spoon in my mouth. Any voyage I dreamed of had to be financed by yours truly. What I found out was that travel could fit a limited budget. For a quick and cheap adventure, I could check out a new area of town or head to a museum on a free day. (I have included a **City for Free** chapter that lists some great money-less adventures). With a little perseverance, library time, and an inquisitive nature, I managed to find work exchange programs, scholarships, cheap fares, and homestays. It was possible, even on my tight budget, to vacation on Mediterranean beaches for a weekend trip while living in Germany, explore the cobblestone walkways of Manchester, UK, and enter a floating temple on the Japanese island of Miyajima. There are ways to afford all kinds of travel. GrassRoutes is more than a guide to a city's attractions; it is a reaffirmation that authentic cultural experiences are not out of reach for anyone.

My first secret is printed right on the cover of this book: take a new view of travel. Try new cities, venture to places that aren't typical tourist destinations. Save time and money by choosing idyllic Rovinj, Croatia instead of over-priced and over-crowded Corfu, Greece for that above-mentioned Mediterranean vacançe. Not only are the next door cities more affordable, but also they bring you closer to the region because they aren't built up as an attraction in and of themselves. Following the same example, in Rovinj, the native cuisine is delicious. Smoky, delicate fish straight from the surrounding waters with handmade lavender goat cheese just doesn't compare to the toast, eggs, and canned beans served at Corfu hostels to keep the many tourists "comfortable."

Along with the sights and sounds, local foods are a window into the uniqueness of each place. By focusing on culinary specialties, GrassRoutes encourages travelers to venture outside their comfort zone.

As you enjoy your travels, you can be satisfied knowing that you are a conscientious consumer. How is chocolate cake, conscientious, you ask? You bought it from an organic, co-operative local bakery that supports school gardening programs and purchases sustainably grown ingredients from nearby farms. When I found out how much fun and, OK, indulgence, could be had while making a positive impact, I chose to be a conscientious consumer. The undeniable facts amassing about the current state of our planet necessitates that more of us make this choice. And with such a bounty of local businesses dedicated to this spirit of positive change, it is becoming easier to support such a philosophy. Each listing in GrassRoutes Travel meets these standards in one aspect or another. Whether re-circulating money into the local economy, supporting community outreach, protecting natural environments, or serving a healthy meal, there are many ways in which these listings participate positively. So while you are venturing out into the world and meeting real people in new places, your dollars are staying in the community, supporting everything from waste reduction to entrepreneurial youth, organic food to zero emissions public transit. Becoming a conscientious consumer gives each individual the power to effect positive change in the world.

I bring you GrassRoutes Travel Guides, created to benefit readers and communities. I hope you will try something new, even if you thought it was not possible. Having a genuine cultural escapade is directly proportional to your ability to let go of preconceived notions. All you need is an inquiring mind, a detective's spirit, and the desire to get acquainted with the world around you.

—Serena Bartlett

Using GrassRoutes Travel Guides

GrassRoutes Travel Guides employ a totally new system of organization that makes searching for activities, restaurants, and venues easy. This guide is organized by situation, with chapters like **Stay Up Late**, **Do Lunch**, and **Hang Out** that pay more attention to your state of being.

Organization by type of venue runs the risk of muddling a six-course meal with a drive-thru, just because both are technically restaurants. Instead, shouldn't guides be organized by what kind of dining experience you are looking for, rather than just that you are hungry?

Of course, there are those times when you are just looking for a restaurant or for a movie theater. It can be tough to kick that traditional categorizing, so we've got you covered in our Index. Here you will find destinations grouped by their respective category.

For practicality, we have also included a handy key that locates each restaurant, movie theater, park etc. in the different neighborhoods of the city. This way, you are still able to find an activity to match your mood but won't have to go halfway across the city to get to it. We've divided Portland into N, NW, SW, SE, and NE.

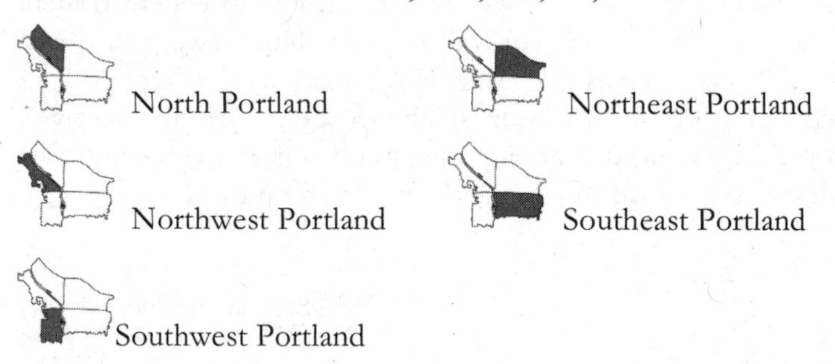

All phone numbers are in the **(503)** area code unless otherwise stated.

There is a price range key and also a "who to go with" key to highlight great spots to go with friends, family, solo, or for romance.

As authors, we want to tell our experiences from our own perspectives, so we use the 'I' perspective. The italicized initials after each review denote the primary voice (*sb*: Serena Bartlett, *dm*: Diana Morgan, *dl*: Daniel Ling, *rrm*: Raina Rose McClellan, *ks*: Kelly Schierholz, *pr*: Perrin Randlette, *ws*: William Schwartz, *nkp*: Nicky Kriara Peterson, *jo*: Jon Ostar, *ec*: Emily Crabtree, *sm*: Sara Miller, *ep*: Emily Picha).

Price Key:

$- Cheap. Entrée prices are under $10.
$$- Moderate. Entrées between $10 and $15.
$$$- Pricey. Entrées are over $15, most are around $20.
CO- Cash Only, no plastic accepted here.

Company Key:

S- Solo. Places and activities that are great experienced alone.
Fr- Friends. Go with one buddy or a group of friends.
Ro- Romance. Great spots to go with that special somebody.
Fam- Family. Places for the whole family to enjoy.
PW- People Watching. Locations that are privy to an outpouring of interesting people. Slow down and take in the atmosphere.
Dg- Dog Friendly. Walk your pooch or settle down on the patio.

Service and Practicality Key:

WiFi- Wireless Internet available free of charge.
R- Reservations recommended
Vn- Vegan entrées available.
Veg- Vegetarian entrées available. If you see Vn, you can assume there are also vegetarian entrées served.

Note: There are very few, if any Kosher and/or Halal restaurants and grocers, so please use Veg and Vn for pareve.

Travel Tips

There are many different kinds of trips: seeing the seven wonders of the world, doing a trek or outdoor-focused voyage, going to a new city, traveling for family or business that may not involve choosing your own destination, or rediscovering your own city when a friend comes to visit. For any given trip there are different ways to plan, but the core remains the same: stay open-minded. I like to remind myself that security is really a false pretense under which humans can never truly live. This is not to say that you should throw yourself to the mercy of the world. Safe travel is smart travel, but judgmental, pre-conceived notion travel can be just as dangerous. I will spare you loads of examples, but suffice it to say, there is a lot out there, and your state of mind is directly related to how much of the world you will explore.

Here are a few tidbits on packing, getting around, trip planning, and safety that I have compiled over my years of world travel.

Trip Planning

My philosophy for trip planning could be considered a tad unorthodox, but let me just say, it has gotten me far. The bottom line is I don't over-plan. I pick dates that make sense and make the fewest reservations I can get away with. It is crucial to take into consideration factors of time, exhaustion, and exploration. Before embarking on a trip, I tell as many people as will listen where I am going and get their feedback and tips. I have the same talkative approach when I am there, meeting locals, and finding out their favorite spots. Look at books and magazines featuring the culture and history of the area before embarking on your trip, and keep a well-organized travel guide and a clear map with you while you are exploring.

Time Allotment

When picking dates, consider what kind of trip you want to have. One game plan is to spread out your time between different sights and get a good introduction to an area. Another is spending prolonged time in one or two cities, and getting beneath the skin.

In my experience, it is good to slow down the tempo of travel enough to smell the proverbial roses.

Reservations

There are a few practical reasons to make reservations, and there are also things to avoid planning too much in advance.

Be sure to reserve a hotel for at least the first night so you have somewhere to go when you get off the plane. Thumbs up to adventure, but even if you travel on a whim, I recommend starting on day two—after you get your bearings.

If your entire vacation will be spent in the same area, I suggest staying in the same, centrally located hotel the whole time, so you avoid carrying your stuff around. After all, you probably didn't travel to see different hotels, but to see the city itself!

In general, and this depends on the city and country, I wouldn't reserve many transit engagements. That way, if you want to extend your stay in a given spot, you can do that without too many trials and tribulations. Local transit arrangements are usually easy to book without much advance notice. As far as restaurants go, they tent to have widely varying reservation policies, so check ahead to see whether your dream meal requires them, or doesn't accept them. That way you can look around, act on a whim, and best of all, get the locals' advice. It is hard to get a good sense of a restaurant from its website.

Regarding hotels, make sure you are aware of each place's cancellation policy. Try to get an idea of the city first, before you book a room, so you can place yourself in the area of town that most interests you. (This is why the **Lodge** chapter is located toward the end of this book.) Be sure to reserve special event tickets and also tables at restaurants that require them. These are noted with an R in this book (see the key in **Using GrassRoutes Travel Guides**).

Packing

I like to have a good pair of pants that can match with different shirts. I bring one dressier outfit and a bathing suit. Bring more than enough underwear, but wear outfits that can keep their shape for two or three days of use, especially pants or skirts. You'll be meeting and interacting with new people everyday, so no one will know you wore the same outfit two days in a row. Buy extraneous items like sunscreen after you arrive. Remember, you will have to carry what you bring, so don't weigh yourself down. Check the climate and current weather conditions of your planned locations and pack accordingly. Try taking your luggage for a stroll in your own neighborhood before hitting the road. Then you'll know right away if you've over-packed, with enough time to do something about it.

Safety

All major cities around the world have some amount of crime. Please use your wits and stay safe. Try to avoid traveling alone to new places at night.

Other Tips

I always travel with the equipment that makes things less apt to bother me. On the plane I have earplugs and headphones, a sleep mask, a good book, and several bottles of water (provided liquid is allowed given new safety regulations). That way even if there is a screaming baby, my voyage will remain blissfully quiet. I find it is easier to make changes myself than ask others to tone it down.

Get enough sleep before you fly. I recommend drinking lots of water the day before traveling and the day of—more if you tend to get dehydrated easily or are prone, like I am, to get headaches from the dry plane air. Boosting your dose of vitamin C won't hurt either.

Don't plan two activity-heavy days back to back. In general, it is good to have a combination of restful, educational, and physical experiences. That is one of the reasons for the organization of GrassRoutes Guides. Traveling can include every type of adventure. Many other Western countries allow for more vacation time than the United States, so Americans risk overdoing it when they actually get time off. Wherever you are from, make vacation time count by balancing your time and not trying to jam in too much activity. Ask yourself what you really want to see, and cut out the rest. Keep in mind that you can always come back, and be realistic about what you and your friends and family have the energy for.

I also recommend breaking into smaller groups when people have different ideas of what they want to see and do. Notations described in the **Key** indicate which restaurants are especially good for family, friends, going solo, and going for a touch of romance. Other activities include explanations that aid in trip planning to keep all members in your party entertained.

Contact Us!

The places and events listed in this guide are ones we thought were outstanding. Cities are constantly changing, so please contact us if you feel there is something we missed or if you find out-of-date information. Updates, new venues, and corrections will be posted on our website. We'd love to hear from you!

info@grassroutestravel.com • www.grassroutestravel.com

About Portland

View of Downtown Portland from the Rose Garden

Brief History

"Keep Portland Weird" is a phrase you'll often see staring at you from the rear bumper of a car driving down Portland's boulevards. This phrase sums up the spirit of preservation in Oregon's largest city, which was designed in order to retain a small town feel. Strange to think that Portland was once a 640-acre plot purchased for a quarter, and even stranger that it was almost called Boston.

The story of how the City of Roses came to be begins in 1843 when drifter William Overton attempted to file a claim for the 640-acre site known as "The Clearing," but lacked the 25¢ to do so. Enthralled by the beautiful landscape, Overton made a deal with Massachusetts Lawyer Asa Lovejoy, who gave him the 25 cents in exchange for an equal share of the land. Overton eventually continued his drifting lifestyle, selling his share to Francis Pettygrove. The new partners concurred that their budding township deserved a name, but they could not come to an agreement. Lovejoy was determined to name it after his hometown of Boston while Pettygrove wanted the honor to go to his native Portland, Maine. Neither was willing to yield, and so the coin toss of the century was held to settle the matter. Consequently, the coin they used became known as the "Portland Penny." In 1851, less than a decade following that fateful coin toss, Portland was incorporated as a city.

Lovejoy and Pettygrove, now namesakes memorialized as streets, predicted that Portland would evolve into a prosperous and popular destination, owing to its prime location on the Willamette River and its abundant natural resources. Indeed, it became a major transportation center during the Civil War, building docks for shipping lumber, fish, and wheat to the rest of the nation and the world. Its popularity as a port city coupled with government corruption resulted in increased abductions of men to work as slave labor on sailing ships. Notorious in this "shanghai trade" was a hotelier by the name of Joseph "Bunco" Kelly, whose deceitful tricks earned him the nickname. Bunco once delivered a cigar Indian wrapped in blankets as another would-be slave to a ship captain, who threw it overboard in a fit of rage upon discovering the ruse. The statue was discovered nearly 60 years later by a pair of dredge operators.

Portland's seamy underground took a turn for the better with the flourishing of the lumber industry and the wealth earned from providing goods for the California Gold Rush. City officials regulated of the waterfront's questionable activities. The subterranean tunnels beneath the city streets that were once used to cart hapless drunks to an unwanted life at sea soon became an historical curiosity. Business owners shifted their concern from making a profit on trickery to improving worker conditions. Lumber baron Simon Benson commissioned 20 drinking fountains when he learned that his employees were substituting alcohol for the lack of drinking water in the downtown areas. Beer consumption decreased 25 percent following the installation of the Benson Bubblers. The elegant fountains are now surrounded by public parks, outdoor art, coffee carts, bookstores, and of all things, microbreweries.

Portland's warm summers and rainy, but temperate winters make it an ideal location for growing roses, as is proven by an explosion of spring blossoms. The earliest known reference to Portland as "The City of Roses" dates back to an 1888 Episcopal Church convention. At the 1905 Lewis and Clark Centennial Exposition, Mayor Harry Lane suggested a "festival of roses" for the city, and the nickname's appeal began to spread. Two years later, the first Portland Rose Festival was held, and it remains an annual tradition. *dl*

Portland Now

Even in European circles, Portland is widely known for its commitment to alternative modes of transportation, land conservation policies and its overall attention to green practices. The city ranked number one in overall sustainability ratings in 2006 and is proud to hold the title of "role model for the nation." Portland has been rated as one of the cleanest U.S. cities and third among the top ten cities making the best use of renewable energy in city operations (the crown goes to GrassRoutes' hometown, Oakland, California). Portland stands as the only American city to be selected by the European Institute of Urban Affairs as one of the "world's most successful cities."

A public transportation mecca, Portland does not follow the trend of the world's most car-dependent nation. Car use is growing at the slowest rate anywhere in the country, and Portland drivers are considered the most courteous to boot. Why drive when you can take a 500-foot high commute over Interstate 5 on the Portland Aerial Tram, one of the first urban trams in the country. Everyone loves Portland's triumphant public transit asset, the free zone on MAX Light Rail through Portland's bustling downtown and Lloyd Center areas. The last couple decades of city planners have looked to European transportation systems in cities such as Amsterdam's for inspiration in keeping with Portland's legacy of a bike friendly city. The city's thriving bike scene and its conscientious urban-growth planning have earned it a high ranking from the League of American Bicyclists. For those who are content to travel by foot, a study by the American Podiatric Medical Association picked Portland as one of the five best walking cities in America.

Approximately 37.8 percent of residents over 25 have earned a bachelor's degree or higher, putting Portland in the top 20 on a list of 70 cities ranked in order of educational achievement. A study found that Portland is among America's top 10 cities for literacy, not only in terms of how many residents know how to read, but also how many actually make a regular practice of reading. It comes as no surprise, then, that Portland's libraries are ranked second in the nation, and why chatting with a stranger on the street can often lead to some interesting topics of conversation.

Doing business in Portland is rife with benefits, owing to its robust economy. *Inc. Magazine* ranked Portland number four among the cities with the most balanced economy and growth. Driving the health of the economy are the estimated 100,449 women-owned firms, making up over 50 percent of the businesses in the Portland area. A 2007 global real estate forecast report has projected Portland to be among the top 10 office markets for investors, and if that is not enough incentive, PDX has been named the best airport for business travel by readers of *Conde Nast Traveler* magazine. Interestingly enough, Portland's educated populace seems to be forever under-employed, with many college grads working the espresso machines around town and lamenting their unpublished poetry. Many city residents seem to collect multiple income generating jobs to make ends meet and to continue intellectual stimulation.

Creativity abounds in Portland, especially since the Dot-com Boom brought a massive influx of young designers. Even after that economic bubble burst, Portland's artistic population has continued to rise, and the last decade has seen a sort of renaissance in the local art scene. American Style magazine ranks Portland the number 10 art destination among cities with populations of more than 500,000. It is also one of the best places for independent filmmakers to make a living. The state of Oregon boasts more than 34 film festivals. GrassRoutes has devoted a section of this book (see **Art House Cinema** chapter) to the best movie houses in Portland. The artistic inhabitants of the city also account for the attractive restaurants, tasteful shops and head-turning public art that make Portland the treasure that it is.

Artistry isn't limited to the high-brow, either. Matt Groening, creator of the television cartoon *The Simpsons*, grew up in Portland. Characters of the show start appearing regularly on street signs in the mid- and north-western parts of the city.

The creative nature of city residents extends to its music scene. Playing a large part in the grunge rock evolution of the late-80's and early 90's, Portland continues to nurture blossoming bands. Most recently, the city has contributed to the indie-rock movement with bands like The Decemberists and The Shins. Portlanders have an ear for good rock and roll.

What about the animals? The Humane Society of the United States evaluated metropolitan areas across the country on a wide range of topics related to pets, farm animals, wildlife, and animal advocacy. The results of this study placed Portland third among the 25 largest U.S. cities for animal friendliness and caring. A high concentration of wildlife rehabilitators, Canadian seafood boycotters, vegetarian dining options, and establishments with cage-free egg policies contributed to this outcome. And for your fuzzy travel friends, Portland is the best all-around city for dogs in America, according to *Dog Fancy* magazine. Annual events include the Doggie Dash and the Pug Crawl fundraiser for the Oregon Humane Society. Doggie day-care businesses are never hard to find, and with thirty-three city-maintained parks, every dog will have his day and then some. There is hardly a house, hovel or apartment without a beloved canine or kitty roaming around. Portlanders have great respect for their pets, and house sitters abound to care for these animals when the explorative Portlanders depart to other lands.

A surprising and distinguishing feature of Portland is the abundance of strip joints. There are more of them in the city borders than any other place in the U.S. Portland is liberal with nudity laws, which is sure to be a contributing factor to the statistic. Mary's Club is the most noteworthy of these establishments, as it was the first topless club and connects with a surprisingly scrumptious Mexican restaurant next door.

Portland is also exceptional in its number of microbreweries that hail the Rosy City as their home. The total is somewhere around 60, with many home brewers contributing to the microbrew culture, as evidenced in the many local beer festivals throughout the year (see **Calendar** chapter). The public agenda of the city is a clear display of environmental sustainability.

Portland is leading the way in sustainability by making a strong commitment to public transportation and conscientious urban growth strategies. The overall conscientious mentality has earned the city acclaim in many aspects of urban life, from business to recreation to just getting around. Portland is an example of the growing concern in the world for restoring the quality of public life.

The public agenda of the city is a clear display of environmental sustainability but individual Portlanders themselves take eco-conscious living seriously as well. By seeking out alternative transportation to work (many workers can be seen on bikes in their business suits during the morning commute), choosing to reduce consumption, taking advantage of recycling, and opting for organic and local foods whenever possible, the personal choices of city residents are a showcase of individual responsibility and dedication to the environment. City inhabitants encourage one another on the path to a way of life with less impact on our planet, and make deliberate choices every day to continue on that path, trying always to fill sustainable living with fun, creativity, and peace.

The sustainable movement is city wide, but it should be noted that the Eastside is where the movement thrives. With less traffic and congestion than downtown, more bike commuters will be found passing by locally owned stores, organic restaurants, and creative enclaves. Pioneering businesses like The ReBuilding Center and Farm Café are plentiful. Wandering the Eastside will showcase lawns-turned-gardens, free boxes galore, and a general atmosphere of conscientious living. *dl*

The GrassRoutes crew had such a cheery time in Portland, we've given it our own nickname, The Rosy City!

Climate

"Temperate" and "seasonal" are the best words to describe Portland's ideal rose-growing weather. Sharing many characteristics of a Mediterranean climate, Portland winters are mild and wet, and summers are hot and dry. The average yearly rainfall is 44 inches, with the rainy season lasting from November to April, so pack a raincoat. Winter lows average 35° F with snowfall uncommon. June to September marks the driest season, with temperatures averaging 80° F, although heat waves exceeding 100° F do occur.

Geographically, Portland is located at 45°60' North, 122°60' West and has a total land area of 134.3 square miles (347.9 kilometers square).

Shopping Districts

Southeast:

Hawthorne Boulevard

This is where the trendy, alternative, and young come out to shop, busk, and beg. Hawthorne gives us a variety of purchasing options from 30th Avenue all the way east past the 40's. A Powell Books chapter, resale clothing stores, niche gift shops, and oodles of coffee and restaurant options add fuel to the consuming on this busy strip. Sometimes the onslaught of canvassers can be a bit much, but they are there for the progressive, moderate price buyers who have opted to shop locally. *dm*

Belmont Avenue

A modestly-sized district, Belmont continues to expand and sprout new shops. I like Belmont because it is not as busy as Hawthorne Boulevard a few blocks to the south and has a slower, friendlier pace. Plus, Belmont boasts quirkiness like boutiques that oddly combine gifts and jewelry with cupcakes all in one space. While there are a handful of unassuming bars and coffee shops here, there is also a bit of a more refined air, with the upscale grocer, Zupan's, anchoring the avenue and rarely an unwelcome loiterer on the sidewalks. *dm*

Burnside, Close-In SE

Portland is always on the move and this district is following suit. With the Doug-Fir lounge anchoring the neighborhood and strips of shops, eateries, and bars springing up left and right, the strip of Burnside from the bridge to the Sandy and 12th Avenue intersection is on the rise. Centrally located, this area is accessible from all parts of Portland and the heavy auto traffic doesn't keep the people from flocking to its many attractions. *dm*

Division Street

Toward 39th Avenue there is a gathering of boutiques and second-hand shops on this long stretch of good food and relaxed people. My friend Sara always exits Village Merchants with amazing finds, and I like to linger on the out-of-my-range goods at Portico. Clearly an established community of families and young professionals, wandering off Division Street proper brings cutely painted and accented bungalows for the aspiring home renovators out there and the idyllic Ladd's Addition is just north of New Seasons Market, west of 20th Avenue. *dm*

28th Avenue

Hugging Burnside Street is a diverse range of shopping options from superb retro duds to a sweet nursery and styling clothing boutiques. This is a hub of a Burnside intersection, which also boasts Laurelhurst Theater and leads to fine dining to the north and south. It is nice that so many contented walkers pass down this street despite its busy automobile traffic. A stroll over to Laurelhurst Park down one of the less busy side streets is a nice follow up to some 28th Avenue shopping. *dm*

Sellwood-Moreland

A bit further south in Southeast Portland sits this district, conjoining the neighborhoods of Sellwood, Eastmoreland, and Westmoreland. Sellwood-Moreland has a *Pleasantville* feel to it, but manages a charming air without the snobbery and false façades despite its adorable shops, coffeehouses and restaurants. This is a nice destination to arrive via the Springwater Corridor, which can be picked up at OMSI and traveled via bike, or for those with the time, two feet. *dm*

North:

Mississippi Avenue

Historically, there has been a strong African American presence in the Mississippi area. The neighborhood has experienced many changes in recent years, drawing the artistic types and first-home buyers to live and the boutiques, restaurants, and coffee houses that accompany this demographic. Clearly a changed district, Mississippi is a great avenue to head for live music, casual dining, and the perusing of unique shops. Because it is far enough from the city center, the pace is even slower and the crowd thinner here. Mississippi is a relaxing place. *dm*

St. Johns

St. Johns catches the city overflow and its businesses are diamonds, though small in number. A trek up north to this neighborhood offers a quieter experience and the beauty of the St. Johns Bridge. *dm*

Northeast:

Fremont

Down the stretch of the 40's, the Fremont shopping districts is a smattering of cute shops and good restaurants. The homes surrounding Fremont are filled with families and 30-something singles, so the vibe around here is not as alterna-hip as Hawthorne can be. Fremont is a nice place for a weekend stroll. *dm*

Killingsworth and 30th Avenue

Killingsworth and 30th Avenue sport a tiny number of businesses, but it is a quiet pause from the alternative bustling neighborhoods. With Cup & Saucer at the corner, the Herbivore Magazine shop, and a bistro or two, this is the area to go for those who want just a handful of options for meals, cups of coffee, and quirky treasures over which to linger. *dm*

Alberta Street

Alberta is jam-packed with some of the best shopping and atmosphere in town. Host of Last Thursday and the Alberta Art Hop, this area distinguishes itself with a vibrant artistic community and funky vibe. Small clothing boutiques, gift shops, celebrated restaurants, and a clown house are all worth a look-see on a weekend visit. With unassuming but adorable homes scattered around the main thoroughfare, the crowd is laid back, fun, and original. *dm*

Irvington/NE Broadway

From MLK Jr. Boulevard all the way to 33rd Avenue, NE Broadway boasts a lengthy stretch of diverse shopping spots. Lloyd Center Mall, just to the south, is the hub of chain store mall shopping, intersperced with locally owned clothing and kitchenware stores. The ritzy Irvington neighborhood, to the north, is a walk through a Norman Rockwell painting. *dm*

Hollywood

With the preeminent feature of the classic Hollywood Theater figured boldly at the center of this district, Hollywood is home to a few good spots for living essentials and maybe a drink at Laurelwood Brewing Co. This area is heavy on the car traffic, with Sandy Boulevard a standout diagonal route for drivers in a hurry, but heading north of the boulevard will give an escape to quieter areas, and heading south on a Saturday leads to the Hollywood Farmers Market. *dm*

Southwest:

University

Portland State University provides the schooling for a number of city residents, continuing ed students and undergrad alike. The student-filled PSU area offers inexpensive eateries and grassy knolls perfect for lounging and reading. *dm*

South Waterfront/John's Landing

The city is rapidly developing the South Waterfront area with condominiums blooming like roses in the spring. Shops and dining are sure to follow, but the John's Landing and McAdam areas already have a handful of bars and restaurants, albeit on busy routes. The waterfront with its walkways and parks is the real centerpiece of this area. *dm*

Downtown

For a big city experience, the downtown area has all the requisite department stores, high rises and big glitzy restaurants. There are a number of gems amidst the activity; performing arts centers, locally-owned shoe and chocolate stores and the Tom McCall Waterfront Park are favorites. Luckily, city blocks are small in Portland, so the downtown can be covered rather quickly and by foot, or by the Max free zone. *dm*

Multnomah Village

'The Village in the Heart of Portland' is situated far in the Southwest, almost outside of the city limits, but still hanging on. It really is village-like; you'll be hard pressed to find WiFi here. This is a nice area for cute little shops and for a small-town feel. *dm*

Northwest:

The Pearl

Once upon a time, this quarter of the city was a raw up-and-coming industrial scene. Now it is a more established area that faintly harkens back to its industrial history—the architecture housing the upscale restaurants and home décor shops makes for plentiful exposed brick and otherwise "roughed up" posh looks. The Pearl also envelops Powell's City of Books, Last Word Books and high-rise, posh condominiums are forever sprouting from these city blocks. *dm*

Nob Hill

Nob Hill is where the snazzy young professionals, fashionable socialites, and established city elite head to romp around. The bars pack 'em in after 5p, reservations are recommended for the bustling gourmet bistros and the weekend sidewalks are an obstacle course of shoppers. This is an upscale district with the 23rd and 21st Avenues framing the area with eating, shopping, and the ever-entertaining people watching. *dm*

Old Town/Chinatown

Chinatown is an idiosyncratic area filled with rundown buildings and questionable establishments, along with destination galleries and music venues. This is home to much of Portland's art scene, catching a good deal of the First Thursday Gallery walk traffic. Head here for some inexpensive eats, a night of jazz or modern dance, or a stroll in the calming Chinese Gardens. *dm*

Maps

The following are maps of the major areas of Portland to help you get around

★ Look for GrassRoutes Travel Guides to these cities.

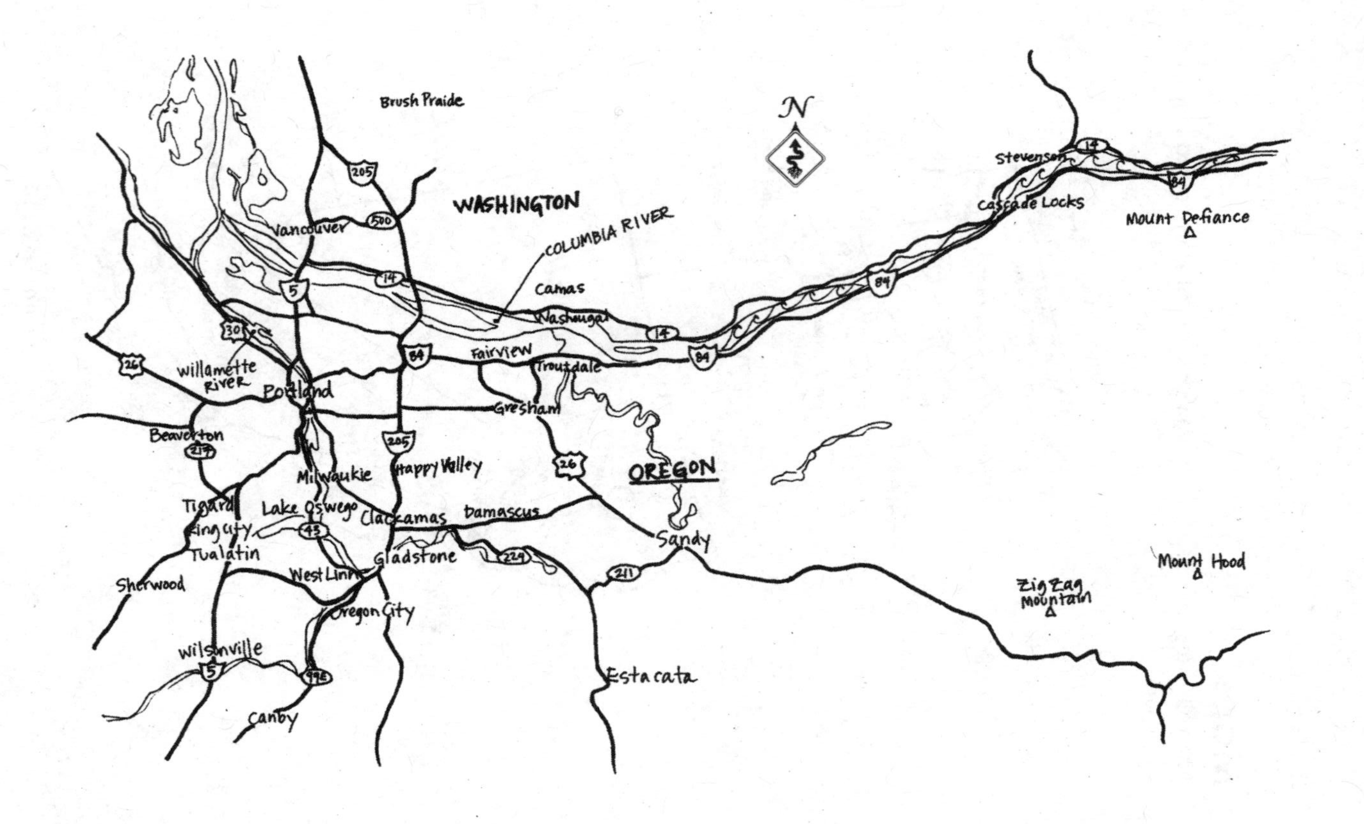
Brush Praide
N
WASHINGTON
COLUMBIA RIVER
Vancouver
Camas
Washougal
Stevenson
Cascade Locks
Mount Defiance
Fairview
Troutdale
Willamette River
Portland
Gresham
Beaverton
Happy Valley
Milwaukie
OREGON
Tigard
Lake Oswego
Clackamas
Damascus
King City
Tualatin
Sandy
Gladstone
West Linn
Sherwood
Oregon City
Mount Hood
Zig Zag Mountain
Wilsonville
Estacata
Canby
205
500
14
5
30
84
26
217
43
224
211
99E

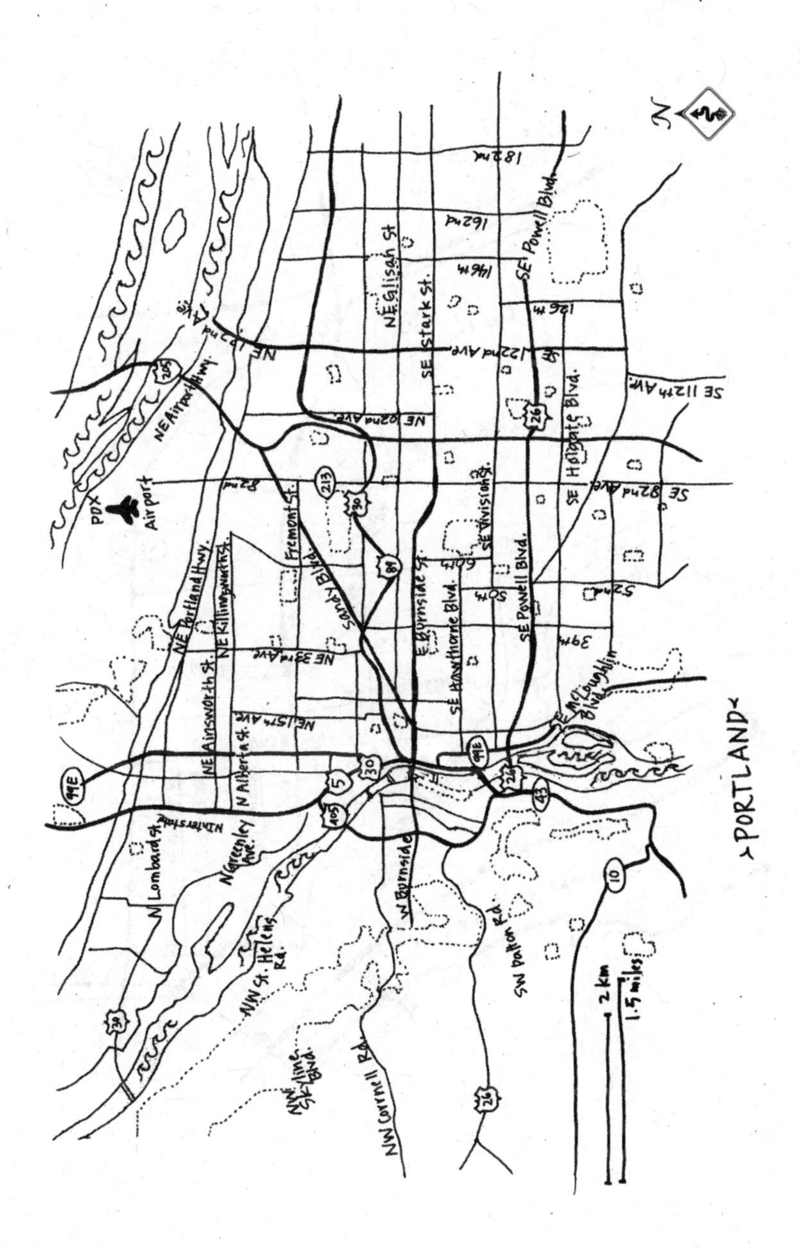
PORTLAND
PDX
Airport
N Lombard St.
N Interstate
N Greeley Ave.
NW St. Helens Rd.
NW Skyline Blvd.
NW Cornell Rd.
W Burnside
SW Dalton Rd.
2 km
1.5 miles
NE Portland Hwy.
NE Airport Hwy.
NE Ainsworth St.
NE Killingsworth St.
N Alberta St.
Fremont St.
Sandy Blvd.
E Burnside St.
SE Hawthorne Blvd.
SE Powell Blvd.
SE Division St.
SE Stark St.
NE Glisan St
SE Holgate Blvd.
SE McLoughlin Blvd.
NE 15th Ave
NE 33rd Ave
NE 82nd
NE 102nd Ave
NE 122nd Ave
SE 122nd Ave
SE 82nd Ave
SE 112th Ave.
39th
50th
52nd
60th
126th
146th
162nd
182nd
N

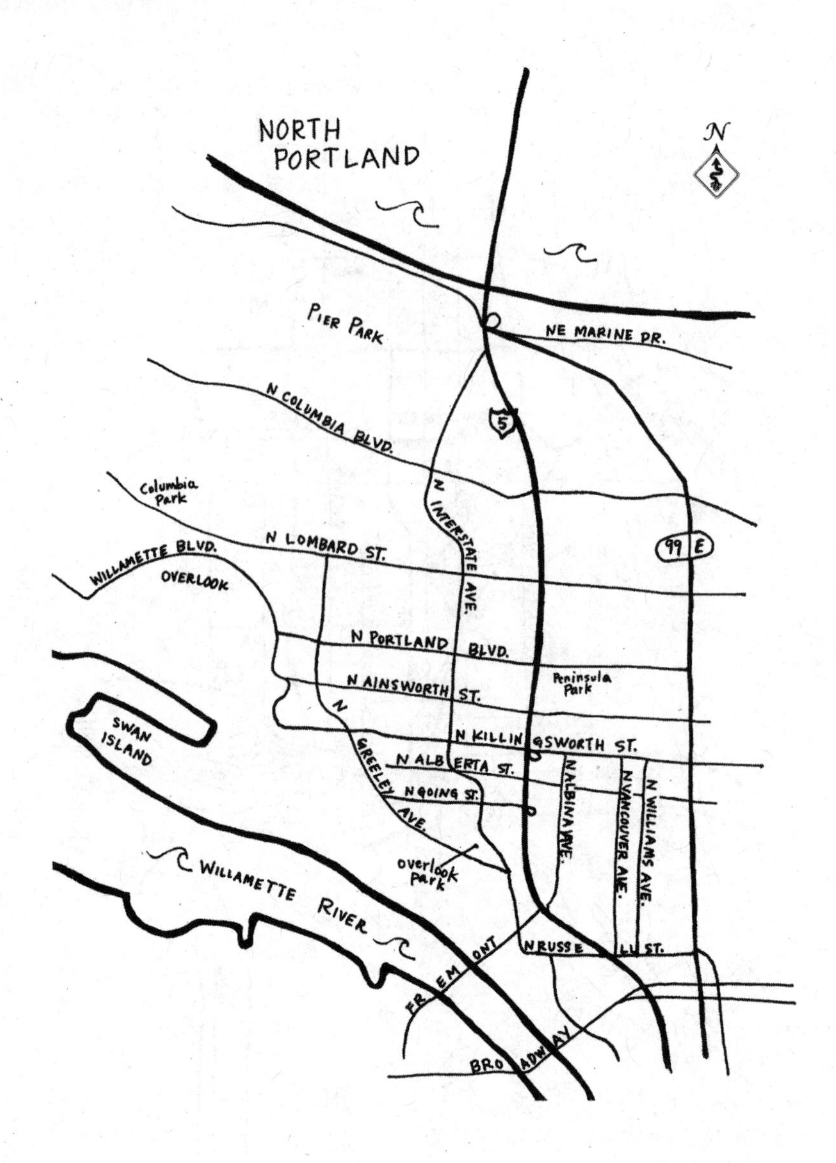
NORTH PORTLAND
N
PIER PARK
NE MARINE DR.
N COLUMBIA BLVD.
Columbia Park
N INTERSTATE AVE.
99E
N LOMBARD ST.
WILLAMETTE BLVD.
OVERLOOK
N PORTLAND BLVD.
Peninsula Park
N AINSWORTH ST.
SWAN ISLAND
N GREELEY AVE.
N KILLINGSWORTH ST.
N ALBERTA ST.
N GOING ST.
N ALBINA AVE.
N VANCOUVER AVE.
N WILLIAMS AVE.
overlook park
WILLAMETTE RIVER
N RUSSELL ST.
FREMONT
BROADWAY

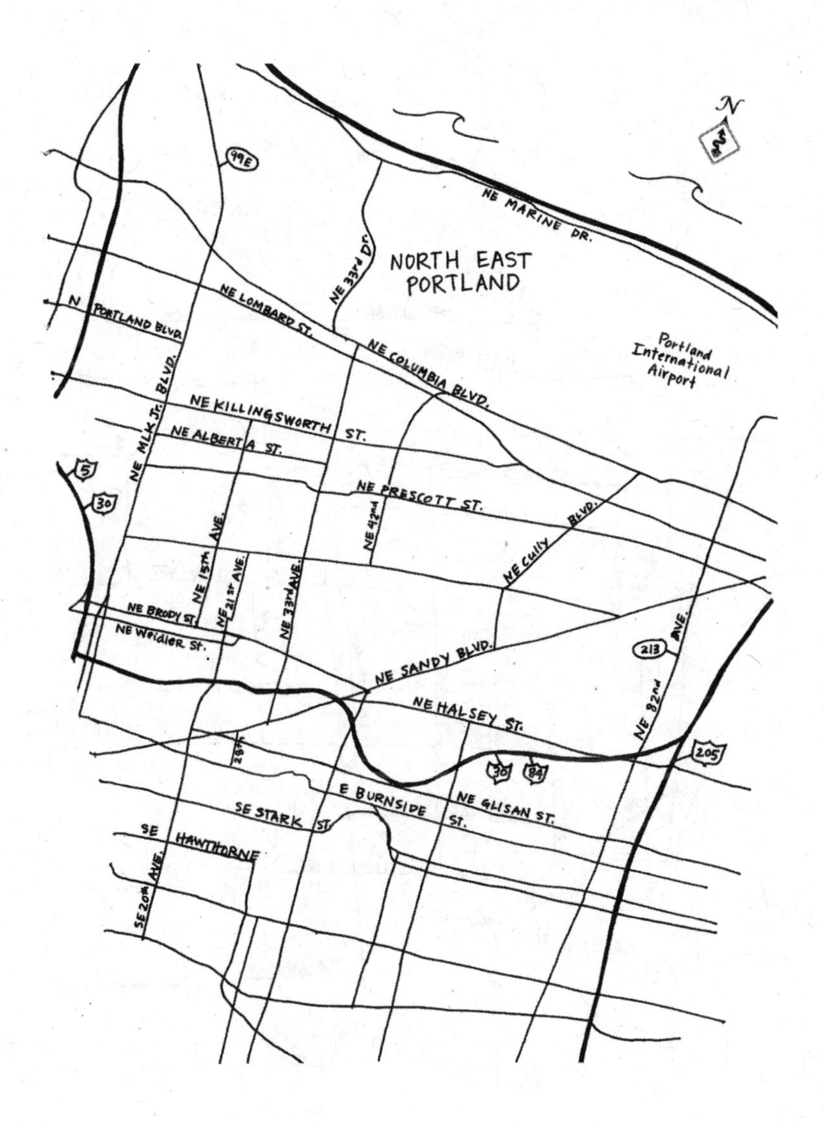
N
99E
NE MARINE DR.
NORTH EAST
PORTLAND
NE 33rd Dr.
N PORTLAND BLVD.
NE LOMBARD ST.
NE COLUMBIA BLVD.
Portland
International
Airport
NE MLK Jr. BLVD.
NE KILLINGSWORTH ST.
NE ALBERTA ST.
5
30
NE PRESCOTT ST.
NE 42nd
NE Cully BLVD.
NE 15th AVE.
NE 21st AVE.
NE 33rd AVE.
NE BRODY ST.
NE Weidler St.
NE SANDY BLVD.
213
NE 82nd AVE.
NE HALSEY ST.
205
28th
30
84
E BURNSIDE ST.
NE GLISAN ST.
SE STARK ST.
SE HAWTHORNE
SE 20th AVE.

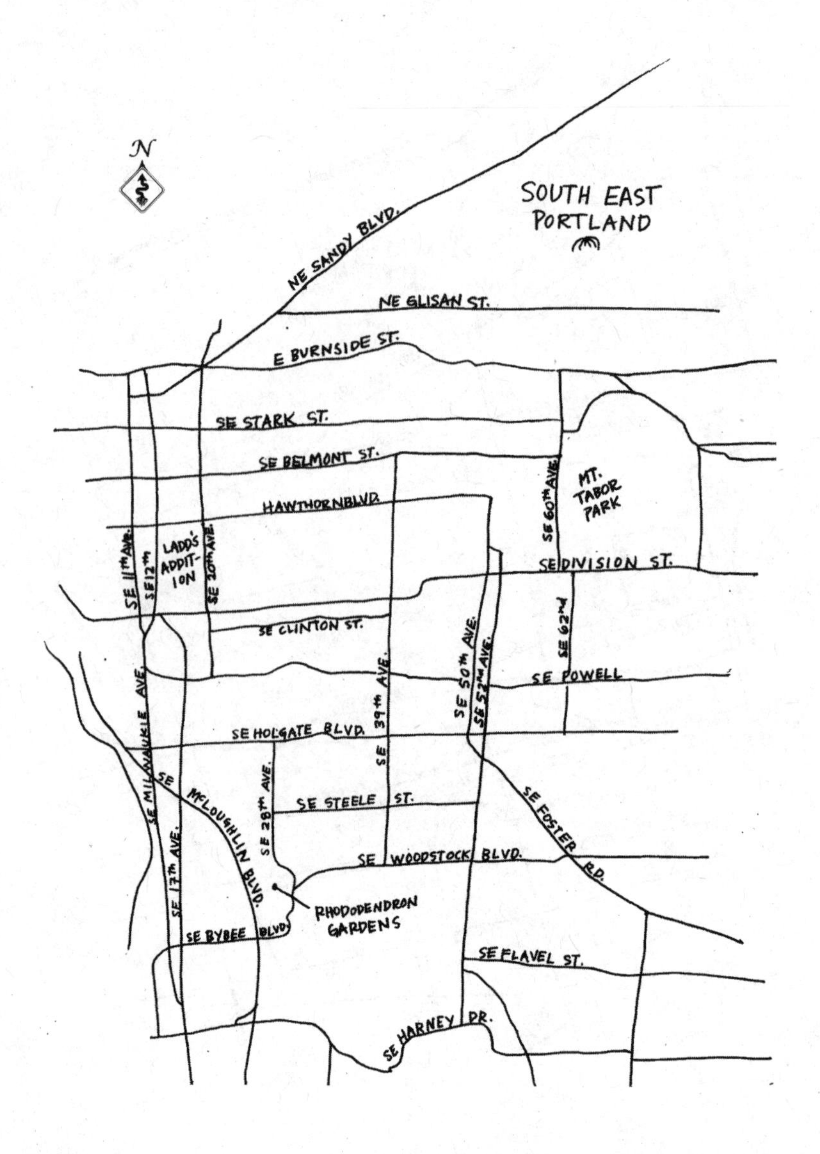
N
SOUTH EAST
PORTLAND
NE SANDY BLVD.
NE GLISAN ST.
E BURNSIDE ST.
SE STARK ST.
SE BELMONT ST.
HAWTHORN BLVD.
SE 60th AVE.
MT. TABOR PARK
SE 11th AVE.
SE 12th
LADD'S ADDITION
SE 20th AVE.
SE DIVISION ST.
SE 62nd
SE CLINTON ST.
SE 50th AVE.
SE 52nd AVE.
SE 39th AVE.
SE POWELL
SE HOLGATE BLVD.
SE MILWAUKIE AVE.
SE McLOUGHLIN BLVD.
SE 28th AVE.
SE STEELE ST.
SE FOSTER RD.
SE 17th AVE.
SE WOODSTOCK BLVD.
RHODODENDRON GARDENS
SE BYBEE BLVD.
SE FLAVEL ST.
SE HARNEY DR.

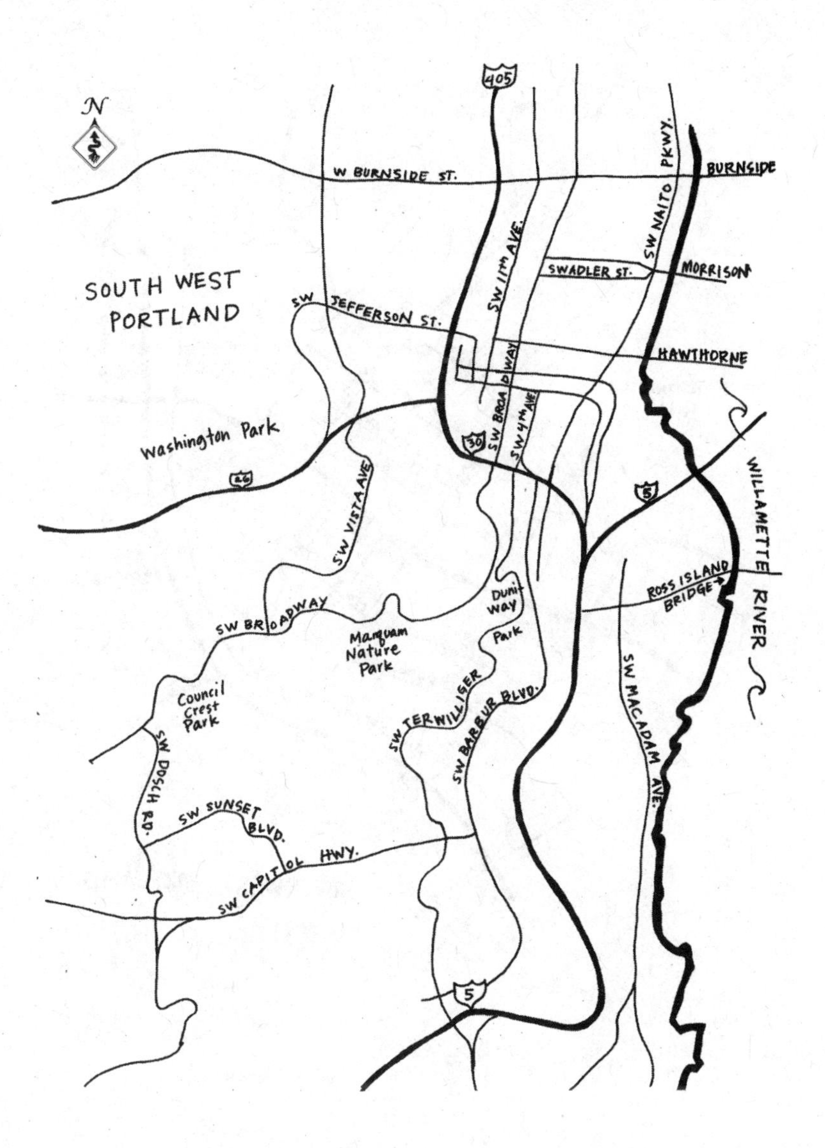
N
W BURNSIDE ST.
BURNSIDE
SW NAITO PKWY.
SW 11th AVE.
SWADLER ST.
MORRISON
SOUTH WEST
PORTLAND
SW JEFFERSON ST.
HAWTHORNE
SW BROADWAY
SW 4th AVE
30
Washington Park
26
5
WILLAMETTE
RIVER
SW VISTA AVE
ROSS ISLAND
BRIDGE
Duniway
Park
SW BROADWAY
Marquam
Nature
Park
Council
Crest
Park
SW TERWILLIGER
SW BARBUR BLVD.
SW MACADAM AVE.
SW DOSCH RD.
SW SUNSET
BLVD.
SW CAPITOL HWY.
5
405

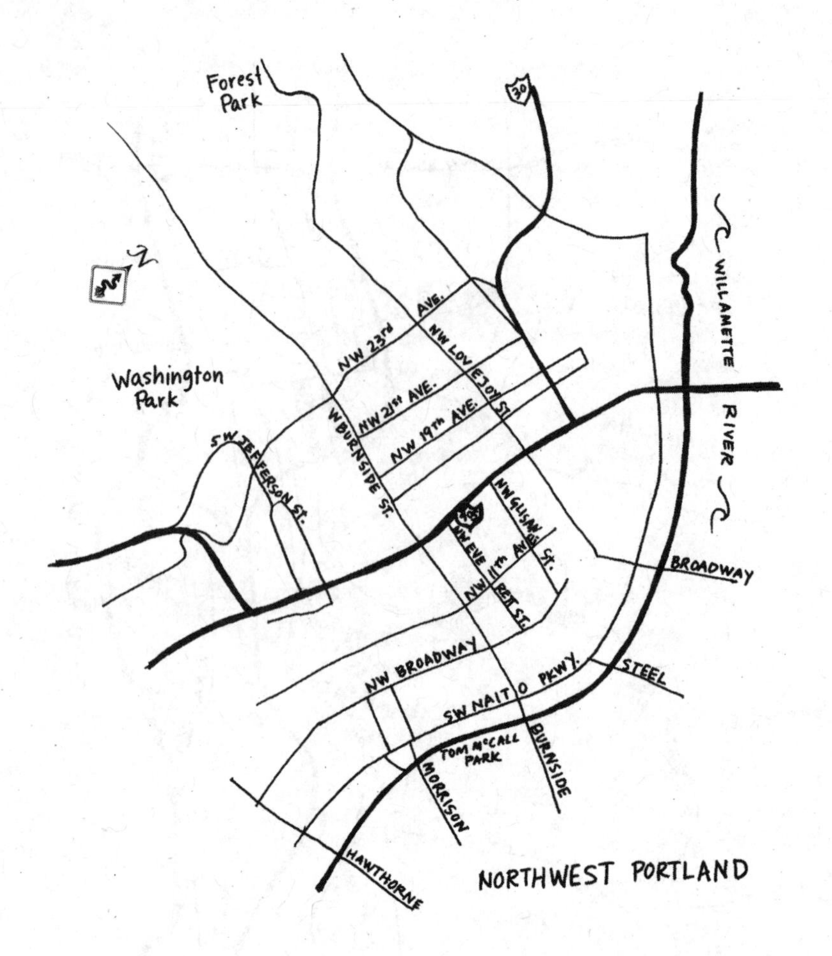
Forest Park
30
Washington Park
NW 23rd AVE.
NW LOVEJOY ST.
NW 21st AVE.
NW 19th AVE.
W BURNSIDE ST.
SW JEFFERSON ST.
NW GLISAN ST.
NW EVERETT ST.
NW 11th AVE.
405
WILLAMETTE RIVER
BROADWAY
NW BROADWAY
SW NAITO PKWY.
STEEL
TOM McCALL PARK
MORRISON
BURNSIDE
HAWTHORNE
NORTHWEST PORTLAND

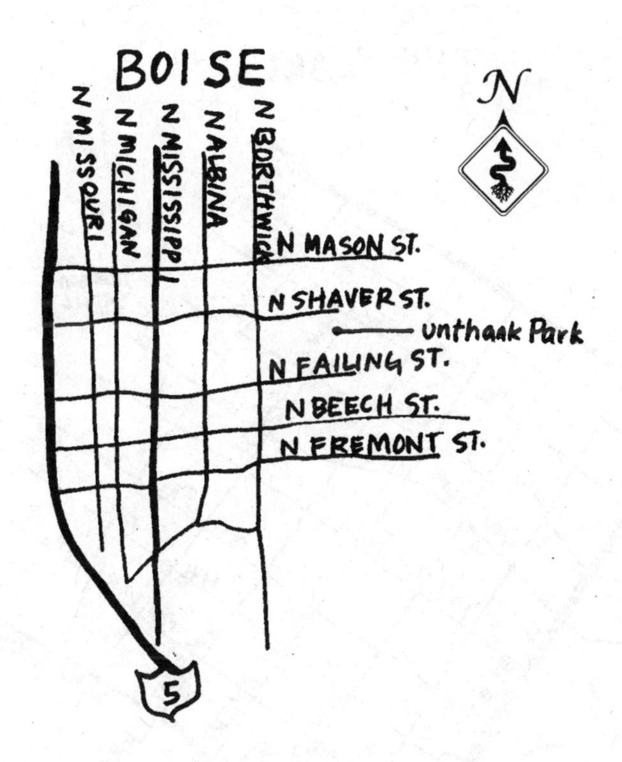
BOISE
N
N MISSOURI
N MICHIGAN
N MISSISSIPPI
N ALBINA
N BORTHWICK
N MASON ST.
N SHAVER ST.
unthaak Park
N FAILING ST.
N BEECH ST.
N FREMONT ST.
5

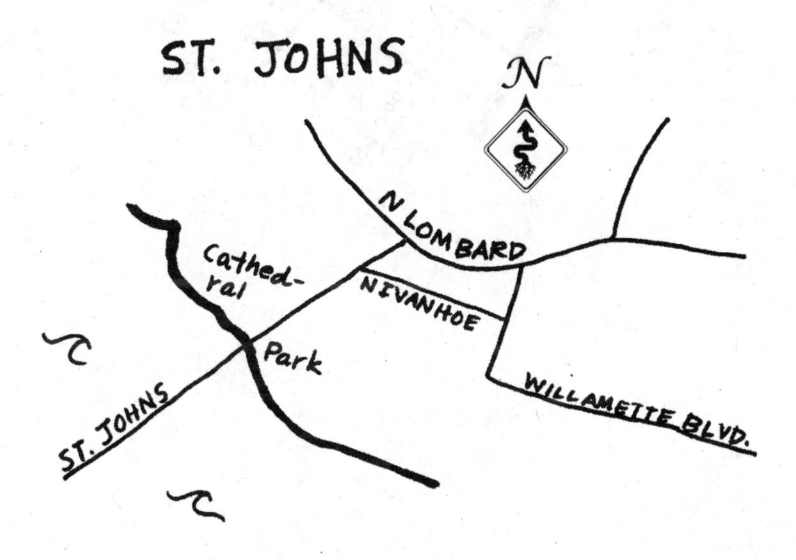
ST. JOHNS
N
N LOMBARD
Cathed-
ral
Park
N IVANHOE
WILLAMETTE BLVD.
ST. JOHNS

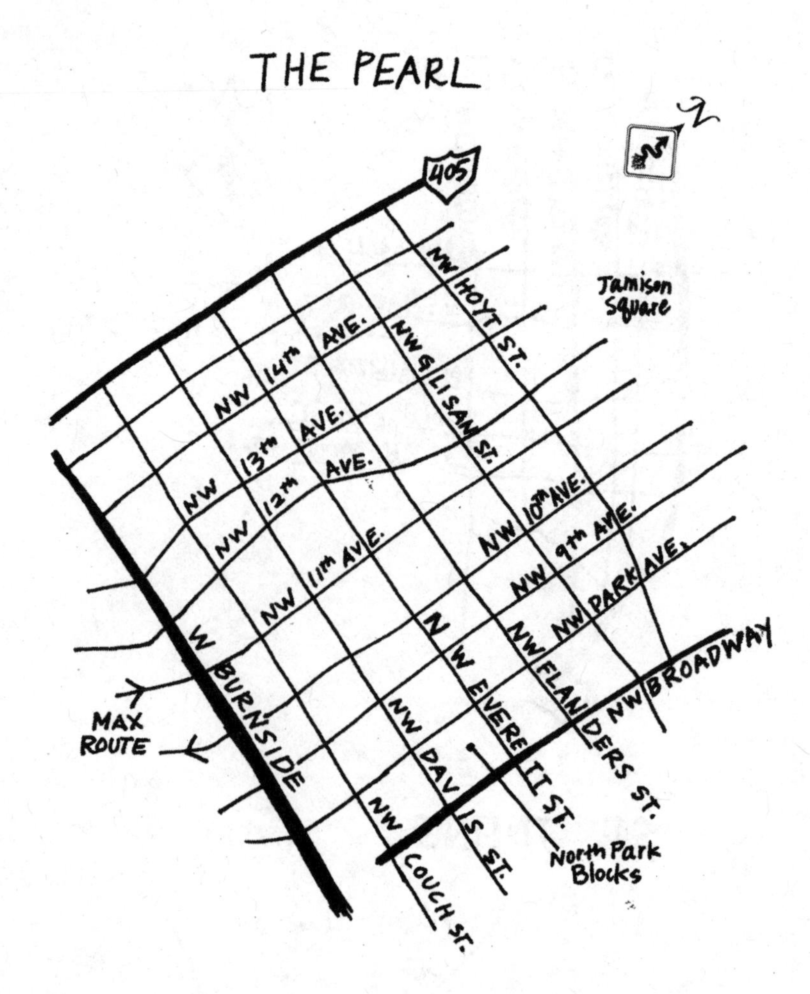
THE PEARL
N
405
NW HOYT ST.
Jamison Square
NW 14th AVE.
NW GLISAN ST.
NW 13th AVE.
NW 12th AVE.
NW 10th AVE.
NW 9th AVE.
NW 11th AVE.
NW PARK AVE.
W BURNSIDE
NW EVERETT ST.
NW FLANDERS ST.
NW BROADWAY
MAX ROUTE
NW DAVIS ST.
NW COUCH ST.
North Park Blocks

Transit Information

Here are some options for travel that include everything from flying to walking. Even we conscientious travelers of the globe must at times make use of transportation options beyond walking! Weigh time, cost, and energy usage to determine which transport choice best suits your needs and the needs of the planet. There is something about the more time-consuming transit that provides a smoother transition to the next spot, though it may take a bit longer. Choose efficient routes to avoid wasting unnecessarily fuel.

Getting Here

Portland is an international destination without the frenzy of a major metropolis. The options below will set you on your way to Portlandia.

Portland International Airport (PDX)

www.flypdx.com

Flying into Portland International Airport (PDX) is a breeze. This place never seems to be crowded, the people who work there are helpful and courteous and the Max train runs right outside baggage claim, ready to scoop you to the city center. There are also shared shuttles that can be hired on the spot. A taxi ride will cost around $30-40 to get you to most places in the center of Portland.

Nearby Sea-Tac Airport

www.portseattle.org/seatac

The Seattle-Tacoma International Airport is about three hours away from Portland, and sometimes there are cheaper flights there. If you are find yourself flying into or out of Sea-Tac, maybe you can score a ride down to Portland on Craigslist. Look under "community," then "rideshare." seattle.craigslist.org or portland.craigslist.org.

Train

800 NW 6th Avenue, Union Station
800.872.7245
503.273.4865, www.amtrak.com

With a big clock tower proclaiming "Go By Train," Union Station is a standout establishment in NW Portland. It is located on the Willamette River and congregates the three Amtrak Train lines that serve the city. The *Coast Starlight* will take passengers all the way from Los Angeles to Seattle, the *Empire Builder* runs a historic route from Portland to Chicago and *Cascades* is a scenic trip from Eugene, OR, to Vancouver, BC. Check Amtrak's website for schedules and rates or call their 800 number. Train-ing from place to place is a great way to utilize eco-friendly public transit while getting to look around you, from a seat with a view not a steering wheel. After a romp in Portland, take the beautiful train route down to Oakland, where you can get fully acquainted with our Soul of the City Next Door, or up to Seattle, the Emerald City, or further north to Vancouver, an open-air city surrounded by lush forests and some of the biggest trees in the world.

Bus

Greyhound
550 NW 6th Avenue, by Union Station
800.231.2222
503.243.2361, www.greyhound.com

Greyhound operates its Portland bus lines into and out of their station located next to Union Station. There are a number of departure and arrival times. Call them up or check out the website for detailed schedules.

Shared Route

800 NW 6th Avenue, Union Station
503.502.5750, www.sharedroute.org

Share Route runs their biodiesel bus from Portland to Seattle and back, passing through Olympia on Fridays, Saturdays and Sundays. Fare is incredibly affordable—only $50 round trip. You're sure to meet some interesting people on board as well!

Driving

Portland is along the I-5 corridor that runs the length of the West Coast, so it is easily accessible to the road tripper. For those arriving from the east, I-84 will get you here. Traffic is not intimidating in the city, so don't be scared to exit off of the safe confines of the highway, find parking, and explore away.

Ride-Share

www.craigslist.org

Craigslist is the online community board of much of the United States and the world. To search the Craigslist of your city, choose from the city list on the right hand side of the page. For the car-less or those seeking to be conscientious carpoolers, Craigslist has a special section under "community" called "rideshare." Often people will post here who are looking for a ride or willing to accommodate passengers. Send a few emails back and forth and have a chat on the good ole telephone to make sure that you are comfortable with the person with whom you will be traveling.

Getting Around

Here's the low-down on your intra-city transit options. Remember, powered transport is plentiful, but city blocks are small in Portland and your own two feet are a viable mechanism to move from one place to the next; this is a walking city. To speed things up, a bicycle is another great alternative with bike routes a-plenty (see **Bike About** chapter).

Portland is mostly on a grid. The Willamette River separates Portland into east and west and Burnside Street separates north and south. Streets running north to south are generally numbered, with numbers increasing as you head east from the river on the east side and west from the river on the west side. Streets are alphabetical as you head north from Burnside (Burnside, Couch, Davis, etc). Check out our maps and locator icons to help get your bearings.

Jay's Garage

734 SE 7th Avenue at SE Morrison Street
239.5167
Open: M-F 7a-7p, Sa 8a-6p
Jay's fills up many ancient Mercedes and sporty Volkswagons with SeQuential Biofuels biodiesel.

TriMet

www.trimet.org
The public transportation arm of Portland is TriMet. In charge of the bus line, Max light rail and streetcar, TriMet keeps the city running and is constantly working on sustainable initiatives, such as alternative fuel for their buses and community development projects. Their online Trip Planner on the homepage of **www.trimet.org** will draw from bus and train options to bring you to your destination efficiently.

A fare of $1.70 will cover most areas (two zones) and can be paid in exact change right on the buses or from ticket vending machines at Max stations. Fares can also be purchased at grocery stores around town. Transfers between buses and trains are good for one hour on weekdays and two on weekends. The "Fareless Square" covers downtown and extends over the Steel Bridge into the Lloyd District. You get a free ride on all lines, buses, the Max, and the Streetcar as long as you are staying within those boundaries!

Bus

With the largest web of lines among Portland's public transport options, there is most likely a bus to get you to where you want to go. This is always a great way to see a nice slice of the city's inhabitants, as buses draw all walks of life. TriMet has fueled many of their buses with biodiesel and is working on more hybrid options as well, so the already sustainable choice of mass transport is becoming even more environmentally friendly.

Max Light Rail

The Max is a way to get to those outer limit destinations. The Max Red Line will bring you and your luggage from the airport to downtown Portland, and the Yellow Line will shoot you up to events at the Expo Center. If the 'burbs are calling your name, the Max also has lines to Beaverton, Hillsboro, and Gresham.

Streetcar

The Streetcar travels between Legacy Good Samaritan Hospital in the Northwest, Portland State University in the Southwest, and the South Waterfront. With much of the line contained within the Fareless Square, this can be an affordable option for the passengers staying in the downtown area. Riding the Streetcar all the way to the South Waterfront will take you to the new Aerial Tram that connects the waterfront and OHSU Center for Health & Healing with the Oregon Health & Science University (OHSU) Marquam Campus.

Portland Aerial Tram

www.portlandtram.org

Oregon Health & Science University (OHSU) and the city partnered to construct and operate this prominent structure that crosses over I-5, and opened its use to the public at the beginning of 2007. Meant to provide a transport option for OHSU patients, students, and researchers, it has also become a destination of its own for the sheer quirkiness of being an aerial tram, and for the view it offers. Take a ride if you want to revel in this unique experience, and get up the SE hill without guzzling gas or resorting to voodoo to find a parking spot.

Flexcar

www.flexcar.com

If a car is simply a must-have for excursions to the city limits or beyond, Portland has Flexcar. This is a national company with at least 10 other cities in their service area. Flexcar is a car share group that serves as an alternative to car ownership, business fleets, and car rental. They do not claim to be a cheaper alternative to renting a car, but they claim convenience (usually there is a Flexcar to be picked up within a five minute walk from your current location), affordability (you pay by the hour, not by the day), lower age requirements (21 years of age and older), and sustainability (they sport hybrids and ultra-low emissions vehicles). Membership is required ($35 one time fee), and the application process can take up to one week, so planning ahead is required.

Resources

Online:

www.portlandpicks.com

This fun-loving website is a weekly update of Portland's newest and coolest shops and inspirations. Check back every Friday for the freshest take on this Rosy City!

www.portlandfoodanddrink.com

Written by honest-to-goodness food lovers, this rather comprehensive and regularly updated blog gives you more opinions on bars and restaurants citywide.

Fresh and Local Blog

http://freshlocalfoods.blogspot.com
A blog for buying local produce, baked goods, wine and cheese.

Green Building Resource

www.portlandonline.com/OSD
One of the projects of the Office of Sustainable Development, this helpful assembledge of information and services gets architects, builders, home-buyers, renters, and land lords more savvy on what they can do to benefit the environment. The LEED certified buildings around town are Green Building Resource groupies! It's all what they call G/Rated, after all!

Portland Chamber of Commerce

200 SW Market Street
224.8684, www.portlandalliance.com

Oregon Business Information

www.stateoforegon.com

Alternative Portland

www.altportland.com/visit
A blog with useful information and some interesting opinion pieces, Alt Portland is focused primarily on Southeast Portland.

Portland Business Alliance, Portland Development Commission

www.pdc.com
For further business information, services and conference support, look up the Portland Business Alliance and their programs.

City of Portland

www.portlandonline.com
All the info on Portland Parks and citywide events and celebrations can be found on this fully-updated website. The city of Portland does an amazing job of organizing information in a useful way, something I rarely see done so well on a city website.

Shopping:

The Virtuous Comsumer

www.thevirtuousconsumer.com
Make each purchase an environmentally and socially responsible one with help from Leslie Garret's blog.

The Chinook Book, $20

www.celilio.net
The Chinook Book is a resource for the coupon-lover in all of us. Look through this book, which can be purchased at many places around town including New Seasons Markets, and you'll find a way to save money doing something good for your body, and good for your family, good for the planet.

ReDirect Guide

www.redirectguide.com
A free directory of Portland's sustainable businesses. Available in many retail locations.

General Information:

Multnomah County Library

Multiple Locations
988.5234, www.multcolib.org
One of the best public library systems in the country.

Small Business Administration

601 SW 2nd Avenue, Suite 950
326.2682, www.sba.gov

Just like every other US city, the SBA is a wonderful resource where classes, information and workshops empower visitors and residents. Being enterprising is so freeing! If you have any business service needs or questions, start your search for entrepreneurship at the SBA.

Portland Business Alliance, Portland Development Commission

www.pdc.com

For further business information, services and conference support, look up the Portland Business Alliance and their programs.

Portland Oregon Visitors Association

701 SW 6th Avenue
275.8355, www.travelportland.com
Open: M-F 8:30a-5:30a, Sa 10a-4p

Newspapers:

The Oregonian

www.oregonlive.com/Oregonian

The statewide newspaper is rather Portland-centric in its local news, and covers major stories and local, community oriented tales with equal gusto. Read it and you'll be able to get through a day's worth of conversations with locals, many of whom read it front to back every morning.

The Portland Tribune

www.portlandtribune.com

Another everyday paper, the Trib is both mocked and adored. It is most notable for being free and available at nearly all bus stops.

Willamette Week

www.wweek.com

The Willy Week is a free weekly paper available in paper boxes and coffee shops. New editions arrive every Wednesday featuring editorials and events around town.

The Portland Mercury

www.portlandmercury.com

The Mercury is another free weekly paper available in paper boxes and coffee shops. New editions arrive every Thursday. A bit more irreverent than the Willy Week; focusing on satirical blurbs and also listing the week's happenings.

Just Out

www.justout.com

This free weekly features articles and events surrounding GLBT life in Portland and is available in paper boxes and coffee shops.

Street Roots

www.streetroots.org

This donation-based newspaper addresses poverty and homelessness. Distributed outside of many retail locations.

Jewish Review of Portland

www.jewishreview.org

A free semi-monthly publication focusing on the Jewish community.

Television:

Oregon Public Broadcasting, Channel 10

www.opb.org

Portland's local public television station—all the Charlie Rose you can handle!

KATU, Channel 2

www.katu.com

Local news and mainstream sitcoms are the name of the game.

Radio:

Portland Radio Guide

www.pdxradio.com

All the information you need for both the FM and AM dials can be found on this site. Tune in to Portland!

KBOO, 90.7 FM
www.kboo.fm
Portland's source for alternative news.

KOPB, 94.7 FM
www.opb.org
Oregon Public Broadcasting station.

KMHD, 89.1 FM
www.kmhd.org
Great jazz, blue and NPR news.

Further Reading

The Portland Bridge Book
by: Sharon Wood Wortman, $24.95

The Zinester's Guide to Portland
ed. Shawn Granton, $5

City of Readers: The Book Lovers Guide to Portland
ed. Gabriel H. Boehmer, $15.95

Reading Portland: The City in Prose
ed. John Trombold and Peter Donahue, $26.95

Fugitives and Refugees: A Walk in Portland, Oregon
by: Chuck Palahniuk, $16.95

City Limits: Walking Portland's Boundary
by: David Oats, $18.95

Portland Monthly Magazine
Available at most news stands

For International Visitors

Welcome—we hope you love Portland a much as we do!

Required Documents

Before you plan to travel to the United States, contact your country's nearest U.S. Embassy or Consulate to determine the necessary documents required for travel to the U.S. You may be required to obtain a visa, passport or to pass certain health requirements, so allow enough time before your desired departure date to obtain this information. Visit **www.usa.gov** for more information for visitors to the U.S.

Customs

You must complete customs and immigrations formalities at your first point of arrival into the United States, whether or not it is your final destination. At this point you will speak with a customs officer and present your forms and documentation.

Travel Insurance

The U.S. has no compulsory government travel insurance plan. It is advisable to purchase private travel and health insurance.

Electricity

The standard electrical current in the U.S. is 110 volts. Most outlets accept two or three pronged plugs. Laptops and other electronic devices should be equipped with a power converter.

Currency

There are a number of large banks that will exchange your foreign currency to U.S. dollars. If you are arriving to the U.S. via an airport, most international airports have exchange bureaus located right at the airport. Portland Airport's currency exchange is called *Travelex,* and it is located in the ticket lobby. Powell's City of Books (see **Explore** chapter) is one of this nations few stores that accepts many foreign currencies!

Here are some banks that will exchange into U.S. dollars:

Wells Fargo Bank

3782 SE Hawthorne Boulevard
800.869.3557
www.wellsfargo.com

Washington Mutual

811 SW 6th Avenue
238.3100
www.wamu.com

Bank of America

3967 NE Sandy Boulevard
275.1301
www.bankofamerica.com

Emergencies

The City of Portland updates its Basic Emergency Operations Plan (BEOP) annually to ensure preparedness for any disaster. There are many emergency resources to support an urgent situation, for English speakers or non-English speakers. There are few natural disasters that can befall Portland; flooding and windstorms are the greatest threats, and earthquakes are an extremely rare occurrence. Mt. Helens is far enough away, and dormant enough not to be considered a volcanic threat.

Emergency Contact Information

Dial 9-1-1 on your phone to stop a crime in progress, report a fire, or call for an ambulance due to a pressing medical emergency. Like most cities, there are a limited number of emergencies that the 9-1-1 lines can attend to at a given time, so determine how urgent your situation is. The Portland 9-1-1 Emergency Communications accommodates the hearing impaired with TTY and foreign language speakers with the AT&T Language Line, which is able to provide translation for over 170 languages.

9-1-1 from Cell Phones

If you are dialing 9-1-1 from your cell phone, you will be connected to highway patrol and need to provide the dispatcher with details about the location of the emergency, your cell phone number, and, as always, the nature of the emergency. The location of cell phone calls cannot necessarily be determined like landline calls can, and sometimes calls can be cut off. If this is the case, call back. If you are in a moving vehicle, stop driving so as to not distance yourself from the location of the emergency. Check with your provider if there is a different emergency number you must dial from your phone.

Know Your Non-Number

Often incidences do not require the immediacy of a 9-1-1 call. For Portland and Multnomah County, the non-emergency number is **503.823.3333**.

City and State Emergency Departments

Here is the contact information for some important city and state emergency resources. Their websites are quite informative and may help you find the information you are looking for:

Portland Fire, Rescue and Emergency Services

283.3700
www.portlandonline.org/fire

Portland Police Bureau

823.4636
www.portlandonline.org/police

City of Portland Office of Emergency Management

823.4375
www.portlandonline.com/oem

State of Oregon Office of Emergency Management

378.2911
www.oregon.gov/omd/oem

Hospitals and Clinics:

Providence Medical Group Gateway Immediate Care Clinic

1321 NE 99th Avenue, Suite 100
215.9900
www.providence.org/oregon

Legacy Good Samaritan Hospital

Main Entrance: 1015 NW 22nd Avenue at 22nd and Marshall Street
Emergency Entrance: on NW 23rd between Marshall and Northrup Streets
413.7711
www.legacyhealth.org

Portland St. Vincent Medical Center

9205 SW Barnes Road, off of Sunset Highway 26 and Highway 217
216.1234
www.providence.org/oregon

Providence Milwaukie Hospital

10150 SE 32nd Avenue
513.8300
www.providence.org/Oregon

Top Picks

Mississippi Studios

Portland has a vibrant music culture, and Mississippi Studios is where many new artists bubble up and realize the full extent of their talents. Seeing an intimate and inspiring show here is your opportunity to say, "I saw it first." In short, we just love this place. *sb*

Pix Patisserie

OK, I'll admit that GrassRoutes writers are happy they are not allergic to chocolate, so if you are, I apologize sincerely because Pix creates the most alluring and passionate chocolate creations. There's a reason they've won competitions, even against the French. And if you can't partake in cocoa, Pix still miraculously has you covered when it comes to the best desserts in town. We beg you, go here, and if you bring a friend along, they'll be forever adoring. *sb*

Laurelhurst Park

In a city where green space is highly valued, this park outdoes them all. Let's make a list: it's beautiful, there are trails, paved and unpaved, sport courts for various games, picnic set-ups by a pond, hilly views… On any given day, there may well be someone from GrassRoutes frolicking here—we just can't help it! *sb*

Kennedy School

The idea of a great cult flick, sipping a beer and just relaxing without moving an inch would have been too thrilling to entertain during high school algebra. But now we can all fulfill our dreams of beer in the schoolhouse on the comfy sofas at Kennedy School. Stop studying, we command you! *sb*

The Farm Café

We always wind up choosing The Farm for dinner out. Even after tasting a city of food (well, several cities at this point), this place has just the right atmosphere, beautiful dishes, a warm and cuddly feel, chocolate soufflé from heaven, and it isn't nearly as expensive as other restaurants in its category. *sb*

Powell's City of Books

There's just nothing like a city block of books. We know we are a bit biased being book writers, but trust me, no matter what your passion, you'll ignite it here. Powell's is what everyone thinks of when they think Portland, and that's OK by us. *sb*

Mt. Hood

When the clouds part, you'll see Mt. Hood towering over Portland, gracing the city with its snow-capped presence. We love being in a place where nature seems so close, so we trek over there as much as possible for winter sports fun, even in the spring. While you're skiing, snowboarding, or snowshoeing around, you can take a reverse glimpse of the Rosy City. *sb*

Redux Reinventions

Here's the story: something breaks, we use up its contents, we simply don't want it anymore, so we throw it out and overflow the landfill. That cycle is broken at Redux, where the discarded becomes the desirable. Get bags, earrings, and generally cute things for life without adding to the trash pile. Pure genius. *sb*

Vendetta

I used to think that bars were where ghosts duked out unresolved issues. Vendetta may be where they get it over with, but let's just say they leave pretty quickly, 'cause this place is too friendly for ghosts. Its cozy feel and friendly atmosphere make it fun for drinkers and non-drinkers alike. It is just a great place to hang out in a bountiful garden without getting dirt under your nails. *sb*

Hollywood Theater

The beautiful mosaics and historic feel bring back memories of the classic movie-going experience. But Hollywood also hosts the best film events in town and is a creative enclave for film students, youth with artistic passion, and a general ambiance of inspiration. Go for a film, but plan for a complete adventure into the world of cinema, brought to you by those who are committed to keeping it quality. *sb*

Hot Lips Pizza

Hot Lips is great pizza that cares. (We know we're corny, but we're also hungry.) They deliver fast, have excellent choices for even the pickiest of eaters and bottle their own grape soda that goes perfectly with a hot slice or one of their huge salads. They are serious about investing in environmental concerns, bringing back bees, using renewable energy, and creating unbeatable community feel. All that and a big, cheesy slice of pizza. *sb*

Malay Satay Hut

Before eating here, we thought, "Malasian cuisine, what's that?" Or maybe, too bad for us, we just didn't consider it. That's all changed now; Malay Satay Hut wins the award for the most wonderful can't fail menu, and easiest way to go to South East Asia without flying. Tropical fruits, saucy dishes, unique meals fit for the king and queen—it is all here. Don't leave Portland without eating here. Trust us. *sb*

Albina Press and Palio's

It's a tie, folks. We're split on our favorite coffee spot. Albina Press is a city place, packed with cool folks who are serious about the divine coffee served up hot cup by cup. Palio's is a cozy spot where one could linger for hours in a Windsor-back chair with a good book and a slice of cake. They're two totally different ways to enjoy a cup of joe, so why not try both? This is Portland, after all, a place driven by the quality coffee craze. *sb*

Portland Calendar

Swine and Wine Dinner Series

Once a month, Olea
Various locations
www.olearestaurant.com

Each month a different chef dives into a new kitchen with the mission to create the best four-course pig menu he or she can. Bring a bottle of your own choice vintage, or trust their pairing judgment as you venture just a little way out of Portland for this big meal. *sb*

Rivercity Bluegrass

First Weekend of January
Oregon Convention Center, 777 NE MLK Jr. Boulevard
224.8499

The premier bluegrass festival of the Northwest sets up shop in Portland every year. Acts like Emmylou Harris and Asleep At The Wheel grace two stages, in addition to workshop offerings and instrument sales. *sb*

O Shogatsu New Year's Celebration

Second Sunday of January, 1-3p
Japanese Garden, 611 SW Kingston Avenue
223.1321, www.japanesegarden.com

The biggest family day and celebration of the year in Japan is New Year's, so come experience a bit of the excitement for yourself in Portland. Ornaments, games, music, and special foods create the perfect atmosphere to ring in the New Year. So sip some sake and shout "O-shogatsu!" *sb*

Oregon Seafood and Wine Festival at Oregon Convention Center

First weekend of February, F 12-10p, Sa 11a-9p
777 NE MLK Jr. Boulevard
360.210.5275

The earliest in the year of many Portland food and wine festivals, this one gets going during Dungeness crab season. Taste the famous local pinots and some hearty seafood concoctions, all to the sounds of regional music. *sb*

Hollywood Luxe

First weekend of February
Hollywood Theater, 4122 NE Sandy Boulevard
www.filmaction.org

Film Action Oregon hosts this student and emerging clothes designer competition where the 15 finalists have their designs modeled down the catwalk. Come see Portland's local fashions go fabulous with these elegant eveningwear collections. *sb*

Annual Chocolate Festival at the World Forestry Center

February, the weekend before Valentine's Day, Sa-Su 11a-5p
4033 SW Canyon Road
228.1367, www.worldforestry.org

The trees in the museum get covered in chocolate ornaments, surrounded by chocolate vendors displaying everything from truffles to chocolate-based facial masks. Learn how to mold chocolate into your own imaginative shapes! *sb*

Portland Jazz Festival

Second week of February
Various locations
228.5299, www.pdxjazz.com

Shuffle down Broadway for this complete festival of jazz performers young and old, novice and Grammy winning. Throughout the week concerts get going at various venues downtown. *sb*

Portland International Film Festival

Two weeks of February
Hosted by the Northwest Film Center at various locations
221.1156, www.nwfilm.org

The predecessor of Portland's vibrant film festival scene, this collection brings together a large number of international screenings from over 30 countries. The opening night is one of the best film parties I've been to. *sb*

Oscar Night America

Oscar Night, usually the end of February
Hollywood Theater, 4122 NE Sandy Boulevard
281.4215, www.hollywoodtheater.org

Get off your sofa and come enjoy America's shining star film night on the big screen. All proceeds go to Film Action Oregon, one of Oregon's premier art advocacy and teaching non-profits. *sb*

Taste of Tillamook County

Second Weekend of March, F 5-9p, Sa 10a-9p, Su 11a-3p
Tillamook County Fair Grounds
842.2236

Multnomah's neighbor county is a culinary destination in its own right, as evidenced in this yearly gathering of professional chefs, clam chowder and oyster maniacs, foodies, and music lovers. Don't miss the timed oyster shucking contest or a front row seat to the "Black Box" cooking competition. *sb*

St. Patrick's Day Festivities

March 17, 1-9p
Holy Rosary Church, 376 NE Clackamas Road
691.2078

A solid tradition in Portland, all ages take part in the St. Paddy's Day celebration. It is far more than just good beer, of which there is plenty: there are Irish bands, folk dancing classes, hot corned beef, and a raffle. *sb*

Oregon Arbor Week

End of March thru the beginning of April, everyday, 10a-5p
World Forestry Center, 4033 SW Canyon Road
228.1367, www.worldforestry.org
Guided hikes, tree classes, tree plantings, and lessons on environmental stewardship make this a classic family outing and a chance to be a little more knowledgeable on the important variety of trees. *sb*

Party for the Planet

Earth Day, April, 12-4p
Oregon Zoo, 4001 SW Canyon Road
226.1561, www.oregonzoo.org
Celebrate Earth Day alongside all the animals with arts and crafts projects and demonstrations on easy, fun ways to give back to our planet. *sb*

Wordstock at Oregon Convention Center

Third weekend of April
777 NE MLK Jr. Boulevard
546.1012, www.wordstockfestival.com
Don't miss this annual literary extravaganza, featuring exhibitors, workshops, over 250 authors, a short fiction competition, and much more. *dl*

Spring Plant Sales at Berry Botanic Garden and Japanese Gardens

Last Saturday of April
Berry Botanic Garden, 11a-3p, 11505 SW Summerville Avenue, 636.4112
Japanese Garden, 10a-3p, 611 SW Kingston Avenue, 223.1321
Get ready to plant your garden by making your rounds at these two coinciding plants sales. At Berry Botanic Garden, you'll find distinct varieties of plants, and native species not easily found at regular nurseries. At the Japanese Garden, there are Asian natives including a rainbow of peonies, camellias, and hydrangea, not to mention Bonsai, Japanese maples, and conifers. *sb*

Astronomy Day and Equinox Star Parties

April 21st, and during vernal and summer equinox
Rooster Rock State Park
www.omsi.edu/visit/planetarium/starparties

Climb up to Rooster Rock to share a view from all manner of telescopes and binoculars of the night sky and the planets of our solar system. Professionals will be there to talk about what you are looking at and guide the experience. *sb*

VegFest

Spring
Location varies
224.7380, www.nwveg.org

Vegetarianism and veganism are all the rage! Jump on board for some helpful tips and head to VegFest, put on every spring by Northwest Veg. There are lectures, cooking workshops, and scrumptious samples. *dm*

Spring Beer & Wine Fest

Spring
777 NE MLK Jr. Boulevard
www.springbeerfest.com

Portland's reputation for having the most microbreweries per capita in the country is showcased at the Spring Beer and Wine Fest. If hundreds of beers aren't enough incentive, you'll find plenty of local vintners, distillers, and cheese makers. *dl*

Taste of the Nation

Last Sunday of April, 6:30-9:30p
Oregon Convention Center, 777 NE MLK Jr. Boulevard
222.4644

All the top chefs of Portland close down shop at their own restaurants and head to the Rose Quarter for this annual feast. A plethora of flavors to tempt any palate match up with local wines and microbrews, all to the beat of live music and a not-so-silent auction. *sb*

Doggie Dash

May
Location varies
285.7722, www.oregonhumane.org/doggiedash

You and your best friend can feel like champions when you participate in this annual fundraising doggie run for the Oregon Humane Society. Portland wasn't rated one of the most humane cities for nothing. *dl*

Pug Crawl

May
Location varies
285.7722, www.oregonhumane.org/pugcrawl

The world's largest gathering of pugs is right here in Portland, complete with a parade and pug kissing booth. Keep it weird! Where's the poodle crawl? *dl*

UFO Festival

May
McMenamins Hotel Oregon, McMinnville
www.ufofest.com

True believer or no, this annual event honoring the famous Trent sighting of 1950, is just plain strange fun. Join in the parade or talk it up with scientists about fact and fiction. *dl*

Forest Film Festival

First weekend of May
www.forestfilmfest.com

Featuring short films from up-and-coming filmmakers, this local festival is a treasure trove of great new flicks and unexpected themes from young directors and writers. It is growing in popularity for good reason. *sb*

Cinco De Mayo Fiesta

First weekend of May, Th-Sa 11a-11:30p, Su 11a-11:30p
Tom McCall Waterfront, SW Naito Parkway at Columbia Street
232.7550

Local crafts people line this riverside park and host live dance shows, musical performances, Mariachi, rides, a carnival celebration, and, like the cherry on the sundae, fireworks over the water. *sb*

Portland Indie Wine Festival at Urban Wine Works

First Weekend of May, Sa-Su 3-6p
407 NW 16th Avenue
595.0891, www.indiewinefestival.com

A stellar collection of craft wineries that produce less than 2000 cases a year make it a point to maintain style and sustainability. Rising stars and popular cellars strut their stuff for chefs and locals alike. *sb*

Annual Shell Show

Mid-May
OMSI, 1945 SE Water Avenue
797.4000, www.omsi.edu

The world's bounty is laid out each year at Oregon Museum of Science and Industry (OMSI) in shells. Come learn about these interesting formations and mingle with top conchologists from near and far. *sb*

Alberta Art Hop

Third Saturday of May
Alberta Street
www.artonalberta.org

The Alberta 'hood teams with artistry, especially during the Art Hop when the thoroughfare is dominated with creativity's invigorating presence. The hop is more like a parade that boasts wackiness of all varieties. Plus your ears won't be jealous of your eyes—cool music completes the inspiring atmosphere. *dm*

Living Green Expo

Second Weekend of May, Sa-Su 9:30a-5:30p
OMSI, 1945 SE Water Avenue
797.6674, www.omsi.edu

Providing information, resources and motivation for a more earth-friendly lifestyle, this annual collage of green ideas is a must-see. Booths and workshops clutter OMSI's floors for this event, a perfect way to celebrate Mother's Day by honoring the mother of all mothers: Mother Earth. Bring in your used batteries and old electronics for recycling. *sb*

Zompire Film Fest

Second weekend of May
Various locations
800.494.8497, www.zompire.com

The "Undead Film Festival" is taking over Portland by storm, but could that be just what the zombies and vampires want? Let's just say the GR illustrator is glued to the screen this time of year, as zombies take over his brain—though we think he likes it that way. Your ticket gets you an all day pass to these startling cult films. *sb*

Mother's Day at the Crystal Springs Rhododendron Garden Plant Sale

Mother's Day weekend
SE 28th Avenue at Woodstock Boulevard

The full bloom of Portland's treasured rhododendrons are on beautiful display for mothers on this weekend, and there is even an opportunity to purchase some plants as gifts. The cost is $3 to enter the garden—worth it for the flowers as well as the serene paths and fountains. *dm*

Sunday Afternoon Summer Concerts

May thru September
Various locations, Columbia Gorge vicinity
509.427.7047, www.skamaniaarts.org

Throughout the summer, the Skamania Performing Arts Foundation hosts a number of Sunday afternoon events ranging from Taiko performances to piano recitals. Most are held in Washington State, across Columbia River. Find detailed schedule information online. *dm*

Festival of Quilts

First week of June
Univeristy Place Hotel, 310 SW Lincoln Street at 4th Avenue
222.1991, www.northwestquilters.org

Put on each year by the Northwest's diverse group of quilter afficionados, this quilt show and expo brings together a close-knit community of skilled craftspeople and takes you on a tour of the history of this American art form. *sb*

Waterfront Village

First week of June
Tom McCall Waterfront Park, SW Naito Parkway and Columbia Street
www.rosefestival.org/events/waterfrontvillage

What better way to kick off the summer than with a good old-fashioned carnival experience, complete with cotton candy and pirate shenanigans? Pick up some locally made crafts in between funnel cake snacking and a ride on the salt-and-pepper shaker. *dl*

Portland Queer Documentary Festival

First weekend of June
Clinton Street Theater, 2522 SE Clinton Street at 21st Avenue
www.queerdocfest.org

Get ready for one of the premier documentary film festivals in this city of film festivals. A vast array of subject matter, presented both tamely and flamboyantly, lights up the screen. Chat it up between flicks at the theater's cafe. *sb*

Rose Festival

First two weeks of June
Various locations
227.2681, www.rosefestival .org

The Starlight Parade, Dragon Boat races, the crowning of the Rose Queen, fireworks, and an onslaught of civic pride infuse this time of the year with many chances at free and fun entertainment. There are numerous events that the whole family will enjoy, so bring the kiddies! My personal favorite is the rose show, where you can choose from a large selection of rose bushes to bring home. *dm*

Pedalpalooza

Middle two weeks of June
Various locations
www.shift2bikes.org

Maybe it's the endorphins released from bike exercise that inspire individuality, but there are some seriously inventive bike folk around town. SHIFT embraces this phenomenon and invites two-wheelers to put together two weeks of unique rides around the city. Naked Bike Ride, Karaoke 2 Karaoke Ride, and Slow Poke Pastry Patrol are just a few of 2007's rides. Who knows what creative cruising will grace the docket of this year's Pedalpalooza? *dm*

Lake Oswego Festival for the Arts

Last weekend of June
368 South State Street, Lake Oswego
636.1060, www.lakewood-center.org

Fine art comes outside and into George Rogers Park, where you can stroll by booths interspersed with breathtaking views of the Willamette River. Bring the whole crew to view paintings, sculptures, and special exhibits of computer art, collage, and modern installations while taking in sounds of local musicians, and eating equally artful cuisine. *sb*

World Music Wednesday Concerts at Oregon Zoo

Wednesdays, late June thru August
Oregon Zoo in Washington Park
www.oregonzoo.org/concerts

Reserve a spot on the lawn, bring a blanket and let the music transport you around the world with something different each Wednesday evening. *dl*

Oregon Lavender Festival

Early July
Portland and outskirts
662.4488, www.oregonlavenderfestival.org

The Oregon Lavender Festival is a celebration not only of lavender, but also of artisan works. With farms participating from Yamhill to West Linn to Sauvie Island, there is an event near you and some lavender waiting to be cut. *dm*

North American Organic Brewers Festival

Early July
Various locations
www.naobf.org

In case you hadn't heard, craft beer brewing is big in Portland and organic brewing takes that art and raises it to the eco-friendly level. This festival is free to enter, with costs per taste. Sip pesticide-free brews on the scene. *dm*

Portland Highland Games

Mid-July
Various locations
www.phga.org

Traditional highland games include athletics, dancing, music, and food, with a hearty scoop of competition, whether on this side of the pond or not. For literally thousands of years, fans have gotten rowdy watching the heavy-weight events and hollering for their favorite pipers and drummers as they duke it out for number one. This is a popular festival for a reason, so don't miss it. You are probably itching to know what the Scottish Hammer is, what they do with the 96-pound Portland Stone, or what it means to "Caber Toss." I'll give you a hint—there's a 120 pound spruce tree involved. *sb*

Oregon Brewers Festival

Last weekend of July
Tom McCall Waterfront Park, SW Naito Parkway at Columbia Street
778.5917, www.oregonbrewfest.com

Craft breweries freckle the city as though they were Irish lasses in summertime. So it follows that such a mecca would draw the finest craft brews for three days of sampling for public enjoyment. This is a non-judged event, and is celebrated solely in reverence for the art and, clearly, for opportune daytime boozing—priceless. *dm*

PDX Pop Now!

End of July, beginning of August
616.4433, www.pdxpopnow.com

In case you hadn't heard, Portland has some long, rainy winter months! Though this characteristic has its downside (seasonal depression disorder, knitting obsession, etc.) a happy side effect is coping with the creation of great music. PDX Pop Now! brings city bands to the public for free for a weekend of rockin' delight. You might just discover the next best thing at this showcase. *dm*

Mt. Hood Jazz Festival

First weekend of August
200 NE Hood Avenue, Downtown Gresham
661.2700, www.mthoodjazz.org

Just outside of Portland, the suburb of Gresham hosts the annual Mt. Hood Jazz Festival. Take I-84 east to exit 16 and you can catch some smooth styling with affordable tickets that range from $10-35. *dm*

Homowo African Storytelling

August
Washington Park
288.3025, www.homowo.org

Sharing the folk story traditions of Ghana, West Africa, Homowo offers an opportunity to glimpse and celebrate the customs of a culture many miles away from the City of Roses. *sb*

Bridge Pedal

Second Sunday of August
www.providence.org

There is a TV commercial out there that portrays an imaginary world where highways are filled with bicycles instead of cars. The Bridge Pedal is the closest we may ever come to making that dream a reality. On this special Sunday, all of the ten Portland bridges that crisscross the Willamette River support only bikers, with some walkers, and the potential of pedaling for up to 36 miles. Borrow, rent or steal (not really, silly!) a bike and join in the festivities (see **Bike About**). *dm*

Iron Art Sculpt-Off

Mid-August
Portland Art Center
www.portlandart.org

Creative re-use goes competitive in this high-energy, team-sculpting race. In groups of ten, local artists have to resurrect beauty out of a box of junkyard scraps, provided by whom else but SCRAP, of course. You'll be mystified, transformed, and in awe at the instantaneous inspiration! *sb*

Festa Italiana

End of August
Various locations
www.festa-italiana.org

This Italian festival lasts an entire week, starting things off with a celebratory mass, then gets into some bocce playing, and wraps up with festivities at Pioneer Courthouse Square (see **City for Free** chapter). *dm*

Soapbox Derby

Last Saturday of August
Mt. Tabor slopes
493.WINK, www.soapboxracer.com

Portlanders like to take amusements from childhood, resurrect them, and lift them up to a higher, less safe, level. The Soapbox Derby calls upon dabbling engineers and mechanics to construct ridiculous soapbox cars and use the gravity of the hills of Mt. Tabor alone to rush them to a hopeful victory. Throngs flock to see which cars are distinguished as the Lame Duck and the Crowd Pleaser. Helmets on! *dm*

TBA Festival

Second week of September
Various locations
242.1419, www.pica.org/tba

Put on by PICA, the Portland Institute for Contemporary Art, the Time-Based Art Festival asks artists from around the world to draw attendees to the here and now with performances that can never be relived. The acts are scattered throughout the city and require tickets, so plan ahead. *dm*

Polish Festival

Last Weekend of September
287.4077, www.portlandpolonia.org

In the midst of the festivities of this weekend, you might have to double check with a fellow polka dancer that you are indeed still in Portland, not Chicago. You wouldn't know it with the full schedule of Polish performances, activities, and food. So, grab a Pole, head to the festival, and eat a pierogi, (or two or three or four). *dm*

Portland Marathon

First Sunday of October
www.portlandmarathon.org

It seems we all aspire to run a marathon one day. Indulge your imaginings as you cheer on those who are undertaking the task—or, darn it, get in there with them. *dm*

Greek Festival

First weekend of October, F-Sa 10a-10p, Su 12-8p
Holy Trinity Church, 3131 NE Glisan Street
www.goholytrinity.org/festival

Finally, you'll be able to pronounce all those mesmerizing Greek specialties by getting your fill of them at this yearly fête. Cooking demonstrations, dancing, and of course baklava make an entrance. *sb*

Apple Tasting

Second weekend of October
Portland Nursery, 9000 Division Street
788.9000, www.portlandnursery.com

During autumn in New England: pretty leaves always led to leaf-rubbing art. It is also apple picking-time and, of course, apple baking, caramelizing, and straight up eating. It used to be that the varieties of apples were McIntosh and Granny Smith, plain and simple. Portland Nursery blew my mind with the variety of apples on their grounds—70?! Beware, apple obsession will result from attending this event. *dm*

Wine Country Thanksgiving

Thanksgiving
Various locations in Willamette Valley
www.willamettewines.com/thanksgiving.shtml

For three days at Thanksgiving, over 100 wineries open their doors for celebrations with music, food, and of course wine tasting straight from the barrel. Everything on the traditional turkey day menu has a wine compâdre. *dl*

Holiday Artisan Market

First and second weekends of December
Pioneer Courthouse Square
222.6073, www.pioneercourthousesquare.com

Peruse through handcrafted jewelry, ceramics, holiday crafts etc., and find the perfect, locally made gift for that special someone. *dl*

Peacock Lane Christmas Lights

Last two weeks of December
SE Peacock Lane between Stark Street and Belmont Street
www.peacocklane.net

My first room in Portland looked over 39th Avenue and Alder Street was right in the thick of Portland's holiday spirit. When Christmas-time rolled around, activity was furious on Peacock Lane, one street to the east. Every house on this street decks out their home with lights and adornments of every sort. There's usually some yummy hot chocolate to sip while you stroll, for the cost of only a couple of quarters. *dm*

Festival of the Last Minute

December 18th-24th
SW Ankeny at Nato Parkway

The Saturday Market is open all week to bail out your holiday season procrastinators from the embarrassment of giving your loved ones another sweater in which they'll never be caught dead. *dl*

Zoolights

Late November-December 31st
Oregon Zoo, 4001 SW Canyon Road, just off of Highway 26
226.1561, www.oregonzoo.org
Open: Su-Th 5-8p, F-Sa 5-8:30p

The holiday bug hits the Zoo during the cold winter months when it is adorned with lights galore. There is limited zoo access with special admission prices that range from $6-10 and can include a train ride on the lit-up locomotive. *dm*

The Grotto's Christmas Festival of Lights

Late November thru end of December
The Grotto, NE 85th and Sandy Boulevard
261.2400, www.thegrotto.org
Open: M-Su 5-9:30p

The Grotto is a Catholic religious sanctuary that is most notable for its large shrine to Mary, carved from a cliff wall with a replica of Michelangelo's Pietà housed inside. During the Christmas season, The Grotto puts on numerous choral performances and lights up everything in site—something a person of any religious or non-religious background will find pleasing. Entry is $7 for adults and $3 for children. *dm*

Up Early

Early bird specials and morning treats

Violet's Café

It is much easier to get up and get out knowing there are fantastic omelets, crépes, and all manner of breakfast fare at the end of the proverbial rainbow. Whether you have to be dragged from your bed, or are the one with that annoying extra morning gusto, follow your nose on a whim and enjoy the early hours of the day. Start the day with simplicity or extravagance. I like taking it easy, stepping back for a moment from all our electronic systems, and letting my feet go for a stroll. Our research assistant poodle has helped us find some great morning walks, all of which end with the best breakfasts in town. *sb*

Violet's Café

NE Sacramento Street at NE 52nd Avenue
281.7933
Open: Th-M 7a-2p
$ Vn Fam S

With an unparalleled friendly feel and healthy, hearty breakfasts Violet's is my favorite breakfast spot in Portland. On mornings when you get up on the wrong side of the bed and need a boost or a bit of cheering up, Violet's out-of-control scones have a way of turning my day around. Beautiful benedicts with heaps of fresh fruit on the side, or blueberry pancakes that come with cheesy scrambled eggs are part of a complete menu of morning fare. Strong coffee is in my hand before I know it, so I can get out from the morning blues by staring at Violet Café's happy purple walls. It is a great place to have a heart-to-heart with family or to come alone to collect your thoughts before starting your big day. *sb*

Riverplace Waterfront and Marina

Westside of Willamette River below Marquam Bridge
S Dg

Walk along the west riverbank past cafés and the marina for a pleasant stroll with excellent bridge views. It's a great spot to take your four-legged friend on a quintessential Portland romp. *sb*

Rose City Park

NE 62nd Avenue and Tillamook Street
www.portlandonline.com/parks
Fr S Dg

The feel of woodchips under my sneakers and the shade of larch trees make the paths of Rose City Park, located in the neighborhood of the same name, a great walk, rain or shine. This Northeast neighborhood has a strong community feel, and you'll often find friends and puppy buddies meeting and talking on the trails. There are also picnic tables, a playground, and tennis courts for everyone to enjoy. *sb*

Zell's

1300 SE Morrison Street at SE 12th Avenue
239.0196
Open: M-F 7a-2p, Sat 8a-2p, Sun 8a-3p
$$ Veg Fam

When Saturday morning rolls around, bellies start rumbling and lines pile out the doors of the best breakfast spots in the City of Roses. Zell's is one step ahead, providing free coffee, mini scones, and a box of sidewalk chalk while you await your table. It's in the upper echelon of Portland's benedicts and scrambles. The industrious staff makes sure the line keeps moving so you can order your Gruyère potatoes and proscuitto-mozzarella fritatta sooner. They're serious about giving back to the community in other ways than hearty breakfasts—their annual food and toy drive benefits local foster kids. *sb*

Cup and Saucer Café

3566 SE Hawthorne Boulevard at SE 36th Avenue
236.6001
Open: M-Sun 7a-9p
$ Vn Fam Fr

Offering a menu of morning staples at several PDX locations, Cup and Saucer is where I go for an early bird face-stuffing session. Scrambles are twice the size as elsewhere, toast is thick and slathered with unsalted butter. There is usually a line of hungry people, so write down your name on the clipboard and hang outside to people watch on Hawthorne Boulevard. *dm/sb*

Redwing Coffee & Baking

1700 SE 6th Avenue at SE Market Street
445.9900, www.redwingcoffee.com
Open: M-F 6:30a-5p, Sa 9a-3p
$ Fr S WiFi Vn Dg

Redwing is a woman-owned café, where everything is made from scratch, and fair-trade, organic coffee is roasted in-house. When I was in a bad mood my mother used to let me have dinner for breakfast and breakfast for dinner to cheer me up. Now I use this trick on my own by ordering a Mediterranean salad for my first meal of the day. Situated in an industrial district across the way from a righteous Goodwill, this café is a perfect opportunity to explore the lower southeast. There is always great rotating art on the walls and a Free Geek computer to check email. There are a few outside tables, so your furry friend can grovel and wait for your leftovers. *sb*

Paradox Palace Café

3439 SE Belmont Street at SE 34th Street
232.7508
Open: M 8a-9p, Tu-W 9a-9p, Th-Su 8a-9p
$ Vn PW Fr CO

With a mostly vegetarian menu (they also serve hamburgers to accommodate meat-eating folks) and a low-key atmosphere, Paradox is the place to go when you want to take the pace down a notch. Chill out over some corn cakes or an unconquerable breakfast burrito (yay for leftovers!), read your *Free Will Astrology* horoscope in the *Willamette Week,* and try not to get too freaked out by the overabundance of mirrors by your booth. For a contemporary architectural foray, take a peak right across the street to the impressive Belmont Street Lofts, erected by well-known developer, Randy Rapaport. Belmont Avenue is the more laid-back version of Hawthorne Boulevard, so hang here to avoid crowds. *dm/ sb*

Bijou Café

132 SW 3rd Avenue at Jefferson Street
222.3187
Open: M-F 7a-2p, Sa-Su 8a-2p
$$ Veg Fr Ro

With the sophistication of Provençal France minus the pretense, Bijou is the perfect sunny joint for an upper end breakfast. The brightly painted and lofty interior spits in the eye of another rainy Portland day and defiantly turns its back. The wait will fade into a distant memory when that freshly baked zucchini muffin is laid on the table, followed by a superbly flavored scramble (the tofu version is also delectable). For the bold, order a breakfast platter of oyster hash. Bijou fits the bill of a jumping off point for a day's exploration of the city's downtown blocks, positing people ideally for a walk up to Powell's or over to the Willamette for a riverside stroll. *dm*

Mt. Tabor

SE 60th Avenue at SE Salmon Street
www.portlandonline.com/parks
S Fr Dg

There is nothing that can match the giddiness that falls with the flakes of a snow day. On one extremely rare occasion, snow shut down Portland, cars slid on the roads with the ease of a curling stone on ice, and my friends and I aimed for Mt. Tabor to sled. While chances aren't good you'll get to sled this hill (snow falal is rare in Portland), there are many other activities in which to participate here. Heading east on Hawthorne Boulevard after the sun has ducked under the rain clouds for a stellar view of a dramatic Portland dusk. There are also hilly trails, paved and unpaved, a dog park, an old reservoir and great city views. A narrow cemented drive winds its way around this extinct volcano, so skateboarders, rollerbladers, bikers and the participants of the annual Soap Box Derby (see **Calendar** chapter) all hold Mt. Tabor close to their hearts. Tennis courts, a wicked playground, and prime peak locales for picnicking make Mt. Tabor one of my favorite places to unwind. *dm*

Ken's Artisan Bakery

338 NW 21st Avenue at NW Everett Street
248.2202, www.kensartisan.com
Open: M 7a-9:30p, Tu-Sa 7a-7p, Su 8a-5p
$ Veg S Fr Dg

My friend Leah would always coax me over the river to meet her at Ken's in the Northwest for a morning bun. It was always worth it. The space is small here and fills up quickly so hopefully the weather will be kind and accommodating for outdoor seating while you enjoy your newspaper and pastry. There is also a selection of sandwiches if something more substantial is required. I would recommend topping off the visit with a canelle—French for cinnamon, these are divine. Ken's is a jump-off point for exploring the goods of the Nob Hill shopping district or trekking up to Washington Park to catch the roses doing their morning stretches. *dm*

J&M Café

537 SE Ash Street at SE Grand Avenue
230.0463
Open: M-F 7:30a-2p, Sa-Su 8a-2p
$ Fr Fam CO

I have many a great morning memory of J&M. It's dangerously near my house, so there's quite a stack of those memories amassing. The area is quirky and somewhat industrial, off the main drag of Grand Avenue, and not yet covered with boutiques or blocks of other cute restaurants. You can't go wrong with any of J&M's short list of menu items, plus there's a self-service coffee, eliminating the middleman between you and your caffine craving. I always love the scrambled eggs and the tasty potatoes here. J&M offers a primo setting to reconnect with a friend or loved one over a crossword puzzle. After your meal, find some discount industrial shelving, sign printing services or oil change workshops around the corner. *dm*

Vita Café

3024 NE Alberta Street at NE 12th Avenue
335.8233, www.vita-café.com
Open: M-W 10a-10p, Th-F 10a-11p, Sa 8a-11p, Su 8a-10p
$ Vn Fr Fam

Who knew that breakfast could be so consciousness-raising? The back of Vita's menu lays out their values with some "Food for Thought" to address organics, global warming, sustainable business, percentage sales donations, and, of course, vegetarianism and veganism—no meat here. Luckily, taste is not sacrificed in the pursuit of a conscientious business. I didn't know that French toast could be made a la vegan, but truth be told, it is better than expected. For a true avant-guard meal, the Thai corn cakes are a welcome shocker with bananas, ginger, cilantro, and coconut syrup. Vita Café is a model for sustainable businesses and restaurateurs alike, not to mention a great place to rub the sleep out of your eyes. *dm*

Core Essence Studio

1028 SE Water Avenue at SE Taylor Street
233.0777, www.coreessencestudio.com
Class times vary, call ahead
$$ Fr Ro

It turns out Pilates and pole dancing have something in common other than starting with a 'P'. They're both offered as kick-butt exercise classes at Core Essence, where an 8-week course will get your confidence and muscles in gear. Start barefoot in some comfy clothes, and work your way up to exercising in platform high heels. Have fun moving even your most tired morning body. *sb*

Coffee Time

Coffee beans: ground, pressed, steeped and served

Palio's Dessert & Espresso House

Speaking as a true coffee person, I am overjoyed to find a city with local coffee roasters who are in-the-know about organic and fair-trade coffee. Plus, they're outdoing the ever-present chains that clutter up our towns and shut out community businesses. Find coffee, tea and snacks, both sweet and savory, at these admirable cafés. Each offers its own unique ambiance and crowd; these coffee shops are indicators of what the surrounding neighborhood is like. *sb*

Palio Dessert & Espresso House
1966 SE Ladd Avenue between SE 12th and 20th Avenues
232.9412
Open: M-Th 8a-11p, F-Sa 8a-12a, Su 8a-11p
$ Vn PW S

When the rain comes down in this lush city, what is better than a prime slice of cake, a hot beverage, and a good book? Palio's is the perfect neighborhood nook for regulars and travelers alike to get comfy in an armchair, tune into a classical music mix, and dive into their favorite pages. Palio's shops for their cakes at all the best places—so relax and sweeten up in this cozy library of a café smack dab in the center of lovely Ladd's Addition (see **Explore** chapter). *sb*

Albina Press
4637 N Albina Avenue at Blandena Street
282.5214
Open: Everyday, 6:30a-8p
$ PW S WiFi

Albina Press is where the beautiful and trendy co-mingle over their laptops, daily newspapers and award winning java. At the northernmost part of the Mississippi neighborhood, Albina is a good place to find yourself for a bit of study and some Stumptown roasts. An espresso won't be served up in one minute flat, mostly because the line is usually long, but also because the adorable Albina baristas take the time to make every pour be perfection. Enjoy your Americano with a treat from their pastry selection. *dm*

The Pied Cow

3244 SE Belmont Street at SE 32nd Avenue
230.4866
Open: Tu-Th 4p-12a, F 4p-1a, Sa 10a-1a
$ Fr WiFi Dg

The Pied Cow is a funky, hip place with vegan deserts, strong coffee, and hookahs for those who want to pretend they are in Morocco. On the bottom floor of a brightly colored old Portland Victorian house, the Pied Cow has a neighborhood feel completed by their outdoor patio (rain permitting), low-to-the-ground couches and tables surrounded by a decadence of kitschy décor. The food is tasty, but more directed toward snacks and desserts. Don't leave without trying one of their clever drinks like the lavender steamer and my favorite, the hot toddy. Come for a first date or with old friends. *rrm*

Stumptown Coffee Roasters

3356 SE Belmont Street at SE 33rd Avenue (one of several locations)
232.8889, www.stumptowncoffee.com
Open: M-F 6a-9p, Sa-Su 7a-9p
$ Vn PW S

Portland has many a moniker, one of the more notable being 'Stumptown,' purportedly originating from the days when city growth chopped the trees and left only the stumps. Stumptown Coffee revitalizes a somewhat morbid name with its prolific coffee presence in Portland. Not only does the roaster have its own four cafés around the city, including a tasting annex, Stumptown blends are also brewed up at innumerable coffee joints around town. Truly a Portlandian staple, Stumptown has helped put the city on the coffee map among connoisseurs and is a must visit for those seeking a more enlightened cup of joe. *dm*

Muddy's Coffeehouse

Muddy's Coffeehouse

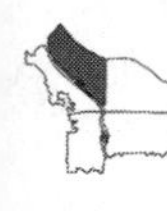

3560 N Mississippi Avenue at Fremont Street
445.6690, www.muddycoffeehouse.com
Open: M-W 7a-6p Th-Sa 7a-9p, Su 7a-3p
$ Veg S CO

Named for the owner's beloved, albeit dirty pouch, Muddy's is a home away from home. Organic coffee and homespun meals keep you company while sitting pretty on a Windsor-back or sofa in the house. Bring a book and laptop, and wax creative while getting some seriously delicious soup to go with your alone time. There's always art on the walls and something sweet to munch on after your breakfast or lunch. *sb*

Crema Bakery & Café

2728 SE Ankeny Street at SE 27th Avenue
234.0206, www.cremabakery.com
Open: M-Sa 7a-6p, Su 7:30a-5p
$ Fr S WiFi

I walk to Crema when I want to affect an air of intellect. i-Book in hand, I order a delectable mushroom and Manchego biscuit from one of the young, attractive baristas, and take a seat on the comfy cushions for an afternoon of tapping away at the keyboard. There is a wide array of treats to choose from (Crema is smartly riding the cupcake wave) and sandwiches to keep you full if you're stuck here trying to finish that paper due Monday. If you are up for it, take a taste of Crema's AM bun, a real challenge to Ken's morning bun (see **Up Early** chapter), with its beautiful hint of orange. *dm*

The Press Club

2621 SE Clinton Street at SE 28th Street
233.5656
Open: M-W 10a-10p, Th 10a-11p, F-Sa 10-12a, Su 10a-10p
$-$$ PW Fr WiFi

Coffee-loving Portland is full of sweet little coffee shops. That is why, when a new one opens, they always step it up a notch. Relatively new to the scene, The Press Club not only has great espresso and personal-sized French-press Stumptown coffee, but also an array of 88 of the most interesting magazines for buying or just browsing. But it's not just java here. A delicious and extensive savory crepe menu as well as a selection of salads and sandwiches are complemented by an admirable array of wine and beers. I recommend the smoked salmon, tomato, spinach, and dill crepe. For something sweet, go for a brie, walnut, brown sugar and pear crepe. While lounging in the spacious Press Club with a good read on a Sunday afternoon, I realized that I could also come here for happy hour, a good art show, well, just about any time. *ws*

Do Lunch

Outstanding mid-day eating of every sort

Besaw's Restaurant & Bar

Lunch is my favorite meal of the day. When I lived in Switzerland, it was an event, with several courses and mandatory attendance by the entire family. In fact, some parts of the world consider this the largest meal of the day, accompanied by a siesta. There are many types of lunches—standing around downtown by the food carts, diving into a platter of momos, (Tibetan dumplings), partaking of a huge hamburger or a raw vegan one, Portlanders run the gamut on tastes and styles of this meal. Even though I've avoided the typical "eat" or "restaurant" sections common in other guidebooks, and incorporated food into various chapters, I had to dedicate a spot for lunch. From business power lunches to lazy afternoon munching, it's a state of mind. *sb*

Besaw's

2301 NW Savier Street at NW 23rd Avenue
228.2619, www.besaws.com
Open: Tu-Sa 8a-10p, Su 8a-3p
$$ Vn Fr Fam

In 1903, on the way to the Louis and Clark exhibition, two Canadian loggers got sidetracked. They stayed in Portland, hammered their last nail in the walnut bar, and opened for business as a saloon and gambling hall. Today, the bar still stands, surrounded by cheery neighbors who come to enjoy Besaw's fabulously comfortable feasts. They serve breakfast, lunch and dinner, but an early lunch of their signature seafood soup and colossal hamburger is what attracts me like glue. Large salads with plentiful chunks of chicken, feta, or house-smoked salmon are healthy and filling. Standards like the Reuben and turkey Havarti sandwiches are made with perfect balance. They are open all day but don't serve breakfast after 11a. Regardless of when you come, Besaw's is bound to cheer you through and through. *sb*

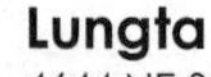

Lungta

4644 NE Sandy Boulevard at NE 74th Avenue
287.1171
Open: M-Sa 12-2:30p, 5:30-9p
$ Vn Fam

As the first Tibetan restaurant to open its doors and heat its ovens in the Pacific Northwest, Lungta has paved the way for mountains of delicacies to be enjoyed by all. The auspicious name, meaning "wind horse", is one of the symbols found on those high-flying prayer flags hung to bring happiness and long life to all in the vicinity. I would liken that reaction to how I feel after a plate of their Momos—they make me so happy. During the Tibetan New Year, Losar, I have stayed up nights making Momos for hundreds of celebrating mouths, and believe me it is no synch. Lungta crafts their handmade dumplings from whole-wheat wrappers, stuffed with just the right blend of ground meats and veggies (or just veggies) and spices. Aside from my obsession with good Momos, the Churul, a cheesy soup, and Lephing, a most interesting mung bean pudding with spicy soy-based sauce, are also outstanding. Most dishes come with Tingmo, a light and fluffy steamed bread great for soaking up the remainder of your curry or Bhaleb pastry stuffing. *sb*

La Buca

40 NE 28th Avenue at E Burnside Street
238.1058
Open: M-W 11:30a-9p, Th-F 11:30a-10p, Sa 12-10p, Su 5-9p
$ Vn Fam Fr

Around the corner from Laurelhurst Theater (see **Art House Cinema** chapter) and along the popular 28th Avenue strip sits La Buca, a corner Italian bistro beckoning for travelers to feel like neighbors. While offering simple and inexpensive pasta and meat dishes, La Buca retains a slight air of fine dining with its high ceilings and simple wall art. Back in the Northeast, on the other side of the U.S., Italian restaurants rule the scene and portions are "gynormous" and heavy with the garlic. I love them, but La Buca spins the theme with more human-size servings and subtle flavors. Their house-made tiramisu is a tasty combination of perfectly soaked ladyfingers and drizzled chocolate sauce. La Buca is simply a comfortable place to have a casual lunch, or dinner for that matter. *dm*

Proper Eats Market and Café

8638 N Lombard Street at N Alta Avenue
445.2007, www.propereats.org
Open: M-Th 10a-10p, F-Sa 10a-2a, Su 12-10p
$-$$ Vn Fr

The St. Johns neighborhood is on the move as many city dwellers are migrating from the more crowded areas of town. Those lucky enough to call this community their home have Proper Eats at their fingertips and its flavorful mostly-vegan, all-vegetarian fare on the tips of their tongues. With music most nights and a small grocery area stocked with bulk items and organic produce for travel fuel, Proper Eats serves hearty wraps, delicious tahini-drenched salads and lovingly-prepared entrées, though their daily specials are always sp intriguing I never seem of order from the regular menu. *dm*

Mi Wa

6852 NE Sandy Boulevard at NE 68th Avenue
493.7460
Open: M-Su 11a-10p
$ Veg Fr

Mi Wa is a modest family-run Vietnamese restaurant that seems to sometimes suffer at the hands of nearby old guard establishments. Yet if you had an old Vietnamese grandmother, this is the type of food you would expect to have grown up on. Pho Tai, the ubiquitous Vietnamese-style beef noodle soup, is rich with fatty beef, while Canh Chua Ga arrives with a pungent sour broth over tender chicken, onions, pineapple, and Bac Ha, the stalk of a taro variety that adds a delicious, spongy texture to the soup. Specialties like Banh Xeo, an egg crepe stuffed with shrimp, pork, sprouts, and cilantro; Goi Ngo Sen Tom Thit, baby lotus topped with pork and shrimp in a balanced nuac mam sauce; and Muc Rang Moi, addictive pieces of pepper-dusted squid, are true to the family's regional roots. Its sister café, Be Van, is next door with Internet stations and delicious Banh Mi sandwiches. With friendly owners, a clean and spacious dining area and very affordable prices, Mi Wa makes a wonderful lunch. *jo*

Pepino's Restaurant

3832 SE Hawthorne Boulevard at SE 28th Avenue
236.5000, www.pepinos.org
Open: Everyday, 11a-10p
$ S CO

Pepino's is a stop down Hawthorne where you can grab a stack of fresh and satisfying tacos for 99 cents each on your way to a relaxed lunch nook. Something always mystified me about the off-limits teaching lounge from back in middle school, so there's a corner of my living room set up like what I imagined it to be. As often as possible I bring a pile of roommates and Pepino's to my very own teachers lounge. If we get to talking and it comes movie time, we forget popcorn and swap it out for a Carne Asada mouthful of joy, or their unbeatable pork Carnitas. Stock up on the yum factor without breaking the bank, or contending with lard and MSG. *ec*

Stanich's

4915 NE Fremont Street at NE 49th Avenue (one of two locations)
281.2322
Open: M-Sa 11a-10:30p
$ Fr Fam CO

Stanich's is the best burger in town, a hard-won title with heavy competition. Even the powerful presence of top quality seafood in the City of Roses has succumbed to America's favorite meal. Get the Special Burger (the works) and fries, and unless you plan to take a couple-hour nap afterward, split one with your buddy. If you are experiencing hunger of epic proportions, grab the aptly named Killer, a Special Burger plus a hearty slice of ham, two fried eggs, and an extra slice of cheese. As the sign in the window says, "relax and stay a while, this ain't no fast food!" *sb*

Kornblatts Delicatessen

628 NW 23rd Avenue at Hoyt Street
242.0055
Open: M-Th 7a-8p, F 7a-9p, Sa 7:30a-9p, Su 7:30a-8p
$$ Veg Fam PW

This traditional Jewish deli is snuggled up in the ritzy Pearl District. Munch on a house-brined pickle from the bucket on your table while you wait for your main dish. My cravings for blintzes, matzo ball soup, and white fish sandwiches are always satisfied here. Friendly service and hot pastrami are sure to brighten your day. Return in the morning for a hearty matzo brei breakfast! Reminds me of my Bubba! L'chaim! *sb*

Thanh Thao

4005 SE Hawthorne Boulevard at SE 40th Avenue
238.6232
Open: M,W,F 11a-2:30p, 5-10p, Sa-Su 11a-10p
$ Veg S Fr

Thanh Thao, right across the street from two smoke shops, serves up a slice of counter culture with tasty salad rolls and scrumptious barbeque. The food is classic yummy Thai comfort food, and the service is always quick, so it is safe to come here when your stomach has already started speaking to you. I have been coming for years to have their coconut soup, but you can choose from 25 main dishes all priced under $5.75! *rrm*

Laughing Planet Café

3322 SE Belmont Street at 33rd Avenue (one of several locations)
235.6472, www.laughingplanetcafe.com
Open: M-Su 11a-10p
$ Vn Fr Fam

A local chain, Laughing Planet specializes in gourmet burritos (I am considering $4-6 a pop to be gourmet in burrito land). Their perfectly packaged burritos are chock full of fresh, organic ingredients in unique combinations with brown rice to tie it all together. Take a peek at their daily burrito offering, which is sure to be both cleverly named and unusually filled. Of their stock choices, my favorite is the Che Guevera; I can stick it to the man and satisfy my sweet tooth with luxurious plantains, sweet potatoes and BBQ sauce. To make it even healthier, and you didn't hear it from me, if you ask for a whole-wheat tortilla they will give it to you at no extra charge. To sip, choose from fresh, dairy-free smoothies (served in a 100 percent compostable container made from corn!) and a great selection of delectable local brews. Dine among the quirky, colorful decorations and play with a toy dinosaur or two. All Laughing Planet Cafés are located in quintessential Portland neighborhoods, so digest with a stroll, some culture and maybe one of their vegan cookies. *dm*

American Dream Pizza

4620 NE Glisan Street at NE 47th Street
230.0699, www.americandreampizza.net
Open: M-Th 8a-10p, F 8a-11p, Sa-Su 9a-10p
$ Veg Fr

This pizza parlor is decorated by creative customers who try their hand at pizza box art while digging in to their custom slices. I like to do up my own design while sipping a Root's Red beer, brewed up at the local brewery across the river (see **Hang Out** chapter). Choose from four different sauces and heaps of toppings—I recommend the pesto-based Goddess Athena slice, featuring chicken and artichoke hearts. They also deliver free of charge, so if you want lunch without moving an inch, just pick up the phone. *ec*

Du's Grill

5365 NE Sandy Boulevard at NE 53rd Avenue
284.1773
Open: M-F 11a-9p
$ Fr

Ask any local where to find the best chicken teriyaki in town and Du's Grill is the answer you'll hear. You could call Du's a bento (Japanese lunch box) joint—but you'd be wrong. Your plateful of chicken teriyaki, rice, and salad sure doesn't look like bento, with nary a partitioned box in sight. You could order something other than the chicken—Du's also serves pork and beef teriyaki, as well as yakisoba—but why? The chicken, expertly grilled right in front of you, is perfectly charred, tender and cloyingly glazed, and Du's leaves you free to add homemade not-too-sweet teriyaki to your liking. The mound of rice and basic iceberg salad, with a surprisingly yummy and creamy poppyseed dressing, add to the experience by not detracting from the sweet and juicy chicken. Portions are large enough for two, and affordable prices leave you feeling giddy and thinking about take-home. Friendly owners and the satisfied smiles of those around you make up for the lack of ambiance in the modest dining area. Just don't call it bento. *jo*

Typhoon!

2310 NW Everett Street at NW 23rd Avenue (one of several locations)
243.7557, www.typhoonrestaurants.com
Open: M-F 11:30a-2p, 4:30-9p, Sa-Su 12-3p, 4:30-10p
$$ Veg Fr

Typhoon! fills the hearts and bellies of Portland's plethora of Thai food enthusiasts and has been awarded a top spot on many 'Best of Portland' lists. In the gourmet line of Pearl District restaurants, this bustling lunch stop has open-air seating for nice days and an extensive tea list to accompany a myriad of classic Thai dishes. Unique curry blends are as plentiful as hairs on your head. I like to try the daily specials, which are always outstanding and make the decision process far simpler. Enjoy the exquisite art hung around the restaurant as you dine on a steamy bowl of fish soup or a noodle-y stew. *sb*

Pok Pok

3226 SE Division Street at SE 32nd Avenue
232.1387, www.pokpokpdx.com
Open: M-F 11:30a-10:30p, Sa 5p-10:30
$ Veg Dg Fr Ro

Pok Pok was once only a stand on Division Street, a perfect place to pop by when the weather was kind or for incomparable papaya salad to go. Now, the shack remains and is complemented by the Whiskey Soda Lounge, located in the basement of the adjacent house, for dining inside the stylish wood paneled rooms. Yes, Pok Pok is a Thai food restaurant, and one that uses the freshest and most local ingredients possible, but you won't find Pad Thai on this menu. What you'll find here is spicey Thai street food, the signature dish being Kai Yaang, a roasted game hen dish. The one I adore is Phat Makheua Yao with the most flavorful and perfectly textured eggplant I have ever eaten. The prospect of whiskey is also a draw; I've gone through a couple "education" sessions here, learning the wonders of this strong drink. After the whiskey or cocktail of your choice, stay for dinner, and remember that the lounge is closed between 2:30p and 5p. Bring a crew and chow down family style to sample a variety of choices, and don't forget to order one or two more than your number; these are not large servings. With an award for Best Restaurant of the Year from the *The Oregonian*, you can't go wrong at Pok Pok. *dm*

Thai Noon

2635 NE Alberta Street at NE 26th Avenue
282.2021
Open: M-F 11:30a-10p, Sa 12-10:30p, Su 12-10p
$ Veg Dg Fr

A front row seat to Alberta Street and on a warm and happy summer day, Thai Noon is my fail-safe for a solid Thai lunch, a Portlander's favorite nationality of food. I usually order up one of the curries, substituting organic brown rice for the usual white—departing from the traditional for a healthier meal. Thai Noon might serve as a gateway to a Last Thursday night (see **Get Inspired** chapter) sanity before diving into the masses and clowns. Thai Noon is clean, fresh, and simple cuisine and that is a priceless commodity in my book. *dm*

Hoda's Middle Eastern

3401 SE Belmont Street at SE 34th Street
236.8325, www.hodas.com
Open: M-F 11a-9:30p, Sa 12-9:30p
$ Vn CO

After picking up *Arabian Nights* from one of Portland's great independent bookstores, head to Hoda's to act out your new role as an Arabian prince or princess. Embrace the perfectly blended hummus or the most delectable stuffed grape leaves. Hoda itself is an Arabic word meaning enlightenment, and this comes through with their unparalleled Middle Eastern fare. Come for Kabobs, grilled meats, hearty salads, or shwarma, but don't miss the plethora of homemade side dishes, including Labne, a hard-to-find pressed cheese that makes fast friends with a crunchy falafel-stuffed pita. Jallab is my drink of choice, a mellow date-and-rosewater combo that will make your belly sing songs of praise. *sb*

Detour Café

3035 SE Division Street at SE 30th Avenue
234.7499, www.detourcafe.com
Open: Everyday, 8a-4p
$ Vn Fr Fam

At Detour, you can munch on an affordable meal (most around $6) that will also be amazingly fresh, made with organic ingredients and served with bread baked in-house. Bringing delicious and sustainable meals to those who can't break the bank, Detour has terrific breakfast scrambles, as well as spectacular sandwiches and salads for lunch at any time of day. The Bortfeld chicken sandwich hits the spot and the Spicy Beef Salad is a treat for the deserving. Have breakfast for lunch by ordering some cardamom toast with your meal—its subtle flavor is the perfect accompaniment to any menu item. Their maple scones are great for the road. *dm*

Nicolas' Restaurant

318 SE Grand Avenue at Pine Street
235.5123, www.nicholasrestaurant.com
Open: M-Sa 10a-9p, Su 12-9p
$ Vn Fr Fam

On a daily basis, Nicholas' leaves many a local with a lifted spirit, glowing in the wake of a Lebanese feast. Fortunately, such nourishment is available even to the tight-budgeted or unemployed. A Mezza for one, available in vegan, vegetarian and meat, is plenty food for two diners with an array of hummus, falafel, tabouli, and pita, but if a bit more is needed, split a Shawarma sandwich; the beef, marinated in a family recipe, is beyond description. Plan to stay and eat and chat and eat some more, the service isn't always speedy but the relaxed atmosphere is a perfect setting for such a royal meal. *dm*

Downtown Food Carts

Rain or shine, the gregarious owners of the downtown foodcarts are here to serve the masses that come down from their skyscrapers and lecture halls for a quick bite to eat. Scattered throughout downtown, two dense concentrations of carts are perched next to parking lots on SW 5th and SW 12th Avenues. Specials from these cart groupings work perfectly for picnicking and people watching at the waterfront or at Pioneer Square. Lunch specials run about $5 at most carts for hefty portions of authentic, homemade grub. My favorites are all located in the SW 5th Avenue area, between Stark and Oak Streets, but look for others on SW 9th and Washington Street and also on SW 12th in that same vicinity. *ep*

La Jarochita

With my snobby taste for tacos, I didn't think I would find seventh heaven in Oregon. After about 600 tacos made by Lupe and Magdalena at this cart, I can attest that I was wrong. I haven't had anything I didn't like, but first try the chicken tamales wrapped in banana leaves ($1.50), or the veggie homemade corn tortilla tacos with black beans ($1.25). *ep*

The Real Taste of India

This cart offers bulging and carb-friendly meat and veggie lunch specials ($5 with naan). The line usually extends out onto the sidewalk, and these people are often too busy to smile, but after chomping down you'll be sure to make up for that. *ep*

Taste of Poland

One of the newest additions to the row, Polish food specials run about $6 for an overflowing clamshell of perogies and sausages with a small salad. If you're pregnant or know a few words in Polish, you might be able to get an extra perogie or at least a charming laugh from the ultra-sweet Polish lady who runs the cart. *ep*

Hang Out

All the best chill out spots, from a cozy reading nook to a relaxed microbrew with your buddies

Powell's City of Books

Sometimes the best way to get a sense of a place is to slow down and stop attempting to see everything and do everything. Try a tapioca-ball boba while hanging out on Hawthorne and give new meaning to loitering. Portland has a relaxed pace; it's a place where you can put life on hold for a moment to enjoy the simple things—see beauty in rain drops and wax poetic in your journal. Bring friends or venture out alone for a moment off the treadmill of usual livelihood. *sb*

Powell's City of Books
1005 W Burnside Street at SW 11th Avenue
228.4651, www.powells.com
Open: Everyday, 9a-11p

In the days before online book sales, Powell's was a healthy, happy giant of a bookstore, with floors of the most fascinating and far-reaching titles. As online shopping made a splash, and an unfortunate dent in many an independent bookseller's pocket, Powell's remains the keystone of indie bookstores. Filling an entire city block, their Portland store is still an absolute must-see, heavily frequented by city dwellers. The bookseller has also been able to adeptly expand into the Internet business world. Prepare to lose yourself on four floors of color-coded books by topic. Enter by the pile-o-books statue and into the shop where there is sure to be a line of locals selling and trading in their old volumes for Powell's credits. Zoom through an epic proportion of graphic novels to the staircase that dumps you at the intersection of travel guides and world philosophy. Up another flight is a meshing of religions from every culture, and further still is the beloved art floor, complete with a small gallery, and every title imaginable from Richard Stella to Stella Macartney. You may not be able to leave the store without a stack of new and used books, so get a hot chai at their ground-floor café and dig in. *sb*

Rimsky-Korsakoffee House

707 SE 12th Avenue at SE Alder Street
232.2640
Open: M-Th, Su 7p-12a, F-Sa 7p-1a
$ Vn Fr

The delightful sound of active espresso machines chimes in over relaxing string music in what is literally the Rimsky-Korsakoffee house. Walk in the rust-colored front door as if visiting a friend and head upstairs to the bathroom when nature calls. The bathroom here really does deserve at least one visit, as it is creatively decked out as if you are in a room underwater; a dock and some fisherman's dangling feet dabble above your head and seaweed creeps up the river-esque floor. Chill out at a living room café table and listen to live music when the classical CD's make way for local performers. Cool your fears of rumored haunted houses and possessed tables by feasting on one of their insanely good ice cream sundaes. *sb*

The Mississippi Pizza Pub/Atlantis Lounge

3552 N Mississippi Avenue at N Fremont Street
288.3231, www.mississippipizza.com
Open: M-F 11:30a-11:30p, Sa-Su 11:30-1a
$ WiFi Fr Ro

There are times when I have just enough energy to go out, but not enough to have a complete nighttime excursion. When I weant it all without parading around town I head to Mississippi to wrap all the evening's merriment into one location. This your local pizza parlor with an adjoining down-home stage to catch some happy bluegrass and a seductive back room lounge for a cocktail and smoldering eyes. Mississippi Pizza is a cornerstone of Mississippi Avenue and has music most nights, my favorite of which is when my very own friends pick up their violins and sing me a song. One time I actually saw a hip-hop performance here, so you never know what will come your way, but you won't be disappointed. There can be a cover for the stage area, but head directly back to the Atlantis Lounge to avoid it and catch the tunes anyway. *dm*

Vendetta

4306 N Williams Avenue at NE Skidmore Street
288.1085
Open: Su-Th 3p-1a, F-Sa 3p-2a
$$ Vn WiFi Dg Fr

A recent addition to the rapidly changing **North Portland** neighborhood (see **Shopping Districts**), Vendetta immediately dove into the souls of area residents and worker bees alike to become the favorite bar for an evening beverage. Despite the slightly antagonistic name, Vendetta is a welcoming place with unbeatable nachos and vegan menu options. On a sunny day, their back graveled lounge has the serenity of a Japanese garden without the silence. When cold or rain pushes revelers inside, hours of fun can be had on the shuffleboard table. Sit under the impressive triptych creation by local artists Nicole Kriara (a GrassRoutes babe, of course) and Alex Robbins. There is no outside signage advertising the name Vendetta, so look for the Rainier Beer cursive red "R" in the window. *dm*

A Roadside Attraction

1000 SE 12th Avenue at SE Yamhill Street
233.0743
Open: Everyday, 3p-1a
$ Veg Fr WiFi Dg

Allure and mystery have surrounded Roadside Attraction ever since it opened. Like a metaphor for this secretivie spot, there is an enormously tall fence wrapping the somewhat confounding façade, but the bar is a relaxing atmosphere perfect for an evening of swapping stories with amigos. I have many a happy memory of this place: the first time my now good friend and I bonded, the setting of a joyous reunion with dear old friends, the site of occasional tipsy fun. There is a vaudevillian feel to the whole décor scheme, helped along by an underground appeal perpetuated by low ceilings and red carpeting. When the weather is right, the outdoor patio has numerous large picnic tables and cozies into the bar with those high wooden fences, but I adore the inside the most because it feels like having a drink in a wacky aunt's living room. *dm*

The Tao of Tea

2112 NW Hoyt Street at NW 21st Avenue, 223.3563
3430 SE Belmont Avenue, 736.0198
www.taooftea.com
Open: W-Su 11a-11p, Leaf Room open until 10:15p
$$ Vn S

Walking into the Tao of Tea is like stepping in a monastery where tea is the deity. The atmosphere is always quiet and reverent thanks to a few small water features, and a knowledgeable staff who seem to be in a state of mediation. The tables are rustic and unique, hidden under bamboo tents and cornered by tall ikebana arrangements. But, oh the tea! This is by far the best tea in Portland with an unimaginably large selection of the best quality leaves and herbs you can find Stateside. You can even buy in bulk at the store, on the web, or at a grocer like New Seasons (see **Buy Me** chapter). *rrm*

Valentine's

232 SW Ankeny Street at SW 2nd Avenue
248.1600
Open: M-Su 7p-late
$ Veg Fr

When I enter Valentine's, it's like I have narrowly escaped the typical Saturday-night bar scene downtown. I feel transformed by a space that has a mature, calm ambiance mixed with the creative playfulness of a clubhouse. The minimalist loft seating over the bar looks like a contemporary tree fort, straight out of the pages of Dwell magazine. The perfect spot for a twosome, my friend and I retreat to the bar, order paninis and some wine from the sole person working, who is altogether the server, cook, and bartender. This is a place to slow down. As we wait for the food, we sift through a large stack of handwritten punch cards, which will determine who wins a free tuna sammy that night (we've pre-decorated our own names, and crossed our fingers already). The bartender complements our newly added illustrations. We admire the quirky and carefree local artwork displayed on either side of the room. This time there are bizarre photographs of a girl imitating specific people in her life, young and old, reflecting back their expressions while dressed in similar outfits. We discuss the ones we like. Our food comes. It's perfectly delicious. Admiring the charming space seems to bring out our own creativity. When I leave, I feel blissful, knowing that I patched up that nostalgic hole I was craving to fill when I set out that evening. *nkp*

Bridgeport Ale House

3632 SE Hawthorne Boulevard at SE 36th Avenue
233.6540, www.bridgeportbrew.com
Open: Su-M 11:30a-5p, Tu-Th 11:30a-10p, F-Sa 11:30a-11p
$-$$ Vn Fr

At the heart of the Hawthorne strip, Bridgeport Ale House satiates both hunger pains and your thirst for one of Portland's local brews. Far more creative than simple chips and sandwiches that you'll find at typical pubs, Bridgeport has a full menu of pizzas, soups, salads, and grilled Brie—all made from scratch with local, organic produce and naturally raised meats. A daily happy hour from 3-6p will tempt every passerby to stop in for a Blue Heron brew. *dm*

Fat Straw

4258 SE Hawthorne Boulevard at SE 42nd Avenue
233.3369
Open: M-F 8a-8p, Sa 9a-8p, Su 10a-7p
$ Fr Dg PW WiFi

After shopping to your hearts content, re-hydrate, and satisfy your body with the best bubble tea in town. Tons of flavors can be paired with different sizes and shapes of tapioca balls served in recycled plastic cups with this rather large (1500-square-foot) spot's namesake fat straws. Although I am partial to jasmine and coffee, here I can safely go out on a limb with pomegranate black tea or a blackberry milky tea. *sb*

Bread & Ink Café

3610 SE Hawthorne Boulevard at SE 36th Avenue
239.4756
Open: M-Th 7a-3p, 5-9p, F-Sa 8a-3p, 5-10p, Su 9a-2p, 5-9p
$-$$ Vn Fam Ro

Bread & Ink is a cornerstone of the Hawthorne, gathering together lunching ladies, studying students and chatty shoppers at sunny little tables. The menu features crab, blintzes, oysters, and lox, so don't go thinking you'll be stuck in diner land. You'll sit easy knowing chefs here use fresh and local ingredients, the option of free-range egg substitution and vegan menu items. Look at the specials board before you make your final decision, or you might miss a scrumptious flat bread or a tasty crab eggs benedict. You'd think you'd be bothered by the extra slpit plate charge, but at Bread and Ink they add bulk to your order, so two can eat their fill of one entrée for only $3 more than the menu price. Linger over shared pasta and floor-to-ceiling views of this trendy couple of blocks. *dm*

Roots Organic Brewing
1520 SE 7th Avenue at SE Hawthorne Boulevard
235.7668, www.rootsorganicbrewing.com
Open: M-Th 3p-11:30p, F 3p-12:30a, Sa 12p-1a, Su 12p-9p
$ Fr S

The organic brews at Roots, together with reggae keeps that keeps on rolling, are a happy match. A Roots concoction on a sunny day or on one of those notorious rannoying Portland days (I call it rannoying when it is annoyingly raining out!) answers your call for a thirst-quencher. While beer and hops go hand-in-hand at most breweries, Roots steps outside the brew box with their Heather Ale, made with Heather tips and zero hops. And that ain't all. I have partaken of their one-of-a-kind Chocolate Habanero Stout and, might I say, it was spicy! Their Island Red is wonderful and if you are around for the North American Organic Brewers Festival (see **Calendar** chapter), Roots hosts a chance for all area organic brewers to strut their stuff. *dm*

Pub Quiz

It's fun to head to your favorite pub for a pint with a good group of friends over some jovial conversation. It's also fun to unite with those friends against strangers and soon-to-be friends in the ultimate test of intellect—the pub quiz! Sometimes this turns out not to be so much a test of intellect as a test of trivial, 1980's cartoon knowledge, but people like competition, no matter how ridiculous, and these quizzes are also an important examination of the effects of alcohol on the brain's ability to operate at full capacity (well, sort of…) *dm*

Bridgeport Brewery

1313 NW Marshall Street at NW 13th Avenue
241.3612, www.bridgeportbrew.com, www.pubquizoregon.com
When: Tu 7p
Cost: $3/person

Alisa Stewart of Pub Quiz Oregon, hosts a number of quizzes around town, including a schedule of events at Biddy McGraw's Irish Pub and Belmont Inn. The largest of these wild trivia nights is held at fancy Bridgeport Brewery, where there are plenty of beers made right before your eyes, plus dining that you'd be surprised to find at a brewpub. Teams are limited to 6 people and there are multiple rounds ending with the champion team winning a cash prize. *dm/ sb*

Billy Ray's Neighborhood Dive

2216 NE MLK Jr. Boulevard at Thompson Street
287.7254
When: Th 8p
Free

'Quizzy' as he is known, is another serial quiz host of PDX, hosting a trivia night at Bitter End Pub also. Quizzy will playfully ridicule players, while soliciting tips as he throws back a few. Good times. *dm*

Peter's 19th Hole

5701 NE Fremont Street at 57th Avenue
460.0544, www.shanrockstrivia.com
When: W 8p
Free

Yet another multi-location trivia night chair, ShanRock, whoops it up with unique quiz events that have participants using capacities beyond their brain (i.e. their physical prowess) to reach the prize. Tipping recommended. *dm*

The Basement Pub

1028 SE 12th Avenue at Yamhill Street
231.6068, www.basementpub.com
When: Su 9p
Free

The Basement Pub is tiny and smoky, but their trivia night is lots of casual fun. Good for the beginner quizzer, The Basement Pub trivia night is not the institutionalized sport of some other establishments. This is a place to keep it real—real trivial. *dm*

Beulahland

118 NE 28th Avenue at Couch Street
235.2794
When: Tue 9p
Free

Another smoky joint, Beulahland draws the hardcore and rowdy for their bout of, er… intellect. Yes… intellect. Yummy ales abound, so why not get your second pint as you adamantly argue that your answer is the correct one. Golly! *dm*

Casual Night Out

Dining and delighting in a relaxed atmosphere

Dan & Louis Bloody Mary

There is always a time when you just want to kick back and have a relaxed evening out. In fact, Oregonians, like Californians are known the world over for their propensity toward all things casual. Go out, but go in comfort, with the divine purpose of repose. Good eats and good laughs galore lie ahead. *sb*

Dan & Louis Oyster Bar

208 SW Ankeny Street at SW 2nd Avenue
227.5906, www.danandlouis.com
Open: Su-Th 11a-9p, F-Sa 11a-2a
$$ Fr Fam

The Wachsmuth Family have been oyster farmers and sailors for generations, and for over 100 years, Portlanders have been packing into Louis and Dan's Oyster Bar for the freshest oysters and most divine smoked salmon stew. The historic dining room and bar is a warm and cozy shelter from any kind of storm. The jalapeno-infused vodka makes their unique Bloody Mary's a perfect pairing for smoke-flavored stew or fried clams. Come before 6:30p and a dozen local oysters on the half-shell are just under ten bucks. *sb*

Wong's King Seafood

8733 SE Division Street at SE 87th Avenue
788.8883
Open: Everyday, 10a-11p, dim sum served until 3p
$ Fam

It is well worth the trek down Division Street and past 82nd Avenue to experience the Hong Kong Chinese food styling of Wong's King Seafood. One of the only Chinese food restaurants in town to serve the traditional full Peking duck dinner, Wong's draws crowds from all around Portland to the area that is rapidly becoming the new Chinatown of the city. Tables are full of celebratory Chinese Americans, a good sign that this is truly a traditional place. For the ravenous in a rush, there is a barbecue take-out window next door to the dining room with delectable barbecue duck for the road. *dm*

Malay Satay Hut

2850 SE 82nd Avenue
771.7888, www.malaysatayhut.com
Open: Everyday, 11a-11p, lunch specials 11a-3p
$$ Veg Fr Fam

Rare is the chance to experience the wonders of Malaysian cuisine on this side of the Pacific. Rarer still it is to find such authentic black and pepper duck, Pampono fish and stuffed handmade bean curd in what looks to be part of a strip mall. But "the hut" has been recognized nationwide for its supernal dishes, outdoing most in the US for flavorful and classic Malaysian dishes. Don't leave without trying the Roti Chanai, a steamy and moist bread served with a buttery, spicy dipping sauce. My favorite menu item is their famous Buddhist Yam Pot, where yam batter is broiled in a bowl shape, and filled with steamed vegetables and an intoxicating sauce that will guarantee your satisfaction. The yummy blended drinks made from exotic fruits are also worth a try, just beware that Durian fruit is what you might call an acquired taste! This family-run restaurant has become so popular that they've opened two more locations in Washington State. *sb*

Alexis Restaurant

215 W Burnside Street at NW 2nd Avenue
224.8577, www.alexisfoods.com
Open: M-Th 11:30a-2p, 5-10p, F-Sa 11:30a-2p, 5-11p, Su 5-10p
$$ Veg Fam Ro Fr

A big huge family-style restaurant is the place to go with your whole gaggle to try some new foods and have boisterous discussions about your comings and goings. Alexis specializes in these festive occasions, with family menus where you pay per person to try all their best dishes, most famously their moussaka (that's mooosaka, not moosaaahka, no long 'A's in Greek) lamb and potato "lasagna," a classic Greek comfort food. Get your kids prepared for some wiggly marinated octopus to go along with their toasty breads and filling appetizers, while you down some Ouzo. Oppah! *sb*

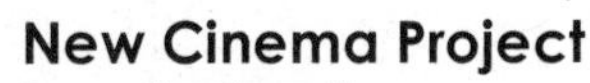

New Cinema Project

Screening Locations:
922 SE Ankeny, New American Art Union
1219 SW Park Street, Northwest Film Center's Whitsell Auditorium
232.8269, www.cinemaproject.org
Admission: $3-6

Film festivals, cutting edge art flicks, and a historical repertoire of silver screen greats are brought to Portland viewers all year long by this important organization. Each season features an average of four themes ranging from Andy Warhol to "First Person in a Globalized World" to documentaries from Lebanese Women. Whether you are a passionate critic or have never been to see an obscure documentary, the moving images this project presents are so diverse and eloquent there is sure to be something for everyone. *sb*

Saburo's

1667 SE Bybee Boulevard at SE Milwaukie Avenue
236.4237
Open: M-Th 5-9:30p, F 5-10:30p, Sa 4:30-10p, Su 4:30-9p
$$ Veg PW Fr

Here's a guarantee: love it or hate it, Saburo's will change the way you think about sushi. Expect seriously long waits, an overcrowded dining area, wait staff that invoke memories of Sienfield's "Soup Nazi," and vertigo-inducing trays of sushi-on-steroids. Saburo's sushi is three times the size of "normal" rolls and cuts—the clean hamachi and fatty salmon belly are standouts. Signature rolls add intrigue to the usual suspects: chopped spicy tuna wrapped in thinly sliced cucumber (Hawaiian roll), and sea eel tastefully paired with tamago (Karate roll) are fanastic. Often overlooked sashimi skips right to the good part without all the rice. I can't help but over-order, and often leave Saburo's stuffed, with a box of leftovers in tow for a midnight snack or an early morning refresher. As long as you're not affixed on the traditional Japanese ideal of "sushi-is-purity," Saburo's will release your inner sushi glutton, who, consciously or not, wants to revel in an orgiastic experience of fresh slabs of fish at affordable prices. *jo*

P.B. & Ellie's Café

4405 SW Vermont Street at SW 45th Avenue
282.1783, www.pbecafe.com
Open: M-Th 10a-8p, F-Sa 9a-9p, Su 9a-7p
$ Vn Fam

Most appropriate for the kiddlywinks, P.B. & Ellie's can also transport the most jaded of adults back to their childhood days. This is a place where parents don't have worry a bit about kids being on best behavior, as P.B. & Ellie's specifically caters to the chlidren with toys, books, a massive chalkboard, train tracks, and birthday party hosting. The Jr. Aidan's is a treat with raisins and chocolate chips accompanying the house-ground organic peanut butter and whole wheat bread. It's cute and healthy, cut in the shape of a flower, served with carrot sticks and applesauce on the side. Though the specialty, PB & J is by no means the only thing happening here. The menu includes burgers, pastas, wraps and even steaks after 5p with a three drink limit on beers and wines—this is an establishment for children after all. To top it off, P.B. & Ellie's uses organic, fair trade and Food Alliance certified ingredients. *dm*

Chaba Thai

5810 NE Sandy Boulevard at NE 58th Avenue
282.3970
Open: M-Th 11:30a-3p, 5-9p, F 11:30-3p, 5-10p, Sa 12-10p, Su 5-9p
$-$$ Veg Fam Ro

In a less-dense block of Sandy Boulevard, Chaba Thai is a wash of color and flavor that people count on for supernal Thai food. Appetizers like fried tofu and spring rolls are both light, not as oily as others you'll find. This warming spot has the best soups in town, also the best Pad Thai in Portland, GrassRoutes writers can agree. From the melted-down rice stew with tender chicken to the ever-present Tom Kha, coconut soup, Chaba's version is stocked with vegetables and flavorful mushrooms. Don't pass up the whole steamed fish, heaping over with natural juices and Thai spices; it is a real crowd pleaser. Plentiful curry and satay options are popular with all, bringing *sanuk*, or good fun-loving pleasure, to all who partake. Chaba is a few blocks away from the main drag but an immediate teleportation to Thailand. *sb*

Nostrana

1401 SE Morrison Street at SE 14th Avenue
234.2427, www.nostrana.com
Open: M-F 11a-2p, Su-Th 5-10p, F-Sa 5-11p
$$ Vn Fam PW

Housed in an airy, yet warm barn-like structure, Nostrana is a happy meeting place of casual sophistication. Come for a beer and a snack-time artisan pizza, or an elegant Italian wine and guinea hen. The simple margherita pizza is best, with the option of arugula and duck egg piled on top. Meats and fish dishes are excellent; halibut, pork and lamb are treated like celebrities, paired with understated veggies like pureed celery root or caramelized cioppino onions. Table bread and focaccia are baked fresh each morning, and greet you at your table with a robust and nutty olive oil. Save room for their supernal panna cotta, my secret indicator of the real heavy-weight Italian restaurant, and their inconceivably good flourless chocolate cake, which you may have to ask for, as it is often left off the menu. Nostrana's chef babies her main dishes, paying less attention to salads and small plates, but has clearly mastered the fine palate of Italian flavors in a restaurant with real ambiance. *sb*

El Palenque

8324 SE 17th Avenue near SE Tacoma Street
231.5140
Open: M-F 11:30a-9:30p, Sa-Su 12:30-9:30p
$ Veg Fam

El Salvadorian cuisine isn't always the first thing you think of for a casual weeknight outing with the gang, but El Palenque is one of the best places for a family feast. Papusas and Salvadorian creamy-style tamales are hearty and delicious. Palenque's guacamole menu includes a Guatemalan mint version, a tequila concoction and the tasty Salvadorian classic served with hardboiled eggs. Everything is handmade in house and served at reasonable prices. With a full list of Mexican favorites, I recommend the family platters that include all of Palenque's kitchen highlights and are certain to satisfy everyone round the table. *sb*

Jo Bar & Rotisserie

701 NW 23rd Avenue at NW Irving Street
222.0048, www.papahaydn.com
Open: M-Th 11:30a-10p, F-Sa 11:30a-12a, Su 11:30a-10p
$$ R Ro

Don't ever disregard a round sofa just because it is different. It's OK to sit close to the stove sometimes. It's OK to have dessert first. Be indulgent when the time is right. Throw out your mother's rules and adopt Jo's for a luscious evening of food and good company at this purplish, reasonably priced wonderland of all things passionate. Perfectly roasted chicken with locally-grown seasonal vegetables and a course of wines or well drinks will mellow out even the most stress-heavy shoulders. Stare into the eyes of those near and dear and share a rich moment without parting with all your dough. These dishes are made to rustle things up, in the best kind of way. *sb*

World Cavalcade Travelogue Film Series

Scottish Rite Center, 1512 SW Morrison Street at SW 15th Avenue
241.2575, www.worldtravelfilms.com
Film schedule varies

For over 30 years, World Cavalcade, hosted by the Scottish Rite Center, has brought the world to the screen with their intimate portraits of filmmakers and their travels. Go see the beauties and bounties of a journey to Slovenia, a co-production including the film and a narrative story by the filmmakers themselves. For a full-scale trek, buy a ticket package to circumnavigate the globe without leaving your seat. After seeing these images and hearing the stories of such open-minded voyagers, pre-conceived notions and generalizations must fade away, and only admiration and curiosity remain. *sb*

Horn of Africa

3939 NW MLK Jr. Boulevard at Shaver Street
331.9844, www.hornofafrica.net
Open: M-F Lunch Buffet 10:30a-3p, Dinner 5-10p, Sa-Su 5-8p
$ Veg Fr

Venturing beyond Ethiopian cuisine to encompass spices of the surrounding region as well, Horn of Africa knows its audience well. The proprietor provides numerous vegan options and uses organic ingredients for many dishes; even for the traditional Injera, a crepe-meets-sourdough bread used for spooning food. The Horn has a pleasant dining area and a hospitable host, and you can find interesting grocery items on the few shelves in the adjacent room. It is a regular addition to the Saturday Market food carts as well. *dm*

¿Por Qué No? TaqueriaPor Qué No? Taqueria

3524 N Mississippi Avenue at N Fremont Street
467.4149
Open: M-Th 11:30a-9p, F 11:30a-10p, Sa 11a-10p, Su 11a-9p
$ Vn Fr S Dg

Mississippi Avenue is lined with opportunities to snack, shop and scope and ¿Por Qué No? contributes generously to the snacking part of that equation. This is the Mexican food you wish you had eaten in Mexico. The fresh ingredients, including local meat and line-caught fish are just the compliment needed for rice and beans. The space is small and comforting with soccer on the tube at all times and outdoor seating to take the indoor overflow if the day is nice. The owner is part of an active initiative to solarize the avenue by grouping businesses into solar-panel power grids, so community investment is strong. When I was living in Mexico, my landlady Sara was always pouring me *jamaica* water, a delectable hibiscus drink, and I recommend some to wash down a Por Qué No beef taco or Bryan's Bowl. There is also Negra Modelo and unblended margaritas for those seeking some extra relaxation at this beloved neighborhood joint. *dm*

Kalga Kafe

4147 SE Division Street at SE 41st Avenue
236.4770
Open: M-Su 5-12p
$ Vn Ro Fr

More restaurants like Kalga should exist. Their organic, local ingredients fuse to create an all-vegetarian, and often vegan, menu with made-from-scratch items. Offered are steeps from the lovely local tea merchants at the Tao of Tea as well as eco-friendly wines. The building is on a graceful corner curve that puts most guests at window dining. Candlelight and water goblets create a medieval atmosphere as an array of international cuisine descends on diners. Watch out, "medium" is spicy at Kalga, and I mean spi-cy, waiters recommend a spiciness rating of 'mild plus' to avoid a tongue burning. A rare experience is stopping into Food Fight! located around the corner in the tiny shopping strip, a vegan convenience store (there can't be too many of those in the world), open 10a-8p everyday, 233.3910. *dm*

Savoy Tavern and Bistro

2500 SE Clinton Street at SE 25th Avenue
808.9999
Open: Tu-Sa 5p-2:30a, Su 5p-12a
$$ Vn Ro Fr WiFi

The low-lit Savoy is a 1950's basement spruced up and hipped out with handsome waiters who casually lay plates of jazzy southern dishes next to your unbeatable whiskey sour—avoid the busy hours, this place is casual and sometimes slow with the service. The owners use local and organic meats and produce whenever possible. Diners can indulge in the classic mac and cheese, popable chicken croquettes, a dependable pork loin and choose from a slew of sides. Look for the amoeba-like Savoy symbol and enter into a haven of sophisticated tunes and mushroom shaped lamps. Open a couple hours later than most other restaurant pubs, this place would also fit in to **Stay Up Late** chapter. *dm*

Horse Brass Pub

4534 SE Belmont Street at SE 45th Avenue
232.2202, www.horsebrass.com
Open: M-F 11a-2:30a, Sa-Su 9a-2:30a
$-$$ Veg Fr

Maybe it is some latent love I have for the motherland, or perhaps it is simply my adoration of beer, but this British pub on U.S. ground speaks to me. With over 50 brews on draught, smoke in the air, Guinness and royal family paraphernalia on the walls and darts in the corner, the Horse Brass hits the mark. They serve breakfast on the weekends, and lunch and dinner everyday, all fairly basic grub, but food is not the forte here—that top spot is reserved for beer. City breweries Rogue, Widmer, and BridgePort are always an option as well as house-brewed and cask-conditioned offerings. The cost of a creamy stout and a corn beef sandwich at this 30-year-old Portland institution is an affordable alternative to that costly plane ticket to England, not to mention that pesky jet lag. *dm*

The Night Light

2100 SE Clinton Street at SE 21st Street
731.6500
Open: Everyday, 3p-2:30a
$$ Veg PW

All local and organic ingredients go into Night Light's adventurous cocktails, and better than ordinary bar food, the clear favorite of which is the Pomegranate Martini and the killer nacho plate. The simple fusion fare makes it another Portland staple eatery and hang out. *ec*

L'Astra

22 NE 7th Avenue at E Burnside Street
236.3896
Open: M-Sa 5:30-11p
$Veg PW Fr

Seasonal specialties and a small but vibrant atmosphere make L'Astra the kind of restaurant whose cozy dishes will keep you coming back for more, especially since they are all under $10. *ec*

The Clinton Street Pub

2516 SE Clinton Street at SE 25th Avenue
236.7137
Open: Everyday, 2p-2:30a
$-$$ Veg Fr

The Clinton Street Pub is the meeting place of Portland's pinball set, the Fierce Flipper Fingers, who have regular gatherings here over pints. Movies play in the background and bartenders become DJ's at this smoky neighborhood bar. *ec*

Rotture

315 SE 3rd Avenue at SE Pine Street
234.5683
Open: Everyday, 5p-2:30a
$ Fr

Located in the East Industrial District, this diamond in the rough has a diverse, queer-friendly bar, great weekend DJ's and a gorgeous patio overlooking the Willamette River. *ec*

Acapulco's Gold

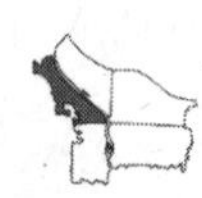

2610 NW Vaughn Street at NW 26th Avenue
220.0283
Open: Sa-Th 11a-11p, F 11a-11p
$ Vn Fr

Acapulco's Gold borders on Portland's NW industrial district and can be easily overlooked, but if you want a pitcher of citrus-y margaritas, a giant plate of nachos with meat, grilled veggies, or soy taco meat, and a place with authentic Tex-Mex feel, look no further. Large nachos can comfortably feed three and you can stay all night laughing and getting a bit on the sloppy side. *rrm*

The B-Side Tavern

632 E Burnside Street at SE 6th Avenue
233.3113
Open: Everyday, 4p-2:30a
$ PW

B-side hosts Portland's laid back, minimalist bar scene. X-Ray lamps adorn the walls, and locals dig into cheap drinks as they ponder which juke box song to pick next. Grab the window seat for the best people watching vantage point. *ec*

Veganopolis

412 SW 4th Avenue at SW Stark Street
226.3400, www.veganopolis.com
Open: M-F 9a-6p, Sa-Su 9a-4p
$ Vn S WiFi

Veganopolis is a meat-free, dairy-free, casein-free zone. Supported by bamboo floors and digested through composts and low-flow toilets, it is probably one of the least ecologically impacting restaurants in the city. Luckily, this vegan "cafeteria" does not sacrifice style or sumptuous dining in the pursuit of its vegan ideals. For feasters, there is a daily lunch buffet and a weekend breakfast buffet, plus the steady menu options, heavy on the sandwiches, with inventive alternatives gracing the bread like raw almond pâté and cashew ricotta. Give them a call to hear their daily specials, then head over to try 'em out. Wrap up your meal with a slice of Brownie Chunk 'Cheese'cake baked by Sweet Pea Bakery, a local, vegan slice of heaven. Veganopolis offers soy jerky and raw bars for the road as well as a selection of vegan cookbooks for those who are ready to test the waters of a plants-only diet. *dm*

Eleni's Philonexia

112 NW 9th Avenue at Davis Street
227.2158, www.elenisrestaurant.com
Open: Tu-Th 5-10p, F-Sa 5-11p
$$ Veg Fam PW

I am lying on a pristine beach in the Adriatic. There are gentle waves washing ashore. Soft whistles rise with the ebbing tide as olive branches flutter in the wind. A kind sir finds me and offers an elegant feta filo treat, dazzled with sweet honey. In the other hand, I hold a glass of incredible Greek house wine. Now I am back on a rainy night off a concrete strip of turf in Portland. But the moment is still there, held up loftily by the strong renditions of Greek fare at Eleni's—sautéed ground beef, mystifying filo creations and of course the seafood—the non-spongy grilled calamari is most notable. Bring back your dreams of the most beautiful waters of Greece as you indulge in these delights. *sb*

Speakeasy Gils

601 1/2 SE Taylor Street at SE 6th Avenue
234.8991
Open: M-Th 11-2a, F-Sa 10-2a
$ Fr

Sundays at the Speakeasy mean dollar beers for all, but on any night trigger-happy bartenders mix some of the strongest drinks in town. Stay busy with their antique shuffleboard set. *sb*

Sagittarius

2710 N Killingsworth Street at N Burrage Avenue
289.7008
Open: W-M 11a-12a
$-$$ Veg Fr PW

A recent addition to the ever-evolving North Portland scene, Sagittarius fills the void in the chill spot category. The walls remind me of a cut watermelon just after the sun goes down, making these some of my favorite wall colors in Portland. A casual happy hour with friends won't leave you longing for the flirtatious eyes of your sweetie, but Sagittarius is versatile enough to accommodate either scenario. With a menu that appeals both to my burger mood or my lighter veggie mood, and a selection of drinks that includes an extensive cocktail menu and some great local wines and beer, I leave happy with the hope that I will return soon. *sm*

Ohana Hawaiian Café

6320 NE Sandy Boulevard at NE 63rd Street
335.5800, www.ohanahawaiiancafe.com
Open: M-Sa 11a-9p
$-$$ Veg Fam S

All around Portland are glimpses of a bountiful Hawaiian community and Ohana is a monument attesting to that fact. Completely authentic, with most ingredients sourced locally, this family joint is a perfect spot for a comfortable bite. The Hawaiian version of ceviche, called Lomi-Lomi, is delicate salmon and bold spices, a nice compliment to one of their meat dishes. Whether you see it as a good thing or a bad things, Hawaiian cuisine exhibits a determined propensity toward all things macaroni salad—this creamy sidedish is a constant companion to every menu item. Kids are certain to enjoy the sunny atmosphere as well. *sb*

Bewon Korean

1203 NW 23rd Avenue at NW Northrup Street
464.9222
Open: M-F 11:30a-10p, Sa 5-10p, Su 5-9p
$$ Veg Ro Fr

Is the sign of a fine restaurant the absence of condiments? At Bewon Korean, the chefs prepare every dish with flawless flavor. A full course dinner for two covers much of the menu, but for the more modest appetite, the expert informer/waiters will suggest some choice dishes. The Japchae starter of sweet potato noodles and cripplingly divine mushrooms is a perfect segueway into Daeji Bulgogi pork. While there are white tablecloths on the tables, the vibe is generally casual here, though dinner will take you beyond that under $10 bracket, so head here for lunch if you are not up for spending around $15 a plate. *dm*

Queen of Sheba

2413 NE MLK Jr. Boulevard at NE Brazee Street
287.6302, www.queenofsheba.biz
Open: Su-W 5-9p, Th-Sa 12-2:30p, 5-10p
$$ Vn Fr Ro CO

If the Queen of Sheba is good enough for Danny Glover, and a framed quote of his gracing the wall behind the register will confirm this, then it's good enough for me. Spicy dollops of divine concoctions adorn a communal platter of traditional Injera flat bread, a crepe-like sour dough mechanism intended for tearing and scooping up healthy servings into your mouth or the mouth of a loved one or family member. The vegan or veggie sampler is the speed-dating entrée of the menu, quickly aiding guests in determining which dishes they'd see again. What a nice thing to walk away from such a spread of saucy and spicy chickpea, mushroom, and lentil masterpieces without dropping all your dough. *dm*

Happiest Hour

The best times to eat, drink and make merry

Gilt Club

Whether you're having a late lunch or an early dinner, the best time to eat for cheap in Portland is during Happy Hour, a trend that's a major asset to this river city. Most restaurants have a special menu for this time of day that is tasty and affordable, to go with signature drinks, in both the alcoholic and non-alcoholic variety. Some of these places make such extravagant gourmet drinks that ordering virgin has become a flavorfully common occurrence. Here is a smattering of our favorite happy hour finds, in all four corners of the city. *sb*

The Gilt Club
306 NW Broadway at NW Everett Street
222.4458, www.giltclub.com
Open: M-Sa 5p-2a
Happy Hour: M-Sa 5-6:30p

Yum is the name of the game at the Gilt Club, where you can splurge on fancy foods without draining your wallet during their daily 5-630p gilded happy hour. The lush interior space hosts fine plates for just five dollars, including Alsatian flammenkueche with melt-in-your-mouth caramelized onions and creamy frommage blanc. Steamed mussels and Angus burgers make a swanky entrance paired with Gilt's most famous drink, the spicy Moscow Mule. Served in a traditional copper mug, this ginger-heavy drink heals your body, mind and spirit. I ignore other drink options here, and suggest you go out on a limb, too. Even if you are usually a one-note samba when is comes to buzzy drinks, I can't hold back my excitement for this true PDX gem. *sb*

Callaloo Caribbean Escape
1639 NW Glisan Street at NW 16th Avenue
517.8220, http://callalooescape.com
Open: M-Sa 11-2a
Happy Hour: Everyday, 3-6p

French fried appetizers and everybody's Caribbean favorite Red Stripe beers arrive on your table for a mere $2 a pop. Marinated hanger steak is priced right during their daily 3-6p happy hour. Grab a beer, or their unspeakably good mohitos (a whopping $4) and take a quick vacation to Jamaica via this rather non-descript seafood stop. *sb*

Corbett Fish House

5901 SW Corbett Avenue at SW Pendleton Street
246.4434, www.corbettfishhouse.com
Open: M-F 11a-10p, Sa 12-10p, Su 12-9p
Happy Hour: Everyday, 3-6p

My dream come true is a place where I can nosh on gluten-free and sustainable fish and chips for under $3 while sitting in the sun sipping a lemon drop. Corbett Fish House, and their sister-in-law Hawthorne Fish House follow the Monterey Aquarium's strict outlines for sustainable seafood in order to keep the oceans healthy and our bellies satisfied. You'll do flips over the fish tacos, yummy calamari, and heaping bay shrimp quesadilla. Bring all your friends and smile because you are supporting a truly conscientious business and eating just about the healthiest version of fried food I can think of. Happy hour menu items are all $2.95 for food or drinks. *sb*

Alberta Street Oyster Bar and Grill

2926 NE Alberta Street at NE 29th Avenue
284.9600, www.albertaoyster.com
Open: Everyday, 4:30p-late
Happy Hour: Su-M, 4:30p-late, Tu-Sa 4:30-6p and 10-11p

Steamed mussels with white wine and fennel seed or roasted beets with dilled cucumbers, blood orange and goat cheese are a perfect compliment to local oysters on the half shell. Go back in time with a four-dollar Whiskey Sour, Old Fashioned, or a Tom Collins. For more modern drink tastes there are Lemon Drops and Kamekazes. You'll feel like royalty with a platter of delectable shellfish and a perfectly mixed drink. *sb*

The Empire Room Bistro & Bar

4260 SE Hawthorne Boulevard at SE 42nd Avenue
231.9225, www.theempireroom.net
Open: Tu-F 11a-3p, Tu-Th 4p-11p, F-Sa 4p-12
Happy Hour: Tu-Sa 4-7p

The Empire Room is a home away from home. Co-owed by three sisters, this cozy joint serves three-dollar Lemon Drops and Cosmos from 4-7p everyday. Pair your drink of choice, whether it is one of their signature martini-style cocktails or a local wine or beer, with an appetizer—all priced at just five bucks. The salami plate comes with smoked Gouda and grainy bread, or pick the beef skewers piled with cool yogurt cucumber dip and toasted pita. Saturday nights, live jazz starts early, so even happy hour goers can get in the groove. *sb*

Purple Tooth Lounge

938 N Cook Street at N Mississippi Avenue
517.9931, www.purpletoothlounge.com
Open: Tu-Su 5p-late
Happy Hour: Tu-F 5p-6:30p

I'm not picky, at least I like to think. I'm happy plopped down anywhere I can imbibe a hot Irish Coffee or whatever my taste buds are craving. I imagine what my own home would be like if I spruced it up and maybe hired a full time staff to wait on me. It is more realistic to pass time at a place like Purple Tooth Lounge. An unmistakable pink house with black trim, this dark and cozy lounge serves up a lengthy cocktail list with some choice chow. Happy hour at the Tooth means $3 well drinks and $1 PBR. Just off the beaten Mississippi Avenue path, you will find it hard to pry yourself from the cozy clutches of this intimate bar. *dm*

820/Mint

816 N Russell Street at N Albina Avenue
284.5518, www.mintand820.com
Open: M-Th 5-10p, F-Sa 5-11p
Happy Hour: Everyday, 5-6:30p

Owned and lovingly tended by the woman hailed as the best mixologist around, Mint restaurant and the adjacent bar 820 serve fresh and beautiful cocktails. House-infused liquors and syrups dapple inventive drinks like the Bella with blackberry puree and sugared lemon-lime juice or the Ad Lib with muddled cilantro. Most drinks are quite sweet, with the exception of the beet vodka lemon Ruby. Chow down on some sweet potato fries or a Cuban lamb burger, both significantly cheaper during their everyday happy hour. Get a bit dressed up and live up the swanky atmosphere, that at first seems snooty but when you realize the bartenders are on a first name basis with so many regulars, you'll see its just an ultra cool neighborhood place. *sb*

Slow Bar

533 SE Grand Avenue at SE Stark Street
230-7767, www.slowbar.net
Open: M-F 11:30a-2:30a, Sa-Su 5p-2:30a
Happy Hour: M-F 3-6p

Slow Bar is equipped with the best jukebox in Portland. At least, that's what our resident metal head thinks. But it's the menu, which serves the best bar food on the east side of the river, and the high-backed round red booths that are the draw for me. With the not too extensive, but thorough menu, you will be able to enjoy your cocktails with both your vegetable and meat loving friends. And, if it's meat you love, the burger, which comes to you dressed with deep-fried onion rings, is a top contender around town. *sm*

Art House Cinema

Movies plus pizza plus popcorn plus suds equals fun

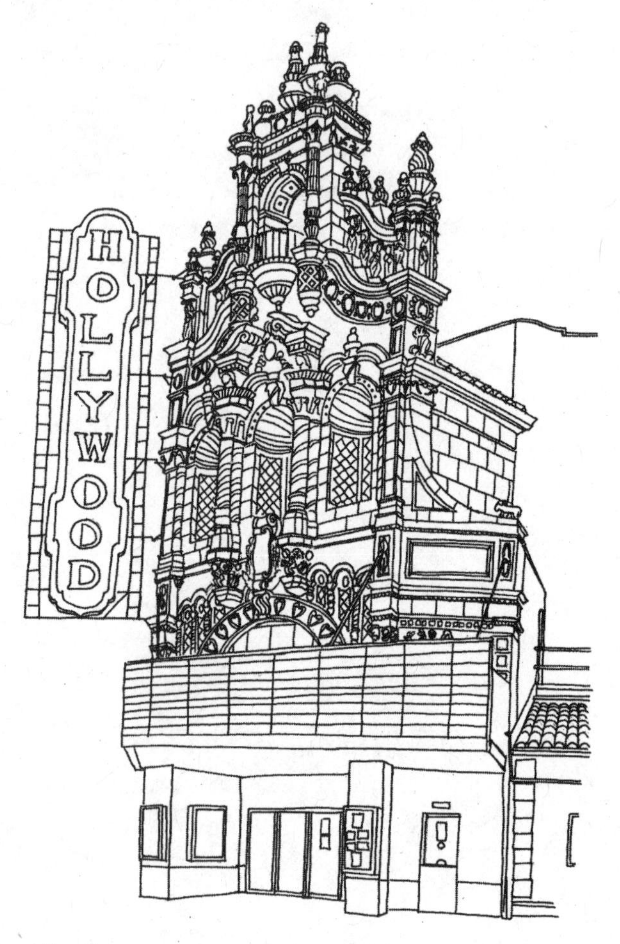

Hollywood Theater

In Portland, there is an unwritten rule that all residents are partial to beer and pizza with their movies. Trust me, it is not something to complain about. There are nearly as many film festivals in this city as there are in New York City, which clarifies my second point, that Stumptowners are happy moviegoers, cinema enthusiasts, and filmmakers. I don't think it is just the rain driving them inside, although when the drops are coming down, it is nice to pile onto a sofa with four friends and eat pizza in front of *Taxi Driver.* Whatever movie magic got sprinkled on these folks, the result is a plethora of great art house cinemas scattered around the city, where tickets are cheap and community presence is strong. *sb*

Hollywood Theater
4122 NE Sandy Boulevard at NE 41st Avenue
281.4215, www.hollywoodtheatre.org, www.filmactionoregon.org
Show times vary, look for film festivals
Admission: $4-6

With the help of Film Action Oregon, the Hollywood Theater has maintained its historic roots while inspiring Oregon filmmakers, young and old, novice and experienced. From the 1926 premier of "More Pay-Less Work," to the underappreciated Cinerama widescreens of the 50's to the Forest Film Festival (see **Calendar** chapter) of today, this landmark theater has honored the film medium and served as a catalyst for engaging ideas. As an aspect of the education programs hosted here, special attention is paid to women filmmakers, and there is an entire film festival dedicated to young documentary makers. Watch the recognizable blinking sign illuminate the night air, waltz to the Wurlitzer, and catch a film from any decade in movie history, classic to current. *sb*

The Academy Theater

7818 SE Stark Street at SE 78th Street
252.0500, www.academytheaterpdx.com
Open: M-F Matinees start at 4:15p, Sa-Su 1:15p
Admission: $2-3

The older, wiser cousin of Portland's teaming mass of great independent cinemas, Academy Theater has the reclining seats and spaciousness of an Orange County (CA not FL) multi-plex at art house prices. The steady $3 adult price can be upgraded with a pizza and beer for a few extra dineros. Monday blues fade into oblivion with a four-dollar double feature. Before 8p you can bring children for one buck—just be careful not to over-stimulate their young minds—video has an enormous impact on youngsters that should be given careful consideration. My parent's didn't let me watch TV until I was a teenager, so that I could develop a full imaginative and creative mind instead of inputting the TV images instead—it has really benefited me. Even now I can notice who watched a lot of movies and TV as a kid. There's a striking impact on them. OK, I'm off the soapbox and we're on with the rest of the **Art House** chapter… *sb*

The Kennedy School Theater

Located inside the Kennedy School Hotel
5736 NE 33rd Avenue at NE Killingsworth Street
249.3983, movie hotline 249.7474 x4, www.mcmenamins.com
Open: Matinees and evening shows everyday, after 5p, 21+
Admission: $1-3

A re-invented elementary school auditorium, The Kennedy School movie-theater, housed inside The **Kennedy School Hotel** (see **Lodge** chapter), puts the typical school performance-art experience to shame. Instead of Johnny's cracking voice feebly reciting a grade school play, Hollywood stars entertain viewers as they cozy up in couches and cushioned seats with beer and popcorn. The McMenamin Brothers revision of our city delivers once again; who wants to sit through a mediocre rendition of Romeo and Juliet anyway (unless it's your kiddo, then no offense!)? *dm*

Mission Theater & Pub

1624 NW Glisan Street at NW 16th Avenue
288.3286, movie hotline 249.7474 x5, www.mcmenamins.com
Open: M-F 5p-12p, Sa-Su 2p-12a
Admission: $1-3

Portlanders have a surprising penchant for local chain businesses, as long as those businesses are sustainable, incredibly clever, and unique. I guess we like the comfort of brand recognition as much as anyone. The Mission Theater delivers with the notorious McMenamin Brothers at its helm. I like The Mission because it never seems to draw too large a crowd even though you can watch movies, *Buffy the Vampire Slayer* episodes and CD release performances from the balcony of an old longshoreman union meeting hall and, once upon a time, evangelical church. Solve the problem of having to get up and go to the kitchen by ordering a veggie burger with your Meryl Streep and, of course, a McMenamin's brew, and it will be delivered right to your seat. *dm*

Laurelhurst Theater

2735 E Burnside Street at NE 28th Avenue
232.5511, www.laurelhursttheater.com
Open: Matinees start early afternoon, everyday
Admission: $3

You want to check out all the cool things this vibrant metropolis has to offer, but right now you just want to dummy up in front of a movie. At the Laurelhurst, you don't have to feel like you are pausing your Portland explorations to gift yourself some downtime. Portland has more breweries per square mile than any other US city, and the locals are expert independent theater seekers, so drinking beer and watching films for cheap is an authentic cultural experience. The Laurelhurst plays more recently released flicks and some throwbacks. I caught *Harold and Maude* here and was happy to giggle with a whole theater full of people, not just the amount of people that fit in my living room. A wit-filled flick is the best pick in PDX—Portlanders are a receptive crowd for clever turns of tongue and subtle drops of humor. *dm*

The Roseway Theater

7229 NE Sandy Boulevard at NE 72nd Avenue
287.8119
Open: Evening showings, matinees on weekends only
Admission: $4-7

The Roseway has been around since the 1920's, when each show began with an organ recital. In the same family-owned, independent fashion, this historic theater blacks all lights during shows, and provides visitors with a neighborhood movie theater feel. *sb*

Avalon Theatre

3451 SE Belmont Street at SE 35th Avenue
238.1617, www.wunderlandgames.com
Open: Matinees begin early afternoon, everyday
Admission: $2-3

Avalon is the answer to the afternoon doldrums, or the whenever doldrums, for that matter. What makes this place unique is the incredible schedule. Movies run in two auditoriums all day, everyday, so any time is the right time for a good flick. Surround-sound invigorates old classics, as well as new releases. Tickets are two dollars for most shows, on occasion a whopping three, but you can still get your candy and popcorn and pile in for less than any mainstream theater. Save up your spare nickels for the vintage arcade games in the lobby. *sb*

Baghdad Theatre and Pub

3702 SE Hawthorne Boulevard at SE 37th Street
225.5555, www.mcmenamins.com
Open: M-Sa 11-1a, Su 12p-12a
Admission: $3

The ever-present McMenamin Brother brew masters have created a slew of pubs, theaters, restaurants, and hotels across the city. A smaller incarnation of their usual grandeur, The Baghdad is Moorish-architecture-meets-hearty-pints-meets-iconic-Hollywood-pictures. Enjoy beautifully restored mosaic work on your way into the ornate theater. This is a great spot for hungry movie-goers, where salads and sandwiches are served to you while you bask in the glow of the silver screen. I recommend indulging in the locally farmed Marionberry cobbler while a thriller gets you scooting towards the edge of your seat. *sb*

St. Johns Theater

8704 N Lombard Street at N Alta Avenue
286.1768
Open: Matinees begin early afternoon, everyday
Admission: $2
CO

Quite possibly the best deal in Portland's movie land—this funky old theater near the bridge of the same name serves up cheap pizza and beer to go along with its cheap tickets, plus there are tables in the theaters. Talk about dinner and a movie! *sb*

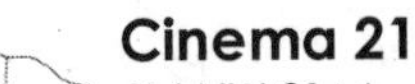

Cinema 21

616 NW 21st Avenue at NW Hoyt Street
223.4515, www.cinema21.com
Show times vary, look for film fesativals
Admission: $4-8

A Portland classic, the locally owned and independently operated Cinema 21 plays host to some of the city's most ravishing film festivals. In addition, they often play rare and unique films other theaters dodge. Check out the weird and wild cosmic hex cult films of the 70's or brash films from today's urban youth and gay activists. This place will push your buttons and make you tick. When you come up for air, it doesn't matter which direction you turn, there will be a great restaurant awaiting your tableside pontifications. *sb*

Clinton Theater

2522 SE Clinton Street at SE 25th Avenue
238.8899, www.clintonsttheater.com
Open: Everyday from 5p
Admission: $4-7
CO

During the hot summer months, the Clinton Theater is a cool venue for catching a vintage flick or a big-screen re-play. On a rainy night I had to keep my coat on, but it was worth bundling up and getting reacquainted with *Buffalo 66* and an overflowing basket of popcorn. As the smallest operational brewery in the state of Oregon, the walk-in closet-sized space yields some high-class suds. Match a monstrous hamburger with your unique brew, and groove to live music playing most nights in the attached café before or after the show. *sb*

Listen

Any auditory experience you can imagine, from concerts, theater, and open mics to headlining shows—it's all here.

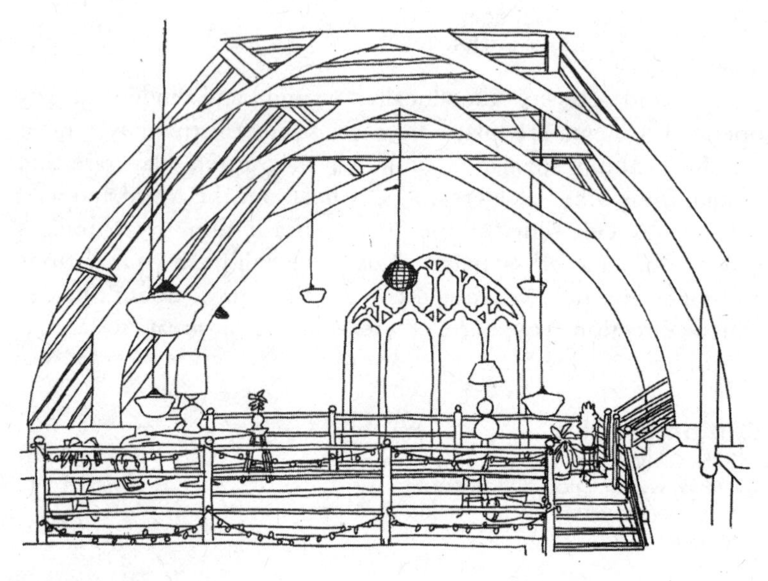

Funky Church

Well-strung notes can carry every shade of human emotion. I like to close my eyes and let my other senses go when I catch wind of some magical melodies. My mother used to say you can't listen with your mouth open. But some of these places promote listening while you eat scrumptious tapas or sashimi. Whatever your ears perk up to, it is essential to enjoy the sounds and indulge in aural distraction as often as possible. *sb*

Funky Church

2456 SE Tamarack Avenue at SE Division Street
www.funkychurch.com
Show times vary

The Funky Church is just that, a church that has been refurbished as a homey theater. Shows light up the stage four or five times a month, mostly acoustic, but occasionally a full band. Funky Church is on the edge of Ladd's Addition, (see **Explore** chapter), a beautiful and vintage neighborhood that has alleyways and rose gardens. The Funky Church even has a bell tower and baptismal font. Check their website to see if something's going on, and it will be a special night! *rrm*

Ozone Records

701 E Burnside Street at SE 7th Avenue
227.1975, www.o3records.com
Open: M-Sa 11a-10p, Su 12-9p

A corner shop of musical treasures, Ozone caters to listeners with particular tastes. They feature off-the-beaten-track records from new and buried artists, many of whom you'd be at a loss to find elsewhere. Employees are geared up for questioning, so you'll find that obscure song or out-of-print album you had your heart set on, but thought was a lost cause. Mostly rock, with lots of local stuff, there's also a good selection of world beats to be found. Whether you go with purpose, or just to peruse the shelves for something unique, you're sure to find something that needs a new home: yours! *sb*

Mississippi Records

4007 N Mississippi Avenue at N Shaver Street
282.2990
Open: W-M 12-7p

Music fiends of all flavors make regular visits to this used record and cassette tape store. Skip out on CDs and iPods and get back to the classic sounds of vinyl and tape. As much as everyone loves the new technology, I've noticed personal music players separate people not only from one another but also their environments. Take off your headphones, disconnect from your devices and get into the sounds around you. Then head to this well-organized, inexpensive, and friendly record store to pick up something you can share with your friends. Last visit produced a 3-record addition to my collection with Miles Davis' *Sketches of Spain*, Pink Floyd's *Dark Side of the Moon,* and an Aretha album. For under $10, I had a tune in my head, a party at my apartment, and an extra skip in my step. *sb*

Portland Baroque Orchestra

1020 SW Taylor Street at SW 10th Avenue
222.6000, www.pbo.org
Office Hours: M-F 9:30a-5:30p, show times and locations vary

To get the real sound of Telemann, Shubert, Scarlatti, Bach, Purcell, or any of the Baroque composer greats, you have to hear their pieces performed on the original instruments. And that's just what this world-class orchestra plays. The evolution of tuning and shaping strings, brass, and especially the variations of the keyboard have changed the way the music sounds. Though there is always personal preference involved as with all the arts, there's no question any listener will have a more intimate knowledge of the life of the music when hearing it in its nascent form. From a young age, these composers have been my close "friends," and I encourage even those who've never been interested in this music to give it a listen and open up to the tapestry melodies. After all, counterpoint and the harmonies thought up by these guys have influenced nearly all music being played today. Get in the know! *sb*

360 Vinyl

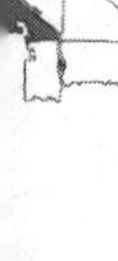

214 NW Couch Street at NW 2nd Avenue
224.3688, http://360vinyl.com
Open: M-Sa 11a-8p, Su 12-6p
Stop what you're doing and perk your ears towards 360 Vinyl, the best underground and hip-hop record store to speak of. For DJ hopefuls or the professionals, or little ole me with my record player keeping me company while I make wild forays in the kitchen, the truth is that music will never be all boxed up with that impossible shrink-wrap. We'll still be making it, singing it, dancing to it, and proudly spinning it on our turntables. *sb*

Powell's Book Events

Various Powell's locations citywide
www.powellsbooks.com/calendar
Schedule varies
Nearly every day of the week Powell's offers a book event. Whether it is Children's Storytime, an author reading, or a discussion group based on a new title, there is something you'll enjoy. Check out the web calendar for current information on who is coming to town. There are local authors, and big names spreading themselves all over their epic list of events. Get behind the pages of your favorite livre! *sb*

Blue Monk

3341 SE Belmont Street at SE 33rd Avenue
595.0575, www.thebluemonk.com
Open: Tu-Sa 5p-1a, Su 5p-12a
It wasn't even 5:30p, and the sky had already blackened, storming so strongly that we had to swerve around fallen tree limbs. We were trying to drive towards Belmont Street, cringing as we swaggered down the road past an eerie cemetery. When the weather persists like this, as it is known to do upon occasion, there's no place I'd rather be confined than Blue Monk. With wicked happy hour deals and an East Coast-inspired menu of classic spaghetti and meatballs and chicken parmesian with a gourmet twist, my belly is always satisfied. On uber-indulgent nights I order the bacon-wrapped scallops before heading into the jazz-filled basement for an intimate concert. *sb*

Pi-Rem

433 NW 4th Avenue at NW Flanders Street
227.5494, www.pi-rem.com
Open: W 8p-12a, most Th 8p-12a, F-Sa 9p-2a

This gallery-meets-bar-meets-music venue hosts intriguing bands and DJ's that represent international sounds. Swanky drinks featuring fresh-squeezed juices combine with an epic sound system. Visitors are furnished with a complete evening of culture at its most modern without ever paying cover charge. Enter through a single door in a non-descript whitewashed brick factory building, with not much in the way of signage, and you are in for a treat. Don't miss Wednesday Jazztronica nights. *sb*

Music Millenium

3158 E Burnside Street at NE 32nd Avenue
231.8926, www.musicmillennium.com
Open: M-Sa 10a-10p, Su 11a-9p

In high school, my favorite record store was called Mystery Train, a place where used albums were plentiful and there was never any rush while you took in your potential new tunes on the CD players at checkout. Music Millennium captures this small town record store feel with a collection of both new and used CD's, a vinyl section, and an adjunct classical music shop. Scattered throughout the store are inserts for Music Millennium's suggestions of the 100 Greatest Albums and for someone wanting to take a blind leap of faith, this is a good way to go. If you want to take a listen, they are happy to pipe in the sounds at the barber chair listening station. This is no pretentious or elitist joint; they just want you to find some great music. *dm*

Tugboat Brewing Company

711 SW Ankeny Street at SW Broadway
226.2508, www.d2m.com/Tugwebsite
Open: M 5-10p, Tu-Th 4p-12a, F-Sa 4p-1a,

The Tugboat is a sweet little jazz and indie venue in southwest downtown. This is the kind of place where you can listen to some obscure jazz musician, while telling the bartender all your troubles. One of the coolest things about this bar is that there is a library worth of books lining the shelves. Go read a book and listen to music and you'll be all the smarter for it. *rrm*

The Goodfoot

2835 SE Stark Street at SE 28th Avenue
239.9292, www.thegoodfoot.com
Open: upstairs pub, everyday 6p-2:30a, downstairs lounge, M 8p-1:30a, W 9p-1:30a, Th-Sa 9p-2:30a, Tu and Su special shows only
Happy Hour: Everyday, 6-9p

The Goodfoot has two levels, and two feels. Upstairs with big 'ole hot sandwiches, ice cold micro brews (and Pabst Blue Ribbon, too), pool tables and that neighborhood bar feel that we all love. Downstairs features some of the best up and coming nationally touring and local jam bands as well as some hip-hop and Friday's dance party, "Soul Stew," with a sick DJ and a packed dance floor. It is a real smoky place though, so if you're seriously opposed to smelling like an ashtray when you get home, you might want to skip this one. In my opinion, the music makes up for it. *rrm*

Chamber Music Northwest

Box Office: 522 SW 5th Avenue at SW Taylor Street
223.3203, www.cmnw.org
Shows times and locations vary

Bringing to Portland the refined joy of classical music, Chamber Music Northwest presents concerts all year long, in addition to an outstanding five-week summer festival. World-reknowned musicians come to Portland venues thanks to this important organization. Chamber music transcends a specific time period. Rather, its defining feature is its intimate instrumental grouping of no more than eight players. During the summer festival, concerts are held at two college venues, Reed and Caitlin, and are built on themes explored through a series of performances. It is like having a vacation into the world of a single composer or time period, a very powerful way to listen to such impressive music. For instance, there has been a four-concert series on Shostakovich, where one concert is billed Russian music before Shostakovich, another focuses on his early years, and so on. My favorite living pianist, Andre Watts, played a similar three-concert grouping, with David Shifrin on clarinet, comparing Beethovan and Brahams. Not only are the musicians of the highest caliber, but the inventive method of organizing concerts makes Chamber Music Northwest one of Portland's most important musical and cultural assets. *sb*

Mississippi Studios

3939 N Mississippi Avenue at N Shaver Street
753.4473, Box Office: 288.3895, www.mississippistudios.com
Box Office: Tu-F 2-6p, show times vary

This is the premier place to see live music in Portland. The room seats no more than 130, with sexy red walls, bottled beer and wine, impeccable sound, and a list of some of the finest touring and local musicians in the country. If you love music, you will love this intimate venue in one of the most hip neighborhoods in town. You never know who is going to be on the schedule, from Rickie Lee Jones to Hot Tuna to Country Joe McDonald to amazing locals, Sneakin' Out and Storm Large. A trip to Portland wouldn't be complete without catching a show, and you can bet that even if you haven't heard of the band, it's gonna be good. Above the music venue is a world-class recording studio, and if you ask nicely, they might let you take a tour. *rrm*

The Red and Black Café

2138 SE Division Street at SE 21st Avenue
231.3899, www.redandblackcafe.com
Open: M-Th 7:30a-11p, F 7:30a-11:30p, Sa-Su 8a-11:30p

Worker owned, The Red and Black Cafe has been a place for music, meetings, reading, web surfing, and revolution for quite some time. Recently a Starbucks opened up across the street, and it is perpetually empty, whereas the Red and Black has steamy windows full of beatniks and hipsters. Read from their packed information board to get ideas for fun activities in the community. Even the most feisty of carnivores amongst us won't miss the meat with heir sandwich combinations. The Heritage combines roasted red peppers, tempeh bacon, cheese, red onion and veggie spread, all melted to perfection. No-guilt food and cozy, there's usually some traveling or local musician with something to say and a sliding scale donation after the sun sets. Don't miss their home-brewed spearmint chai. *rrm*

Portland Fret Works

3039 NE Alberta Street at NE 30th Avenue
249.3737
Open: W-F 12-6p, Sa 10a-2p

Portland Fret Works is the place to get your guitar fixed if you're in town and you need a bridge pin or a strobe tuning real quick. The people who work here are guaranteed to do a great job with your axe. *rrm*

Albert Street Pub

1036 NE Alberta Street at NE 10th Avenue
284.7665
Open: M-Th 5p-12a, F 5p-1a, Sa 5p-2a

A staple of the Albany district, this neighborhood pub has music year-round. Choose from local suds, reasonably-priced well drinks or the ever-present free hot cocoa next to the stage as you get a happy ear-full of strummy music. Homey pig décor flies from the ceiling and can be found throughout the two side-by-side pub halls. Friendly bartenders complete the scene. *sb*

Chopsticks Express

2651 E Burnside Street at SE 26th Avenue
234.6171
Open: M-F 11a-2a, Sa-Su 5p-2a

On Friday and Saturday, this is the hip place to get dolled up, drink a cocktail or five, and convince all your friends to get on stage and sing Elton John's *Tiny Dancer* or some fall back Salt N' Peppa. This karaoke bar also has Chinese food in case you're hungry, but the real attraction is the microphone and the person who's behind it. *ec*

Jimmy Mak's

300 NW 10th Avenue at NW Everett Street
295.6542, www.jimmymaks.com
Open: M-Sa 4p-2a, music usually begins at 8p

Jimmy Mak's has a good collection of some of Portland's most respected jazz musicians as its regular players. It is always a good bet if you want to spend an evening in the Pearl and "be seen." Decently priced drinks and low door cover make it a cheap date for downtown. *rrm*

Portland Center Stage: Gerding Theater at The Armory

1111 SW Broadway at SW Main Street
274.6588, www.pcs.org
Show times vary

Portland Center Stage relocated in 2006 to the renovated Armory, a stone's throw away from Powell's on Burnside. Revamping this historic building was done in sustainable style and The Armory was awarded LEED Platinum certification. I am always amused by the imposing façade of this building smack dab in the city. Portland Center Stage puts on wonderful plays and musicals and, obviously, the atmosphere can't be beat. A dinner at one of the Pearl's many notable restaurants is a perfect foray into one of these performances or a great way to cap off the night. *dm*

Back Door Theater, at Sowelu Stage

4319 SE Hawthorne Boulevard, behind Common Grounds Coffeehouse (see **Coffee Time** chapter)
230.2090
Showtimes vary, call ahead

Accessible by its own outside entrance or, oddly enough, from inside Common Grounds Coffeehouse, lies this lowly publicized theater. Small productions are put on here and you might just happen upon a gem of a show some month. To find out what's on stage right now, grab an Americano and a Voodoo Doughnut (see **Stay Up Late** chapter) at Common Grounds and check out the board between the mens and womens facilities. *dm*

Brody Theater

1904 NW 27th Avenue at NW Upshur Street
224.0688, www.brodytheater.com
Show times vary

I once had a roommate who participated in an improv class at Brody Theater and, let me tell you, it is fun to have that stuff around. There is a certain therapeutic element to the uninhibited immediacy of an improv performance; we could all use a bit of it I'm sure. If you are not up for it at the moment, head to Theatersports at the Brody to watch two teams have a competitive go at an improvisational performance and let the idea of your own future in spontaneous acting begin to germinate. *dm*

Portland Center for the Performing Arts

www.pcpa.com
A network of five theaters that house six theater companies, including the Portland Ballet, Oregon Symphony, and several other musical organizations, the Portland Performing Arts Center is the place to head for an evening of the arts. But this place is far from snooty. PCPA hosts ballets and operas, but it also brings acts like Sleater Kinney and Pearl Jam. So, a night at PCPA can beckon for a tux or some casual slacks. The theaters are scattered around downtown, and each have an air all their own. *sb*

Portland Opera at Keller Auditorium

222 SW Clay Street at SW 2nd Avenue
274.6560, www.portlandopera.org
Show times vary
It might be sad that an evening at the opera always makes me think of *Pretty Woman.* Who can resist the idea of a sexy Richard Gere whisking you away to an evening of such fanciness and smiling lovingly at you as tears trail down your face from the overwhelming emotion emanating from the stage. I guess some could resist that idea. For those who imagine creating their own memorable nights, Pretty Woman-esque or otherwise, plan to ticket in an evening at the opera. The performances are seasonal, so check to see what's on stage now. *dm*

Arlene Schnitzer Concert Hall

1121 SW Salmon Street at SW 11th Avenue
228.8476
Show times vary
Oh, the Schnitz! It is the Carnegie Hall of Portland. Everyone wants to attend a performance at or, better yet, perform at the Schnitz. This beautiful concert hall was expertly restored in the 80's, thanks in no small part to its namesake and her hubby, and is a gem of a venue. Though the symphony makes its lovely music here, there are a slew of surprising acts that pass through the doors of this hall, so you can feel classy even as you listen to your favorite contemporary rock act. *dm*

Newmark Theater

1111 SW Broadway at SW Main Street
796.0132
Show times vary

This intimate, Edwardian-style theater is the baby brother of PCPA, and the perfect place to experience dance performances or improv. Their yearly schedule of productions focus on plays and dance. Pretend you are in Europe a century ago, attending a royalty-only viewing of some talented writers new play. No matter where you sit, you'll be no further than 65 feet from the actors. A recent choral performance filled this acoustic gem with the symphony of voices in the Aurora Chorus. *sb*

Oregon Symphony

921 SW Washington Street near SW 8th Avenue
228.1353, www.orsymphony.org
Show times vary

Tchaikovsky, Rachmaninoff, Stravinsky, Shostakovich, Sibelius, and Strauss. Do you know these names? Do they live in your heart? Try as I might, I can't avoid being a bit pushy here. Classical music is cooler than you think, and brings me to tears quicker than watching *Life is Beautiful.* I am always bringing new friends to the orchestra and watching as their shoulders drop back, their eyes glaze over, and their skin covers with goose bumps. Whether you are familiar with this foundational form of music or not, hearing the full symphony sound is sure to inspire and move you. Classical music isn't just for background music at a café or a massage, it is intellectually stimulating, emotionally pulling, and a powerful experience that can be enjoyed universally. If this message is already your own banging drum, you'll be dumbfounded by this spectacular symphony's rendition of Mendelssohn's *Mid-Summer Night's Dream.* And those who've never been to the orchestra will, too. Give me a call if your friends won't go with you! Recently appointed concertmaster Jun Iwasaki has gotten off to a riveting start leading this already mellifluous group to new heights. *sb*

Get Inspired

Museums, installations, awe-inspiring exhibits and anything that aims to enthuse

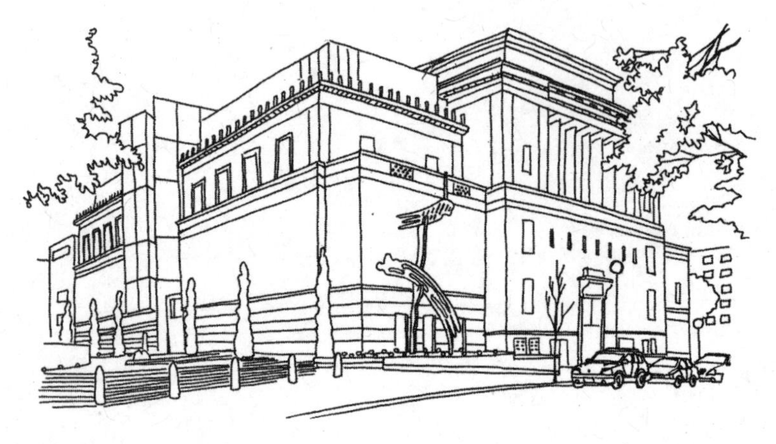

Portland Art Museum

Portland's lively art scene is ever growing. Underground filmmakers and modern sculptors have found a steadfast community of equals here. With regular citywide gallery crawls, and a strong commitment to sustainability and reuse in art, Stumptown is evolving some of its very own art trends. At any time of year, with a little searching you'll find theater, comedy, and musical acts from the most sophisticated to the most improvisational. Here is a listing of galleries, stages and museums that bring to the surface the artistic integrity of this part of the world. *sb*

Portland Art Museum
1219 SW Park Avenue near SW Main Street
226.2811, www.portlandartmuseum.org
Open: Tu-W 10a-5p, Th-F 10a-8p, Sa-Su 10a-5p
The oldest art museum in the Pacific Northwest, PAM's permanent collections are rich with Native American artifacts, African sculptures, and centuries worth of paintings. Los Angeles artist Kehinde Wiley shows his modern takes on Renaissance portraiture, right down the hall from his inspirations. Regular events and interesting exhibits deck the halls and walls, one of the highlights of which is Museum After Hours that features local wines and bands with a strong community feel. *sb*

Portland Art Center
32 NW 5th Avenue at NWCouch Street
236.3322, www.portlandart.org
Open: W-Su 12-6p
There is always plenty of visually-stimulating artwork at PAC. This young gallery space encompasses a nice variety of mid-range and emerging artists. Artists submit entries each year for both the main space and a sound and light gallery. The two-story building adapts its space to showcase works in endless mediums. I have viewed exhibitions that included experimental installations (like axes hanging overhead and packaged political candy), mind-altering soundscapes, and plenty of sensually stirring sculptures. PAC is boastful of supporting the artist community and has an area for posting creative events near the entry. Most of their crowds come through on the bustling First Thursday opening night. *nkp*

Working Artists

2211 NW Front Avenue, #102 at NW 17th Avenue
445.1268, www.workingartistsonline.com
Open: M-F 11a-4p and by appointment

As I walk into the quiet warehouse headquarters of Working Artists, I felt slightly adventurous. The quiet hallway curves towards the entrance of a seemingly secret world. As I pop my head into the office looking for signs of life, the room lights up with colorful artwork strung along the walls. A friendly woman, busily typing away at a computer, excitedly whisks me on a tour of the facilities. I am led up a charmingly rustic staircase and into the extending rooms, which include a low-key classroom, a large room where multiple artists share a studio space, a dance studio, and a gallery equipped for installations. Along with classes in belly dancing, collage-making and life drawing sessions, this non-profit's strongest attribute is the desire to educate and empower artists with business skills and resources to manage new and emerging artists' careers. They are also big on fundraisers and supporting community outreach. The possibilities for involvement seem limitless. Check their website to see what kinds of opportunities are taking place within this good-natured artists' network. *nkp*

Grass Hut

811 E Burnside Street at SE 8th Avenue
445.9924, www.grasshutcorp.com
Open: W-Su 12-7p

Walking into Grass Hut is like entering a magical little world filled with enchanted creatures and metaphors for mushrooms. This playful gallery will make you smile as your attention jumps from humorous paintings by local artists to silk-screened prints, colorful cards, and even pre-packaged underwear. They have a nice selection of indie-published E-zines, including their own annual publication called Pencil Fight, filled with poems, writings, and inky images. Owners Bwana Spoons and Justin "Scrappers" Morrison use the space as their studio, gallery, retail shop, and every once and a while host "Doodle Clubs" that are open to everyone to come in and draw. The space has a fun energy, the kind that makes you want to rush home and let all your bottled up ideas out onto anything that's too crisp and too white. Grass Hut rotates artists frequently; new shows open the first Friday of every month. *nkp*

Velveteria

518 NE 28th Avenue at Glisan Street
233.5100, www.velveteria.com
Open: Th-Su 12-6p

So, you saw one painting of Elvis on velvet and now you think you've seen 'em all? Well, the Velveteria will make you think otherwise. Periodically rotating works from their personal collection (that includes over 14,000 paintings), Owners Carl Baldwin and Caren Anderson are now fulfilling their dream to open a velvet painting museum. With a three-dollar admission fee, you can take your time wandering through a space filled with leopard-print carpeting, wall-to-wall pink, and a glorious medley of velvet images. Featuring both amateur and famous artists—it seems the really good ones have a sort of ominous glow to them. They range from mesmerizing Polynesian nudes and animals to political figures and cheesy cartoons and a spinach-eating Popeye. You'll definitely leave with a smile on your face. *nkp*

New Renaissance Books

1338 NW 23rd Avenue at NW Overton Street
224.4929, www.newrenbooks.com
Open: M-Th, Sa 10a-9p, F 10a-9:30p, Su 10a-6p

The second you walk into New Renaissance Bookstore, you feel calmer. There is quiet instrumental music playing, the singing of chimes, and essential oils in the air. They have any book you could want on spirituality, metaphysics, and the occult, plus alternative calendars, gorgeous hand-made jewelry, music for meditation as well as a series of healing arts classes, past life readers, gurus, and many other paths toward self-betterment. *rrm*

Street Level

909 N Beech Street at N Mississippi Avenue
493.9750, www.streetlevelpdx.xom
Open: Whenever the owner/resident is there

A living gallery (quite literally as the owner lives in a loft above the storefront) Street Level directs our eyes toward the art of daily life. Graphic design inspired paintings and installations feature street art, acrylic-painted vinyl, graffiti and political poster art. Take a piece of the gallery home—art is reasonably priced, and pillows, bags and t-shirts bring a little pizzazz into your every day. *sb*

Reading Frenzy

921 SW Oak Street at SW 9th Avenue
274.1449
Open: M-F 10a-6p, Sa 11a-7p, Su 12-6p

Although Reading Frenzy is across the street from Powell's City of Books (see **Explore** chapter) it is another world away, carrying items that even a place as big as Powell's doesn't carry. Located on Oak Street since 1996, Reading Frenzy offers the best selection of independent and alternative media around, plus service with a smile. Reading Frenzy is mostly volunteer-run, so I always ask whoever is working about their favorite zine, or about upcoming events. (My favorite event is the Portland Zine symposium, every summer.) My favorite part of Reading frenzy is the local zine selection. Look for *Invincible Summer* by Nicole Georges. The walls of RF often showcase local talent. Once you have browsed the printed material, move on to the baskets of cheap jewelry, tiny buttons, and novelties like handmade View-Master reels. With the focus on arts, culture, politics, comics, girls' stuff, queer notions, and quality smut, Reading Frenzy has the key to my heart. *pr*

SCRAP

3901A N Williams Avenue, Building 9 at N Failing Street
294.0769, www.scrapaction.org
Open: W-Sa 11a-6p

Visiting SCRAP is like going to a thrift store for art supplies; you never leave with exactly what you came for, but you always find goodies to spur your creative imagination. The School and Community Reuse Action Project (SCRAP) is a volunteer and donation-based organization. This non-profit promotes sustainable reuses of materials, provide workshops, and offers it all up at affordable prices. Friends of mine find cork and foam cutouts to insulate the walls of their recording studio. I have picked up stickers, zippers, 3-ring binders, glitter, and beer cozies. Businesses around town often pair up to support SCRAP, resulting in deals from cheap haircuts to recycled paint. During their annual fundraiser, the **Iron Artist Sculpt-Off** competition (see **Calendar** chapter), teams duke it out to see who can creatively promote waste reduction in the ultimate sculpt-off. Stop in and see where it leads you! *nkp*

Orlo

2516 NW 29th Avenue at Nicolai Street
242.1047, www.orlo.org
Open: By appointment only

Orlo is like a rare old gem, partially buried under the settling dust of newer, glitzier galleries in Northwest. This volunteer-run organization complements my curiosities by combining environmental issues with visual arts. They put together a quasi-annual publication called The Bear Deluxe, whose brown paper covers can be discovered in most grassroots coffee shops around town. Out of their headquarters, they scheme up gallery exhibitions, political puppet shows, hilarious video slams (like poetry slams but with camcorders and environmental themes), and "Junk to Funk" fashion shows. They also rent a small amount of equipment such as printers and projectors for community use. This group is fun and intimate with an underground sort of feel. Check their website for events and opportunities. *nkp*

Launch Pad Gallery

811 E Burnside Street, Suite #110 at NE 8th Avenue
231.7336
Open: W-F 1-7p, Sa 12-7p, Su 1-6p

Launch Pad is one of the hippest, hottest galleries in PDX, a place where the artists go to check each other out. Each First Friday there is a new show of cutting edge paintings, sculptures, or installations. Shows are a mix of mediums, with artists of varied backgrounds and experience levels, bringing art to the people in a new way. The alternative style of the gallery makes art more accessible for all. *sb*

In Other Words

8 NE Killingsworth Street at N Williams Avenue
232.6003, www.inotherwords.org
Open: M-F 10a-9p, Sa 12-6p

In Other Words bookstore has a beautiful collection of books about, for, and written by women. They carry CD's by local and national touring female musicians, zines by women, art by women—you get the picture. They also host live music and poetry readings on random special nights. This is the kind of place to get a cup of coffee and hang out for hours of inspiration. *rrm*

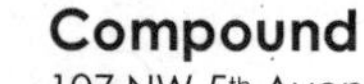

Compound

107 NW 5th Avenue at Couch Street
796.2733, www.compoundgallery.com
Open: M-Sa 12-8p, Su 12-6p

Compound Gallery resides within the "Just Be Complex." This Japanese-owned retail store features plenty to delight your urban senses. Upon entering the space, you are greeted with an impressive selection of "serious" toys ranging from Godzilla to collectable figurines and mutant stuffed animals. Nearby is the DVD corner where you can peruse through an international selection of live-action and animé flicks. Rows of vibrant sneakers line the front windows, directing your gaze toward hoodies and t-shirts enhanced with street graphics. Making your way upstairs, the airy loft-type gallery space features silk-screened prints, art books, and foreign magazines, along with rotating artists' works. During First Thursday, this colorful corner gallery drips with art aficionados. *nkp*

Ogle

310 NW Broadway at NW Everett Street
227.4333
Open: Tu-Sa 11a-6p

It's no wonder this gallery has a sophisticated eye for art—they sell high-end eyeglasses as well. This combination gallery and optical venue showcases cutting-edge work by local Portland artists. Whether the exhibit is small or large, the expansive windows and vast cherry-colored wood floors invite viewers into a warm and well-lit space. I observed coastal artist Anne R. Archer's works twice in the gallery and both times she captured my sensory cravings with her unique fondness for mapping places in Oregon using found objects, natural elements, and painted images. Ogle is located in Old Town, surrounded by fourteen experimental live/work galleries called the Everett Station Lofts. The gallery is pleasant to browse during daylight hours, but I suggest heading out on a First Thursday. *nkp*

Regional Arts and Culture Council (RACC)

108 NW 9th Avenue, Suite 300 at NW Everett Street
823.5111, www.racc.org
Open: M-F 8:30a-5p

This is the kind of place where dreams can come true. The RACC is a strong supporter of local artists, non-profit organizations and educational programs. They have funded many of the public sculptures and murals around the city. Look for their walking-tour brochure, featuring all the public artwork in Portland. Their website is a great resource for art-funding opportunities, cultural events, job postings and calls-to artists. I took a fantastic grant-writing workshop they offered—it was cheap, informative, and most importantly inspired me to pursue my art-making intentions! *nkp*

First Thursday Art Walk

NW Portland
Hours: 6p to about 9p, hours vary

Like a choose-your-own-adventure book, the first Thursday of each month offers alternative opportunities for a fulfilling evening. Overall, the spirit of the night may entice one into aesthetic discussions at a bar, making new friends, taking home some artwork, or racing towards pen and paper to let out freshly inspired thoughts. From mattress stores to mechanic shops, it seems as though every business in **Old Town** and the **Pearl District** (see **Shopping Districts**) transitions into a gallery for one glamorous night, often celebrating with wine and cheese. This year-round event generates a mesh of old and young—from the very posh to the scruffiest of creative type, the streets swell with bodies curious to view each other as much as the artwork. Parking spaces fill up fast, so taking public transportation or biking is a more pleasant way to arrive. Since the galleries in the Pearl District close earlier, I like to start out near the Pacific Northwest College of Art (PNCA) on Johnson Street and wander along the bustling row of art vendors on 13th Avenue. Then I tend to zigzag through the streets of Everett and Glisan, popping into galleries here and there. I teeter between the popular highbrow galleries such as PDX, Pullium Deffenbaugh, and Elizabeth Leach on 9th Avenue. From there, I cut east towards 5th and 6th Avenues in Old Town, and pause for a while at the Everett Station Lofts (a block of 14 live/work galleries), the Portland Art Center, Compound, and Motel. There are many routes to take and plenty to satisfy your visual needs. This is a great opportunity to let yourself get lost and see what kind of adventure you can create! *nkp*

Create

From beads to seeds, fabric to photos, these spots will enable your creative side for sure

Dava Bead

I switched colleges my sophomore year to go to art school. I wanted to draw and paint and take photos all day instead of calculating chemical equations and studying political systems.

Later, I changed my mind and went back for international studies and English, but what I learned from the experience was something that hadn't crossed my mind before: everyone can create beauty; everyone can be an artist. I saw people who had never taken their pencil out of the lines on a steno pad draw impeccable contour figures by the end of one semester. Their eyes and their hands had become one unit. With a little drive, anyone can contribute to the beauty in the world. I also feel that it is important to maintain a connection with handwork. If you haven't ever tried something like this yourself, the satisfaction of eating something you have grown or cooked, wearing a dress you made, or a scarf you knit is astonishing. Your hands are the greatest machines. *sb*

Dava Bead and Trade

1815 NE Broadway at NE 19th Avenue (one of two locations)
288.3991, www.davabeadandtrade.com
Open: M-F 10a-6p, Sa 10a-5p, Su 11a-4p
Discounts: 10% off purchases over $100, 15% off purchases over $300

Ever since I first started getting an allowance from Mom and Dad, I've been hooked on cool bead stores. Now I mix the stuff I get here with found objects, piecesof old jewelry and flyfishing materials. Dava has from around the world, in all shapes and sizes, colors and variations can be found in boxes and on strands at this designer's paradise. New findings, specialty metals and chains give your jewelry creations new flair. The staff are all talented designers, and can help give you options and inspire your ideas. Dava Bead is locally owned and operated and has reasonable prices. *sb*

Fabric Depot

700 SE 122nd Avenue near SE Stark Street
252.9530, 800.392.3376, www.fabricdepot.com
Open: M-Sa 9a-9p, Su 9a-7p

One of the largest fabric and notion stores in the Western states, when I go to Fabric Depot it is impossible for me to leave empty-handed. Even browsing their website to find the correct phone number, I couldn't help but make a fabric purchase. The amazing array of fabrics, continual sales, and unique prints get the creative gears going. Any aspect of a given project, from clothing patterns to quilts, are housed here and explained to you by the friendly and helpful staff. I challenge you to enter without coming up with a treasure chest of new and interesting projects of your own. *sb*

Yarn Garden

1413 SE Hawthorne Boulevard at SE 14th Avenue
239.7950, www.yarngarden.net
Open: M-Th 10a-7p, F 10a-6p, Sa 10a-5p, Su 12-5p

Truly a garden of colors and materials, this knitters' wonderland has three rooms of threads from all over the globe. Run your hands over their huge cashmere selection, or find something new like soy-silk or *chitlin*, a soft, yet strong yarn made from crab and shrimp shells. Every Wednesday morning at 11a a professional is in house for their free knitting clinic. Bring your project with you and chum with other shoppers over some tea and scones in their in-store café, complete with comfy sofas. *sb*

Collage

1639 NE Alberta Street at NE 16th Avenue
249.2190, www.collageonalberta.com
Open: M-F 10a-8p, Sa-Su 10a-6p

Although this store is geared toward the scrap booking craze sweeping the country, the crafty tools, hard-to-find art supplies, and complete rubber stamp collection can be used for any possible collage project, as the name suggests. Choose a wide-brush marker in vermillion to go with some handmade paper and a marigold rubber stamp to make unique stationery. Whatever your idea, talk it through with the creative salespeople while perusing the tidy booths of art-making treasures to find exactly what you're looking for. Get busy in their workroom or take a creative class; check their website for current offerings. *sb*

Trade Up Music

4701 SE Division Street at SE 47th Avenue (one of two locations)
236.8800, www.tradeupmusic.com
Open: Everyday, 11a-7p

Need a noisemaker for an impromptu parade down Hawthorne Street? Did you run out of money and are forced to sell your guitar? Locally owned Trade Up Music is the best spot to find new and used instruments and get expert advice and repairs from local musicians. You can also get the low down on some lesser known and possibly free concerts in Portland. Bonus: this is the kind of place where no one cares if you sit and play the mandolins and pianos for hours. *ep*

Broadway Floral

1638 NE Broadway Street at NE 16th Avenue
288.5537, www.broadwayflroal.com
Open: M-F 8a-6p, Sa 8:30a-5p, Su 11a-5p

To go along with a rainbow of floral distraction, Broadway Floral is chock full of silk ribbons, fun ornaments, and classy yard décor. Housed in a historic greenhouse structure in the cozy Hollywood district, the buds and blossoms are another cheery addition to this lovely neighborhood. Arrangements in every shade, designed for any season or occasion can be delivered by request, like the miniature cymbidium orchids, with elegant ikebana-inspired lines. *sb*

Mabel's Café and Knittery

3041 SE Division Street at SE 30th Avenue
231.4107, www.mabelscafe.com
Open: M-Th 10a-9p, F-Sa 10a-8p
Discounts: 10% off for students taking a knitting class here

Coffee, beer, music, and knitting are some core survival tools for a rainy Portland winter. This city specializes in all four and Mabel's takes the knitting to that next level. A low ceiling cozies crafters into coffee and couches, after a seductively soft merino wool purchase and a new project plan. Mabel's website lists the current class offerings, but fellow knitters and the wizened ladies behind the counter are generous with pointers as well. *dm*

Paperdoll

7909 SE Stark Street at SE 79th Avenue
408.6867, www.paperdoll-co.com
Open: Tu-Sa 10:30a-6:30p

Paperdoll's walls are lined with handmade cards and invitations, examples that get your fingers itchin' to make one of your own. With all the tools to do so, this small store is quaintly packed with pretty papers, rubber stamps, glitter, and even acrylic paint. If you need help getting inspired, they offer classes like watercolor boot camp, eco-collage, and how to make your own sassy stationery. If you just don't have the time to make one of your own, they sell elegant ready-made cards and invitations as well. I appreciate their chic selection of reusable gift bags. *nkp*

Pistils Nursery

3811 N Mississippi Avenue at N Beech Street
288.4889, www.pistilsnursery.com
Open: Tu-Su 10a-6p, M 12-6p

Whether on a stroll down Mississippi or as a predetermined destination, Pistils is always a worthwhile experience. From Turkish Spike Poppies to Pineapple Guava fruit trees, this quaint little nursery is bursting with unique varieties of flowering flora. My favorite reason to visit is to inspect the selection of whimsical succulents and admire the fuzzy baby chicks for sale by the register. Along with bulk organic fertilizers, bee pollen, and second-hand garden books, this place has the tools to get your country livin' on, right here in the city. *nkp*

Bolt Fabric Boutique

2136 NE Alberta Street at NE 21st Avenue
287.2658, http://boltfabricboutique.com
Open: Tu-F 10a-6p, Sa 10a-5p, Su 11a-4p

For the "oh and ah" in all of us that we've been holding back until the moment was just right, Bolt is the spot to let it out. Cotton prints are carefully selected from companies that are careful not to participate in some of the atrocities for which the fabric industry is known. Fabric patterns from Free Spirit, Robert Kaufman, and Japanese favorite Kokka fill the dainty shelves. Sit in the back and flip through designs from Amy Butler and Kaffe Fassett, and if you don't already know how to follow a pattern, stay for a sewing class, (see **Learn** chapter). Don't miss their one-of-a-kind notions and buttons. *sb*

Muse Art and Design

4224 SE Hawthorne Boulevard at SE 42nd Avenue
231.8704, www.museartanddesign.com
Open: M-Sa 11a-6p, Su 12-5p

For any creative endeavor, having good tools makes all the difference. Design to your heart's content after finding all the necessary objects at this local artists treasure. For inspiration, stick your nose in a book at their free visual art library, or follow it into the commission-free exhibit space, where customer artists are encouraged to show their work. *sb*

The Office

2204 NE Alberta Street at NE 22nd Avenue
282.7200, www.officepdx.com
Open: Tu-F 11a-7p, Sa 11a-5p, Su 12-4p

This ain't your ordinary office supply store. Owners Tony Secolo and Kelly Coller happen to be award-winning graphic designers, so you are guaranteed to find visually-stimulating and functional office goods. The pair fused a 1950's era, blue-collar space with contemporary product designs that include modern Japanese aesthetics. Re-creations of vintage furniture, laptop bags, waterproof notebooks, ergonomic tape dispensers, and arrays of organizers will get you excited to head to work and finish your tasks with style. Their selection of reference materials for sale includes eco-design books, do-it-yourself publications, and swanky magazines. The Office also has a gallery exhibition space and partakes in Alberta Street's Last Thursday (see **Get Inspired** chapter) art walk. *nkp*

Portland Nursery

5050 SE Stark Street at SE 52nd Avenue (one of two locations)
231.5050, www.portlandnursery.com
Open: Everyday, 9a-6p

For seasoned gardeners and budding enthusiasts alike, Portland Nursery plants the seeds of urban farming with two delightful city locations. It can't just be the oxygen radiating from the potted plants that brings calm and content to the weekend wanderers in this century-old establishment; an eager-to-aid workforce, and an array of tools and starters enthuse every person who stops in. If you happen to be around during the nursery's fall Apple Tasting (see **Calendar** chapter), don't miss it—there are as many varieties of apples to try as there are coffee shops in Portland. *dm*

Explore

Places where science is explained, nature abounds or adventure is to be had

Portland Classical Chinese Garden

Curiosity can lead down many a path; we've all seen our friend Curious George getting in over his head. But fostering a healthy curiosity about the world is as important as taking our very first steps. If we fill our imagination with programmed images and digital friends, games and life, we miss out on all there is to explore for ourselves. History and science, nature and adventure are waiting around the bend to expand your knowledge of the world around you. Seek out the big questions, ask your own, and most of all, enjoy the ride! *sb*

Portland Classical Chinese Garden

239 NW Everett Street at NW 2nd Avenue
228-8131, www.portlandchinesegarden.org
Open: Everyday, November-March: 10a-5p, April-October: 9a-6p
Admission: $5-7

Set back in the somewhat defunct Chinatown area, the Portland Classical Chinese Garden is an oasis of serenity even given its surroundings. Whether it is raining or sunny out, the five classical elements (water, stone, literature, the arts and plants) embodied in the layout here is an escape I seek out again and again. I go for tea from the Tao of Tea's (see **Hang Out** chapter) international teahouse nestled within the gardens, or I head here to sit in the "Knowing the Fish Pavilion" for a while and take a stroll by the lake to forget about time. I always leave feeling content and calm, hoping to return sooner than later. *sm*

Independent Publishing Resource Center

917 SW Oak Street #218 at SW 9th Avenue
827.0249, www.iprc.org
Open: M 12-10p, Tu-Th 4-10p, F-Sa 12-6pm
Youth Only: Su 12-6p

Located above Reading Frenzy, the IPRC Small Press Library is one of the largest and best-organized collections of rare zines and small publications in the country. There are big comfy chairs beside the windows and walls of zines to look through. It is always a nice way to spend the afternoon. *pr*

Architectural Heritage Center

701 SE Grand Avenue at SE Alder Street
231.7264, www.visitahc.com
Open: W-Sa 10a- 4:30p
Admission: $5

Historical archaeology combines the study of artifacts and other media to reveal how everyday people in the past interpreted their world. The Architectural Heritage Center presents a window to Portland's earlier generations with a collection of salvaged architectural materials among the most extensive in the United States. Motivated by the tragic destruction of historic buildings throughout the city, Jerry Bosco and Ben Milligan spent twenty-five years gathering the pieces now on display. The center includes two galleries, two classrooms, a workshop, storage space, and a comprehensive library. Bring out the historical archaeologist in you. *dl*

Portland Parks and Recreation Main Office

Portlandia Building: 1150 SW 5th Avenue at SW Main Street

Portland's incredible knack for organization spreads beyond beautifully situated neighborhoods and a spectrum of well-attended festivals and fêtes throughout the year, and into the Parks and Recreation Department, where it makes a real splash (or two or three). When you're scouring the streets of downtown, be sure to duck under the beautiful Portlandia sculpture and into the building of the same name to gather up all the information you'll need to explore. In the main office there are maps and brochures of all the parks and recreational facilities, in addition to hiking and tours out of town, and sports and hobby clubs within the city. This little office is a wealth of information, and the key to the local side of Portland. At the main desk, just ask for the Parks and Recreation Office, or follow the signs. *sb*

Oaks Park

7805 SE Oaks Park Way, in Oaks Pioneer Park
233.5777, www.oakspark.com
Hours vary throughout the year, call ahead

"Oh my god, the Scream-N-Eagle is soooo scary!" Clearly, Oaks Park is a day of pure bliss for the fifth grade girls in my after school program—no school, plus ride coupons galore. Awesome! Open for some 100 years, this is one of the oldest amusement parks in the country. Located right off the Spring Water Corridor and next to Oaks Bottom Wildlife Refuge, Oaks Park is the place for an interlude of juvenile fun for you or the kiddos of your crew. Be sure to head to the skating rink to skate like it's 1988, or get your aggression out with a healthy round (or two) of bumper cars. *dm/ sb*

Sculpture Garden

Northeast corner of SE 50th Avenue and SE Madison Street

Portland embraces the artist, whether she displays her creations in the gallery, the museum, or a city corner. There are various intersections around town adorned in pretty paint with community boards and benches. This particular corner is not a high traffic area, but houses an interesting assortment of rusted saws and other woodworking paraphernalia, including an old planer, collaged together throughout the yard of a private home. There is also a shadow box with rotating artwork. The entire display is modest, but is a nice taste of art after an afternoon taking in the busy happenings of Hawthorne Boulevard. *dm*

Forest Park

NW 29th Avenue and Upshur Street to Newberry Road
www.portlandonline.com, search 'forest park'
Open: Everyday, 5a-10p

Forest Park is a giant of a park. Covering the peaks above Portland's northwest neighborhoods, it is the third largest city park in the U.S., and includes a magical grove of old growth redwoods. Whether you're heading here for a jog, some gapping at the tallest trees in the world or a classic Portland walk, I like to plan my trip so it ends at sunset. The best time to explore the twisting trails of Forest Park is when the mist descends, right as the last ray of sunlight tucks behind the hills. Dusk here is miraculous. This place has helped me work through stress and a number of life's conundrums. I hope it does wonders for you as well! *dm/ sb*

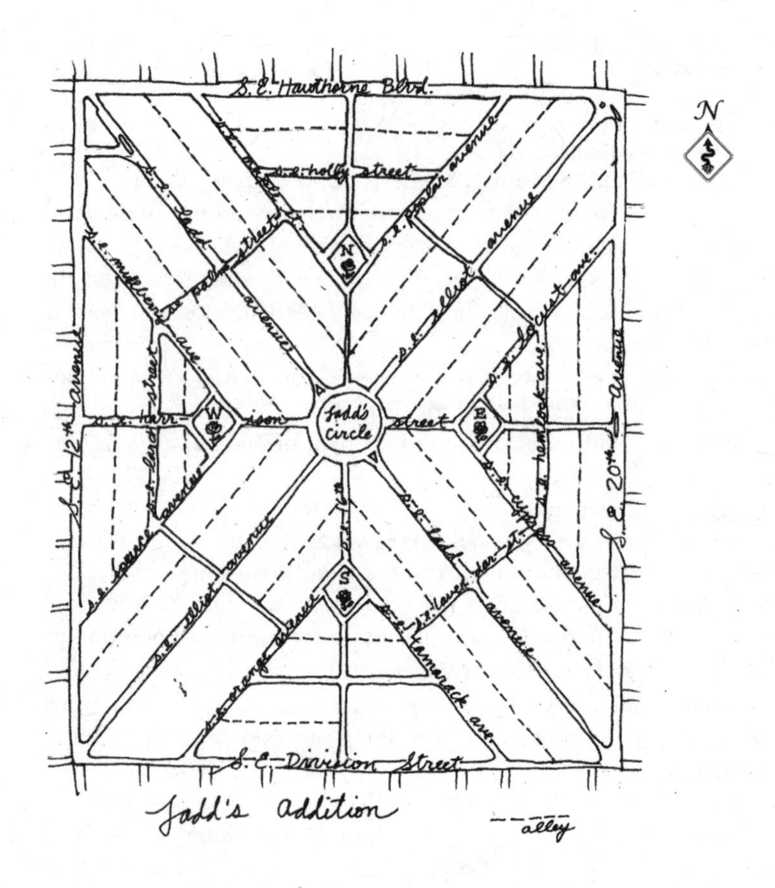

Ladd's Addition

Bordered by SE Hawthorne Boulevard, Division Street, 12th Avenue and 20th Avenue

From a bird's eye view, Ladd's Addition is Portland's most recognizable collection of city blocks. Configured in a lattice reminiscent of an English rose garden, hedges perfectly trimmed, this complete neighborhood has five community rose gardens, with Palio's (see **Coffee Time** chapter), a video store, Funky Church (see **Listen** chapter) and The Movement Clinic (see **Get Active** chapter) at its core. Families and dog walkers mingle and catch up, welcoming you into their geometrically-balanced world. Head here for a yoga class and a slice of cake, then stow away your map and get lost for a while amoung the roses and elm trees lining this criss-crossing streets. You can find your way but can you find your way out? *sb*

Oregon Museum of Science and Industry (OMSI)

1945 SE Water Avenue at SE Clay Street
797.4000, www.omsi.edu
Open: Everyday, 9:30a-5:30p
Admission: $7-9, extra for shows and certain exhibits

Located right on the Eastbank Esplanade, a waterfront bike and footpath, OMSI is a family-friendly hands-on museum. They have extensive standard and rotating exhibits, a zero-gravity chamber, an IMAX movie theater, a planetarium that features laser light shows, and a working submarine. My favorite of the permanent exhibits is the preserved specimens of every stage of a fetus' growth, even though I had a somewhat frightening experience camping out in their presence with my Girl Scout troop when I was young. OMSI is available as a conference center or just for a day trip. Educational and highly entertaining to even the most exuberant, kids (and adults) will never tire of OMSI. Take a date to a laser Pink Floyd show after eating at Produce Row Café on SE 3rd and Oak in the Central Eastside Industrial District (CEID). *rrm*

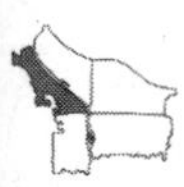

Pittock Mansion

3229 NW Pittock Drive, directly below Washington Park
823.3623, www.pittockmansion.com
Hours: Everyday, 12-4p, Summer 11a-4p, closed in January
Admission: $4-7

Standing high above downtown Portland is the stunning Pittock Mansion, a monument of local craftmanship and a living memorial to the Pittock family's contributions to the blossoming city around the turn of the century. Motifs from French, Turkish, and English design emerge, as you make your way through the elborately decorated home; each room takes on a life of its own. The mansion, having sustained heavy damage from a storm in 1962, was rescued from a dire fate when concerned citizens—perhaps inspired by Henry and Georgiana Pittock's life of community service—gathered in its defense. The family were publishers, most noteably the force behind *The Oregonian* newspaper. The estate was purchased by the City of Portland in 1964 and, following a 15-month restoration, became a community landmark for posterity. *dl*

Portland Walking Tours

Various times, starting points, durations and prices
774.4522, www.portlandwalkingtours.com

Take one of these award-winning tours from a neighborhood expert. Dig deeper into Portland's history, underground tunnels and food scene with one of their themed walks through the City of Roses. On the Epicurean Excursion, you'll get to sample the tastes of an array of restaurants as you tour the kitchens, dining rooms, markets, and bakeries. *The Willamette Week* even called it "the best way to fake being native," guaranteeing that locals and travelers alike will learn something new. Have a laugh and discover some juicy inside secrets. *sb*

Rocky Butte

Take a drive east, all the way down Fremont Avenue until the road winds left and up. This incline will lead to Rocky Butte and a 360-degree view of the city and its surroundings. The view is basically unobstructed and might be the only of its kind. It is a great way to get one's bearings and point out different landmarks of the area: the airport, the Gorge, Mt. Tabor, Willamette River, etc. Bring a sweater in case the wind is strong and choose from one of the restaurants around the avenues of the 40's on Fremont to catch a bite before or after the sightseeing. *dm*

Eastbank Esplanade

SE Water Avenue and SE Hawthorne Boulevard

This one and a half mile riverside paved path leads walkers, hikers, runners and bikers past four of Portland's famous bridges and by a collection of outdoor art. The riverbank you walk by has been re-shaped to promote fish hatching and a rejuvenated habit for native wildlife. Hundreds of trees and shrubs have been planted to reflect what this inner city area was like before the city was here. Take notice of the inventive structures by local artist group, RIGGA, that are a permanent asset to the riverbank. The floating walkway leading to the boat dock is the longest of its kind in the country, and transports you to the water taxi, a fun alternative transit. All in all it's a great walk that gives you city and country all at once. *rrm*

Mill Ends Park

SW Naito Parkway at SW Taylor Street

452 square inches (yes, inches) of pure wonderment, Mill Ends Park holds the Guinness Record for the world's smallest park. Dick Fagan grew tired of seeing a weed infested hole from a failed light pole installation outside of his office window, so he planted some flowers and gave it the name of his column in the Oregon Journal. Named an official park in 1976, the park received many contributions, including a tiny swimming pool (for caterpillars, I guess) and a miniature Ferris wheel installed by a normal-sized crane. Mill Ends receives its share of attention with concerts by the Clan Macleay Pipe Band and rose plantings by the Junior Rose Festival Court. *dl*

Hippo Hardware & Trading Co.

Hippo Hardware & Trading Co.

1040 E Burnside Street at SE 11th Avenue
231.1444, www.hippohardware.com
Open: M-Th 10a-5p, F-Sa 10a-6p, Su 12-5p

Nowhere else in the city will you get such a behind-the-scenes view of Portland. Hippo Hardware is the city deconstructed into all its little pieces. Bathtubs that look like Airstream trailers sit side-by-side classic ceramic tubs with claw feet down a line of other bathing receptacles. The light fixture section is mind-boggling—a mix of stained glass shades and hanging lamps on the same shelf as hanging globes from another era. Picture a typical Portland bungalow and fill it from floor-to-ceiling with imaginative nuts and bolts all found in the hippo-laden structure and now you can picture what lies within those adorable abodes without having to peer through un-curtained windows. *sb*

Washington Park

Washington Park is the setting of such attractions as Hoyt Arboretum, the Japanese Garden, the Rose Test Garden, the Zoo, and the World Forestry Center, but on a clear day, it is worth a visit just for its westerly view that showcases the city and beyond, all the way to Mt. Hood. There are some wooded trails to amble, and if a tennis racket is handy, head to the courts; each one is enclosed in its own fence, weaved with vines and flowers. (Look for Hoyt Arboretum and Rose Test Garden in the **City for Free** chapter). *dm*

Portland Japanese Garden

611 SW Kingston Avenue off SW Kingston Drive in Washington Park
223.1321, www.japanesegarden.com
Open: Tu-Su 10a-7p, M 12-7p
Admission: $3-6

At the foothills of Washington Park, entering this garden is like a jet lag-free passport to Japan. The deliberate growing, cultivating, and sculpting of the foliage in this serene garden is done in the traditional style to enhance the ambiance with what is termed "borrowed scenery." For more than forty years the plants have been trained to form a series of miniature landscapes, originally designed by a Japanese professor and maintained by experts. Volunteer docents are great tour guides who will gladly take you behind the scenes of specific plants and the meanings of their placement. Each visit, I get the sense that I am being fast-fowarded towards enlightenment just from the calm this place brings me. *sb/ dm*

The World Forestry Center

4033 SW Canyon Road in Washington Park
228.1367, www.worldforestrycenter.org
Open: Everyday, 10a-5p
Admission: $5-7

Drawing you inside with its dramatic Cascadian-style architecture, the World Forestry Center boasts tons of interactive exhibits about the importance of sustainable forestry practices, especially to the Northwest. The exhibits are primarily intended for family audiences, but that didn't stop me from testing my skills at the controls of the harvester simulator. You'll also find displays showcasing the planting and use of trees in many cultures around the world. *dl*

The Oregon Zoo

4001 SW Canyon Road off of Sunset Highway
226.5161, www.oregonzoo.com
Open: Everyday, May-September 9a-6p, October-April 9a-4p

Just hop on the MAX and within 20 minutes tops, you emerge through a tunnel under Portland's Zoo at Washington Park. A step above the standard Zoo fare, this center for community gathering also has a world-class ampitheater with a terrific Summer Afternoon Concert Series (see **Calendar** chapter), spring and summer camps for kids, and late-night holiday fun at Halloween and in the winter. Don't forget to check out the Stellar Cove, an exhibit featuring sea lions, otters, and a tide pool—all natives to the Oregon Coast. *rrm*

Children's Museum

4015 SW Canyon Road off of Sunset Highway
223.6500, www.portlandcm.org
Open: M-Sa 9a-5p, Su 11a-5p, closed September-February
Admission: $6-7

The Children's Museum shares a parking lot with the Washington Park Zoo, which are both easily accessible by Portland's light rail, the MAX, for pennies on the dollar. The Children's museum is an active experience with water play, puppet shows, and a pirate ship on which to climb. All sorts of fun for younger kids abound, though children over 10 might not be engaged. *rrm*

Portland Farmers Markets

Farmers markets offer fresh and local finds that put us in touch with the source of our food. They are also a great way to connect a community and get out on a sunny day. Support Portland-area farmers with this selection of superb markets. *dm*

Hollywood Market

www.hollywoodfarmersmarket.org

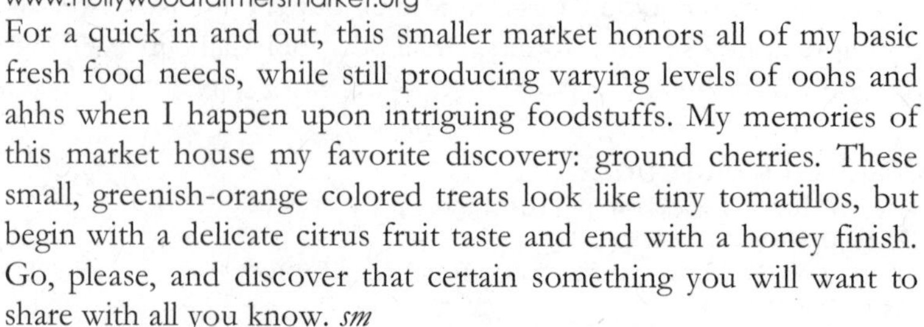

For a quick in and out, this smaller market honors all of my basic fresh food needs, while still producing varying levels of oohs and ahhs when I happen upon intriguing foodstuffs. My memories of this market house my favorite discovery: ground cherries. These small, greenish-orange colored treats look like tiny tomatillos, but begin with a delicate citrus fruit taste and end with a honey finish. Go, please, and discover that certain something you will want to share with all you know. *sm*

Hillsdale Farmers Market

www.hillsdalefarmersmarket.com

If Sunday finds you craving crisp greens and easy access to the freshest fruit around, make your way to the Hillsdale Farmers Market in SW Portland. I love Deep Roots Farm where I can get all of my organic vegetables for the beginning of the week. Nonna's Noodles offers homemade, one minute pasta, which is so good it has me wishing for weeks full of Sundays. *sm*

Portland Farmers Market

www.portlandfarmersmarket.org

With these four locations on four different days, and a vendor list so extensive and diverse to have me believing that I could be the next Alice Waters by simply reading it, the Portland Farmers Market is a "must do." These markets are seasonal, running in the summer months with some stretching into spring, fall, and even winter. Check the website for the months of each market: *sm*

Portland State University

Sa 8:30a- 2p
Downtown's South Park Blocks
Between SW Harrison and Montgomery Streets

From its shady location, to the array of local vendors that includes bakers, farmers, chocolatiers, florists, fisherman, mushroomers, canners, and more, the PSU Portland Farmers Market always makes me feel like I've died and gone to foodie heaven. I like to dive into a seasonal fruit cobbler made onsite in Tastebud's wood-fired brick oven and make my way around the market collecting all the fruits and vegetables I can carry (I usually hurt myself). Pick up some purple asparagus, mustard greens, and morel mushrooms, or begin your weekend with a homemade HoHo from Blue Gardenia. Either way, you get a tasty cross section of the gastronomic bounty Portland has to offer. *sm*

Shemanski Park

W 10a-2p
Downtown's South Park Blocks, SW Park between SW Salmon and Main Streets

Ecotrust

Th 3:30-7:30p
Pearl District NW 10th Avenue between Irving and Johnson Streets

Eastbank

Th 3:30-7:30p
Close-in Southeast at Hinson Church
SE Salmon Street and 20th Avenue

Learn

Courses, classes, and seminars of all sorts, and places to take on new challenges

Flexing your brain muscle is a great way to enhance a vacation, or a prolonged visit to a place. Classes are also a great way to meet locals. My grandmother was never bored; at the ripe old age of 82 she took Chinese language classes, having no background in it at all. She always inspired me to listen up, and see what I could learn. *sb*

Wine Tasting and Pairing Classes

Hip Chicks Do Wine, 4510 SE 23rd Avenue at SE Holgate Street
234.3790, www.hipchickdowine.com
Open: Everyday, 11a-6p

With wine classes and events filling up their calendar, I don't know how these gals manage to create so many vibrant vintages, but it is clear they know their stuff. Traipse around town for a tasting event, or take a class at their Pearl District urban boutique winery, where the goddess and maven of wine will guide your senses toward spellbinding combinations of cheese and wine, chocolate and wine, even truffles and wine. Start with the basics of wine tasting, holding the glass correctly, taking in the "nose," giving it a swirl, and admiring its color. Then sip away city-side, 'cause with such close proximity to acres of heavenly pinot and chardonnay grapes, the vineyard is coming to you. *sb*

Sewing Classes

2136 NE Alberta Street at NE 21st Avenue
287.2658, http://boltfabricboutique.com
Class times vary

Swing by Bolt (see **Create** chapter) for a brush up on your sewing skills. Different classes feature a variety of patterns including tote bags, PJ's, and quilts. Look around the shop for ample choices of fabrics and notions to work with. Check their website for current class listings. *sb*

Pacific Festival Ballet

4620 SW Beaverton Highway at SW 45th Avenue
Box Office: 977.1753, Academy: 245.5269
www.pacificfestivalballet.org, www.portlanddanceacademy.com
Show times vary

Master classes, performance opportunities—at the Schnitz (see **Listen** chapter), no less—and season-long programs make a complete ballet school that turns out a stellar annual Nutcracker show. Join in and learn how to make your body move like the instrument that it is. Check the website for current workshops, classes and intensives. *sb*

The Center for Movement Arts

1734 SE 12th Avenue at SE Hawthorne Avenue
236.1007, www.cmadance.com
Class schedules vary

The Center for Movement Arts is a relaxed and comfortable atmosphere where you can hone your dance skills. Try Ballroom, Jazz dance, the Lîmon method of modern dance, or a Pilates mat class with one of their professional, confidence-inspiring instructors. Build both muscles and self-esteem while dancing to your hearts content. *sb*

Swim Lessons

At these Portland City Pools: Southwest, Sellwood, Columbia, Montevilla, Creston, Mt. Scott, Peninsula Park
www.portlandonline.com/parks/finder/index

I have to make a point about the wonderful aquatic facilities in Portland, many of which come complete with water features, great lap pools, and even whirlpools. Enjoy the watery paradise of each of these hooked-up community centers by taking some lessons, or getting the kids started on feeling being comfortable in the pool. For less than fifty dollars, you can schedule 10 group lessons, offered many times a day in the summer and also throughout the year. Whatever your skill level, you can get started, or improve your stroke at a clinic. Other fitness classes fill out the activity book, a PDF version which is available online. *sb*

Community Music Center

3350 SE Francis Street at SE 33rd Avenue
823.3177
Class and recital times vary

For more than 50 years, Portland's Community Music Center has been teaching students to appreciate and master different forms of melody. If you aren't taking a class your self, come and enjoy a free or low-cost recital from a chamber group, choir, or orchestra. Both private and group lessons are available in guitar, music appreciation, voice, piano, violin, and more for reasonable prices. *sb*

Portland Freeskool

http://freeskoll.ofsafety.net/index

The lessons we have to teach and learn are infinite. With the mission to give everyone access to all sorts of classes, Portland Freeskool is a virtual resource where you can check current class offerings at many locations and even opt to host your own class. Sign up for the newsletter by emailing: **portlandfreeskool-subscribe@lists.riseup.net** or go online for the most up-to-date calendar. *sb*

Portland Rose Society

www.portlandrosesociety.org (see **Calendar** chapter)

This collective of rose enthusiasts is a wealth of information for anyone interested in roses or learning more about them. With loads of fun volunteer opportunities, there are also regular events and classes on rose feeding, new types of roses, and arranging. Check their website for current class offering and meetings. Because Portland is the City of Roses, this club seems to be forever planning some major rose planting around town. *sb*

Knit Purl

1101 SW Adler Street at SW 11th Avenue
227.2999, www.knit-purl.com
Open: M-W 10a-7p, Th 10a-9p, F-Sa 10a-6p, Su 12-5p

This fashionable downtown yarn shop always provides tea and water for their parched shoppers. Mingle with a full spectrum of yarns in all textures, and stop by for one of their ongoing drop-in knitting classes. Check their website for class offerings and times for all manner of topics, from a difficult sweater pattern to baby hats to how to cast on. *sb*

Bead Classes

Various times and locations

To learn the ways towards your own fabulous jewelry designs, head to one of Portland's bead stores for classes in practically every medium. Art Clay Silver, Victorian lace cuffing, soldering, and beaded flowers are some of the classes offered at my favorite bead store, **Dava Bead** (see **Create** chapter) at either of their two locations. Find out current information at **www.davabeadandtrade.com**. Other bead stores like Beads Forever (**www.beadsforever-portland.us**) and Let It Bead (**www.letitbeadportland.com**) offer a variety of beading class choices. For amulet bags and fringe bracelet classes check out DMB Designs at **www.dmbakke.com**. *sb*

The Herb Shoppe

2410 E Burnside Street at SE 24th Avenue
234.7801, www.theherbshoppe.net
Open: Tu-W 11a-7p, Th-F 11a-6p, Sa 10a-6p, Su 12-5p

The Herb Shoppe is a shop of education more than anything else. Owner J.J. Pursell will guide any novice explorer through the extensive array of organic and ethically wild-crafted herbs to arrive at a blend to cure what ails you. For those seeking an extended tutorial in herbalism, there are free lectures every Wednesday evening. Check the website to see the offerings for this week. *dm*

The Attic Writer's Workshop

4232 SE Hawthorne Boulevard at SE 42nd Avenue
963.8783, www.atticwritersworkshop.com
Class schedules vary

For small classes with exceptional and accomplished writing teachers, sign up for a workshop at The Attic. You may find yourself being taught by a contributor to *The Oregonian* or *The New Yorker* who can help send you on your way to the same grandeur. Know before you go that your classmates are contemporary writers, so challenging and elevating critiques are a part of the process. *dm*

Get Active

Hikes, runs, rides, bikes, boats—anything and everything to get you moving

North Portland Bike Works

Whether you are simply getting from A to B, or seeking some good sweaty fun, getting active always has a refreshing result. I started on swim team at a young age, and have been known to go through various ski bum phases now and again. I've also been challenged by Pilates and yoga, and bouldering walls and rocks, indoors and out. Whatever thrill level you're seeking, from scaling cliffs to jogging by redwoods, Portland is the kind place that offers all manner of sport and non-sport ways to jam. *sb*

Yoga Bhoga

1401 SE Morrison Street #B at SE 14th Avenue
241.5058, www.yogabhoga.com
Rates and class schedules vary

Yoga Bhoga is one of Portland's most favorite spots for downward dog, triangle pose and other relaxing movements. Take a slow-paced class focusing on exact poses that are held for extended time. Alternately, get in the groove with a faster course that runs through sun salutations until you are breaking a sweat. There are several beginner classes, but the skill levels also runs to expert. Yoga Bhoga has a great deal; for $20 they offer an entire week of unlimited classes, but you can also purchase drop-in classes and multi-week passes. *dm/ sb*

Portland Rock Gym

21 NE 12th Avenue at N Burnside Street
232.8310, www.portlandrockgym.com
Open: M, W, F 11a-11p; Tu,Th 7a-11p, Sa 9a-7p, Su 9a-6p

Portland Rock makes muscle-building more fun than ever. The walls are higher than other gyms and there's even a tiled element that mimics the technical nature of popular Scott's Rock, a few hours outside of the city. Try your hand at the Slab or the Corkscrew Slab, both matrixed with taped routes for all levels. My only peave is the lead climbing area is almost exclusively overhang, where my preferences are chimneys and arêtes. But luckily, there is an extensive bouldering section for me to practice those overhang moves, including the impossible but addictive mushroom boulder where you have to climb down before you climb up. *sb*

Nelson's Nautilus

8333 NE Russell Street off of Knott Place
254.7710, www.nelsonsnautilus.com
Open: M-F 5a-11p, Sa-Su 8a-8p

The local fitness center Nelson's offers the best physical trainers around. Go to their website and sign up for a free week-long trial so you can test out their top-of-the-line equipment and take a dip in their lap pool. Sports medicine and physical therapy are also part of these centers, scattered around the area, so all your needs are met in one spot. *sb*

Powell Butte Trails

Entrance at SE Powell Street and 162nd Avenue
Public Transit: take TriMet #9, Powell Boulevard

Whether hiking, biking or horseback riding, this wooded tangle of trails even has wheelchair accessible routes. From Ellis Street, wind around Mt. Hood Trail to Orchard Loop Trail where there is a beautiful picnic area. Bikers will love the Springwater Corridor entrance, where they can have access to the 40-Mile Loop around the park, one of the most scenic inner-city bike rides I know. Stables are located near the service road beyond the parking lot. *sb*

Lower Columbia Canoe Club

17005 NW Meadowgrass Drive, Beaverton
www.l-ccc.org

This club is a staple of the outdoor recreation community in Portland. Membership dues are collected annually, and bi-monthly potlucks are hosted at members' houses. Check out their trip schedule online and get in touch with a member ahead of time to join in. Regular day trips include the Wilson River, Kalama, and Washougal, as well as a monthly Coordinator's Choice that could be a class 2 up to a class 5. If you live in Portland or will stay for a while and join the club, you'll receive their friendly monthly newsletter with all the updates and outing information. *sb*

Waterpolo Intramural

Buckman Pool
320 SE 16th Avenue at SE Pine Street
823.3668

Learn the skills of this exciting sport by practicing sculling, swimming, and shooting with locals and an experienced coach. The clinic is the place to start, Mondays and Wednesdays, to learn the techniques, then bring your friends and play at the intramural on weekends. There's no charge to learn a new, watery team sport. *sb*

WOW Walk Club

Wonders of Walking, hosted by REI
1405 NW Johnson at NW 14th Avenue
221.1938, www.wondersofwalking.com
Every Sa, 9a, free guest visit, then $35 annual fee

This community walking club includes fun walks all over the city, at every pace from leisurely to judged racewalking. The most natural healthy exercise is more fun in the company of locals. The founder of the club is an expert on walking, a master racewalker, and she's started quite a group—fun, relaxed, and fit! *sb*

Mt. Scott Community Center and Portland City Pools

5530 SE 72nd Avenue at SE Harold Street
823-3183, www.portlandparks.org
Admission: Drop in $2.50-4, 20-visit pass $36-60, annual pass $210-350
Hours: M-Th 5:30a-9:30p, F 5:30a-9p, Sa 8a-7p, Su 12-6p

There is nothing more exciting than a whirlpool on a rainy day. Inside the spacious Mt. Scott Community Center is an incredible indoor pool, complete with lap pool, 2-story waterslide, and what else but a whirlpool. Get your suit on, take a sit in the locker room sauna, and splash down the slide before you do your laps. I like trying to walk against the whirlpool, and taking breaks floating around in circles with the current. Each neighborhood in Portland has their own park or recreation facility, many of which have excellent pool facilities. For more information, look at the parks website or www.portlandonline.com. *sb*

Monday Night Dodgeball

Colonel Summers Park
SE 20th Avenue at SE Belmont Street

You know Portland is a unique place when rivalries exist between tennis players and dodgeball players. Forget the Crypts and the Bloods, this stuff is heavy. OK, so not that heavy. But most Monday nights, the dodgeball contingent of the Zoo Bombers (see **Weekend** chapter) steps onto the courts at Colonel Summers Park for a game of dodgeball that refuses to accept only the standard issue bouncy ball, using balls that range from tennis to yoga. This is an impromptu, albeit established, event, so you might be able to sneak a throw or two if you play your cards right. We were extended an invite, but only because they muscled us off the tennis court. Dress in black and ride up on a trick bike and you'll have a better shot. *dm*

The Movement Clinic

1994 SE Ladd in Ladd Circle
475.3079
Class schedules vary

Pilates is a subtle exercise with strong results. By practicing individual muscle movements, balance, strength, and stability are attained. Group classes run Tuesdays through Fridays, and semi-private lessons are available by appointment, anytime. Afterwards you can head to Palio's (see **Coffee Table** chapter) for a nice après-Pilates cup of tea. *sb*

Vega Dance Lab

1322 SE Water Avenue at SE Main Street
235.1400, www.vegadancelab.com
Class schedules vary

I have a secret…I took a hip-hop dance class. It was a goal of mine, so I struggled my pride to the ground, tied it to a fire hydrant, and ran to Vega. The owner and master dancer and choreographer, Evie, helped me feel confident despite those chicas who can throw down a move after one go-through. If you are one of those women, more power to you. Head to a Tease + Tone or Burly Q, a class that will bring out the sexy and sassy in you. Vega is a drop-in studio, so don't worry about lovin' and leavin'—that's what it's all about! *dm*

Laurelhurst Park

3601 SE Oak Street, bounded by SE 33rd Avenue, SE Ankeny Street and SE 39th Avenue
www.portlandparks.org
Open: dawn to dusk

Laurelhurst Park is an idyllic respite from the cars of the city streets. Up knolls, around a winding bend in the path, passed a dog park and a duck pond—ancient and enormous trees shelter merrymakers from any outside noise. Add to the beautiful green landscape some tennis and basketball courts, picnic benches, horseshoe pits, and a few rogue middle school mountain bikers trying new jump tricks and you have everything our heart desires in a park. Yes, Laurelhurst is a GrassRoutes numero uno choice for dog walking, tennis and general meandering. The Laurelhurst neighborhood to the north of the park does not adhere to the regular grid-style of the streets of PDX, so enjoy a minute or two of confused wanderings among the *Leave it to Beaver* homes. *sb/ dm*

Burnside Bridge Skatepark

Under the east side of Burnside Bridge
www.skateoregon.com/burnside/burnside.html

For all you skaters out there, Burnside is a venerable landmark. Pioneering the idea of 'skatepark,' the creators of this historically-significant structure were essentially skateboard squatters under the east side of the Burnside Bridge, appropriating an area formerly filled with homeless, junkies, and prostitutes to make a home for the then-suppressed skateboard culture. Eventually gaining legitimacy and city approval, this park is known the world around and even featured in a Tony Hawk video game, remarkable not only for its origins, but also for its difficulty. Head under the bridge to check it out and maybe even take a ride. *dm*

Wilshire Park

4116 NE 33rd Avenue, bounded by Shaver and Skidmore Streets
823.2223, www.portlandonline.com
Open: Everyday, dawn to dusk

Wilshire is a party of a park. Play for hours on end in the horseshoe pit, after splattering your face in barbecue sauce. Jog off the gallon of lemonade and the stack of brownies you just downed on one of the paved trails or gather up your buddies for a volleyball match. All the games you could ever want at a picnic with friends and family are here—an inner city playground for all ages. *sb*

Leif Erikson Trail

In Forest Park, NW 29th Avenue and Upshur Street to Newberry Road
www.portlandonline.com, search 'forest park'
Open: Everyday, 5a-10p

Back when I was running 6 miles a day, I would go to the Leif Erikson trail in NW Portland around sunset. As I jogged in one of the largest city parks in the country, the quarter mile markers tracked my progress. My slow rise above the NW industrial area and the Willamette River kept me motivated as the city completely disappeared. Bikers take this trail all the way to its 11th mile or divert into Forest Park's many connected and small wooded trails. This epic trek through the urban wilds can be taken rain or shine and is best at sunrise or sunset. *ws*

Mt. Hood Skiing, Snowboarding & Snowshoeing

Mt. Hood Meadows
337.2222, www.skihood.com
Exit 16 off of I-84 East to Highway 26 to Government Camp
Timberline Lodge
622.0717, www.timberlinelodge.com
Exit 16 off of I-84 East, to Highway 26, left onto Timberline Road turnoff

Among the many perks of Portland are winters free of back-breaking snow shoveling. We want snow on our time table, and no shoveling at inconvenient times; we like to have our winter wonderland fun sans responsibility, thank you very much. Enter Mt. Hood. Like a frozen oasis, this "potentially active" volcano is a noticeable fixture on the eastern horizon, with its year-round snow topped peaks. Here you'll find three ski resorts, snowshoeing outlets and cross-country skiing trails. Mt. Hood Meadows and Timberline are the resorts that catch the most snow, with Timberline's glacial top able to accommodate skiing and snowboarding into the summer. Meadows is great fun at night, when lift tickets are cheap, and is a special treat if the moon is full to shed light on some woods explorations. Equipment can be rented at either resort. If a downhill rush doesn't strike you, snowshoes and cross-country skis can be rented in town at The Mountain Shop (288.6768, www.mountainshop.net) and you can take them for a spin at Trillium Lake or one of the other stops on the way to the ski resorts. As Highway 26 passes through the town of Sandy, you will notice a number of ski shops at which you can stop to purchase a National Forest parking pass and avoid a pesky ticket. Most of these shops also rent winter gear. *dm*

Bike About

www.BikePortland.org

The cycle culture in Portland reigns supreme. Most residents own bikes and a large proportion of them use them regularly for transit and adventure. Whether you have a second-hand mountain bike, a single-gear handmade road bike, or a bike made of hemp-welded bamboo and cattle horns, you will be in good company in this city of cyclists. This blog is one-stop-shopping for your bike needs. It includes events, missing and found bike notices, and handy tune-up tips. *dl*

North Portland Bike Works

3951 N Mississippi Avenue at N Shaver Street
287.1098, www.npdxbikeworks.org
Open: M-Sa 11a-6p

This collectively run non-profit bike shop is committed to bringing all members of the community together with tons of workshops and volunteer opportunities. Women and Transgender Nights keep the shop open every Wednesday 6-8p and youth workshops are offered during the summer. Get active in your community and put some elbow grease into it! *dl*

Bike Gallery

1001 SW 10th Avenue at SW Salmon Street (one of several locations)
222.7017, www.bikegallery.com
Open: M-F 9:30a-6p; Sa 10a-6p, Su 12-5p

With its four conveniently located Portland stores, Bike Gallery is always just a stone's throw away so you can fix that leaky tire and be back on the road. The business has remained family-owned since it began in 1974, and is dedicated to lending support to organizations for bicycle awareness. In addition to its comprehensive repair and fitting services, Bike Gallery offers a wide range of clinics, from basic repairs and maintenance to proper gear-shifting technique. *dl*

Coventry Cycle Works

2025 SE Hawthorne Boulevard at SE 20th Avenue
230.7723, www.conventrycycle.com
Open: Tu-Sa 10a-6p, Su 1-5p

Excuse the pun, but it can often be an uphill ride for enthusiasts of the unconventional recumbent (lounge-chair-looking seated or supine position) bicycle. Coventry caters to the specific needs of recumbent riders, offering products and services that can be difficult to find elsewhere. Consult these experts for special repairs, accessories, and proper fitting (i.e. no more "recumbent butt"). *dl*

Veloce Bikes

3202 SE Hawthorne Boulevard at SE 32nd Avenue
234.8400, www.velocebicycles.com
Open: M-F 11a-7p, Sa 10a-5p

Whether you desire a practical commuter or high-end road racer, Veloce Bikes will piece together your ideal frame using "a sophisticated ruler" designed to meet each customer's size and riding habits. Man-powered transportation meets high tech at Veloce. *dl*

Citybikes Workers Cooperative

734 SE Ankeny Street at SE 7th Avenue
Repairs: 239.0553, Sales: 239.6951, www.citybikes.coop
Open: M-F 11a-7p, Sa-Su 11a-5p

For no-nonsense repairs and maintenance, Citybikes—a worker owned cooperative since 1990—offers a variety of tune-up options or a complete overhaul for your 1-speed, 3-speed, or you-name-it. Classes and apprenticeship opportunities are available for the amateur mechanic to take his or her skills to the next level. *dl*

River City Bicycles

706 SE Martin Luther King Jr. Boulevard at SE Alder Street
233.5973, www.rivercitybicycles.com
Open: Winter M-F 10a-7p, Sa 10a-5p, Su 12-5p; Summer M-F 10a-8p, Sat 10a-6p, Su 12-5p

Advocates of bike commuting, these guys specialize in pro builds, hand-built wheels and fenders for all of those rainy non-summer days. A team of fitting experts and an indoor test track will ensure you a comfortable and satisfying ride for your money. I highly recommend taking the time to admire their impressive display of historic bikes, which includes one made of bamboo! *dl*

Dress Up

Don your shiny shoes and head out to one of these fancy places, not all come with a huge price tag

The Farm Café

There are those occasions where you just have to dress up—something inside you wants to put your good foot forward and go all out. These spots are as fancy as Portland gets, and that isn't that fancy! The laid-back dress code has spread all over the West Coast, and has been especially relaxed in the north. But if you are looking for an opportunity to take your new dress shoes out on the town, these places are your best bet. Not everywhere requires big bucks, though some are pricier. Remember, drinks are usually the culprit for amping up your dining bill, so if you are careful in that department you can make even the more expensive places affordable. *sb*

The Farm Café

10 SE 7th Avenue at E Burnside Street
736.3276, www.thefarmcafe.net
Open: Everyday, 5p-12a
$-$$ Veg Ro

Off of Burnside, there is an itty-bitty farmhouse you might miss if you're not paying close attention. Take care to make a stop there, preferably with a loved one with whom you feel comfortable gushing over fine organic meals, tasty drinks, and the best chocolate soufflé ever. Here I go with my own gushing… I started one congratulatory evening happily with a Snowflake—a frangelico, Kahlua, and cream dream served in a martini glass with dark chocolate shards covering the white liquid. That warmed me up considerably so I could dive into crab risotto, slow-cooked to perfection, a few of their ravishing salads and a pork dish that drove me, the non-pork person, to exclamations of bliss. That was before we had the chocolate soufflé, so rich and creamy we had to have another round of snowflakes and take our sweet time. It is a small place, but doesn't feel crowded. It is also the kind of place you can go knowing the other people there are pretty groovy, like they've passed the first indicator test by having discerning taste and interesting intellect. Quite simply, I love this spot. For the kinds of refined dishes served here, the prices are astonishingly low. The food is warm and comfortable, cooked with good karma and without a rush. Few things make me happier than another chance to come to The Farm for a full-course meal. *sb*

Park Kitchen

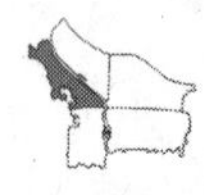

422 NW 8th Avenue at NW Flanders Street
223.7275, www.parkkitchen.com
Open: M-F 11:30a–2p, M-Sa 5p-late
$$-$$$ Veg Fr Ro

Half of my conversations at Park Kitchen sound something like this (please read out loud for the full effect), "Oooo, thmmismmm, soommoo gommood! Did you try this?! Oh my god…" Then there's the setting, which is charming and cozy, and surprisingly without pretense, something I almost expect from a restaurant that selects its ingredients on a daily basis. Spectacular meal options include my favorite indulgence, green bean tempura with bacon; there's a dessert menu so full of attractive options that it may take a while to order. All of this coupled with a chef that will come to your table and take you through the workings of his magical creations, This little gem gets my vote for Portland's best menu. *sm*

Saucebox

214 SW Broadway at W Burnside Street
241.3393, www.saucebox.com
Open: Tu-F 4:30-late, Sa 5p-late
$$$ Veg PW Fr

Enter Saucebox and come into the world of this chef and owner power team, Chris Israel and Bruce Carey. If you're not just stopping in for a swanky drink—and that wouldn't be a misstep, I name them the best cocktails in the city—wind around the bar, passing by Mr. Mumu, the DJ of Portland DJs, and into a muralled room, hung with protruding statues in vibrant hues. Now calm down, sit, breathe, relax, take your eyes off the glass-enclosed closet where booze gets infused, and get to the menu. Can I butt in here and order for you? Well, I think I will then. To get a mix of their appetizers, order a Pupu Platter to split so you can sample the gooey goodness of the tapioca balls and the tasty sauce on the baby back ribs, this place is called Saucebox, after all. Following that same thread, the Javanese sauce on the roasted salmon makes it one of the best renditions of this favored fish I've ever had. Green curry with duck breast and other seasonal main courses are worth a try, but if the salmon's on the menu, then look no further. Go ahead, take yourself on a mini-vacation to Saucebox, where it's possible that you could be in any great world city. *sb*

Apotheke

1314 NW Glisan Street #2A at NW 13th Avenue
241.7866, www.apotheke-nw.com
Open: Tu-Th 5p-12a, F-Sa 5p-2a
$$ Ro PW

Apotheke is the German word for pharmacy, but Apotheke feels more like a secret laboratory. It is hidden in an upstairs loft with a completely white interior in one of the Pearl District's many classy historic buildings. There is a constant supply of experimental music playing as the technicians serve up new and ancient herbal cocktails. Trying the legendary Chartreuse liquor is a must, as it has been developed over hundreds of years by French monks and contains over 130 different herbs. Many others are available to tickle the palette such as star anise Pernod, Glayva, Benedictine, and St. Hubertus. There is a healthy array of Belgian beers, both secular and monastically-produced, as well as a typically Baltic assortment of foods, which includes the classic Belgian fries but also more unique hors' devours like the Norge—cucumber medallions topped with crème fraiche, smoked herring and caviar, and a side of rye crackers. For something a little more substantial, there is always German sausage. *ws*

Wild Abandon

2411 SE Belmont Street at SE 25th Avenue
232.4458
Open: Su-M, W-Th 5:30-10p, F-Sa 5:30-11p, Sa-Su 9a-2p
$$ Veg R Fr

Have you walked along the Willamette River mystified by the beauty, then started to hear a grumble coming from your belly? When you've got to get off your feet and into a grand meal take yourself for a dress-up, yet wallet-friendly meal at Wild Abandon, where their Willamette Dream salad will allow you to continue your pretty ponderings. Oregon blue cheese is perched atop wild-harvest greens and bursting currants with a light bite of vinagrette. The pasta main dishes are the stars: ravioli and polenta lasanga, with noodles made in-house, will give you renewed comfort. All local, all lovely, this may sound like a personals add, but I am not messing about when I say these dishes are one fine lady of a meal. *sb*

Andina

1314 NW Glisan at NW 13th Avenue
228.9535, www.andinarestaurant.com
Open: M-Th 11:30a-2:30p, 5:30-9:30p, F-Sa 11:30a-2:30p, 5:30-10p, Su 5:30-9:30p
$$ Ro Fr

Statistically, Portland is not very ethnically diverse. However, I begin to doubt the figures when I find myself sitting in an authentic Peruvian restaurant enjoying a blend of traditional ingredients and contemporary culinary style. Andina's bustling dining room is elegant, lit with dozens of candles on white tablecloths, and the bar is a more relaxed option with padded benches, big chairs, and a full stock. To complement the atmosphere, live jazz or Latin music plays nearly every night. The food is the crowning point, as it should be. I go straight to the Tapas menu and grab "5 elementos," a clean, traditional ceviche accompanied by yams and fresh corn on the cob. You can't miss the "Causa Mixta Nikkei," a crab salad cake, topped with tuna, avocado and crispy shrimp, or the "tabule de cereals Andinas" with quinoa, olives, avocado, and oils. For drinks, try "the elixir of life," the Acai-Pirinha, a blend of Brazilian liquor and berries, or the even more exciting "Sacsayhuaman" habanero-infused vodka shaken with passion fruit and cane sugar topped with a cilantro leaf garnish. By then your senses will be overwhelmed for the entire night. *ws*

Hurley's

1987 NW Kearney Street at NW 20th Avenue
295.6487, www.hurleys-restaurant.com
Open: Tu-Sa 5:30-10p, Sa-Su 10a-2p
$$$ Ro S

Often, diners head to 23rd Avenue or The Pearl for a night of fine feasting. Hurley's is a welcome escape from that trendy hullabaloo, located just to the side of these busier haunts, on the sleepy intersection of NW Kearney and 20th Avenue. When in bloom, the restaurant is enveloped in leaf-covered vines that give the feel of entering a hobbit hole. The menu is heavy on the meat dishes, with Kobe Beef and foie gras as signature features, and French-inspired preparation the modus operandi. The Chef's Tasting Menu offers a prix fixé chance to try five or eight courses. Ingredients are seasonal and the space is often quiet and uncrowded, suitable for you and your sweetie, or for supping solo at the small bar. *dm*

Higgins

1239 SW Broadway at SW Jefferson Street
222.9070, http://higgins.citysearch.com
Open: M-F 11:30-12a, Sa 4p-2:30a, 4p-12a
$$$ Veg Ro Fr PW

Under the pressed tin ceiling, between the wall tapestries, onions turn into a part of a sensuous salad, cucumber and jalapeno granité tops local oysters, and Oregon Pinot Noir gets poached into pears to top duck confit. Transformations are what this fine restaurant is all about, so sustainable flavors, created with organic small farm produce and meats are the main dish. Each season brings a completely new menu, though autumn is my favorite time to come, when roasted root vegetables set the stage for maple-spiced hazelnut and farro salad. Vegetarian plates are as divine as the sustainably-caught seafood and free-range meat ones. Make a complete night of it, by not missing the wine course, the salads, and the desserts. Follow your nose around the neighborhood to find a concert, a play, or just a walk along the river while reminiscing about the other-worldly meal you've just enjoyed. *sb*

Paley's Place

1204 NW 21st Avenue at NW Northrup Street
243.2403
Open: M-Th 5:30-10p, F-Sa 5:30-11p, Su 5-10p
$$$ Veg Ro Fr R

There are fine dining restaurants in New England that are farm chic. They may be situated in what once was a barn or maybe an old farmhouse, but all the wood has been superbly refurbished and the décor is tastefully cozy, obviously costing someone a pretty penny to install. Paley's Place has that same East Coast farm chic feel. Walk past the porch diners and into the intimate restaurant where you'll be greeted by Nina Simone coming through the speakers and the whiff of a fresh, seasonal menu in the air. Reservations are a definite must for table seating, though a free seat at the bar gives access to the full menu as well. Pick what strikes your fancy from the array—Paley's does everything well, though it is costly and comes in small portions. If there is room for after-entrée enjoyment, Paley's has an impressive cheese menu and some tasty sweets like a chocolate soufflé cake with toasted hazelnuts. This is the restaurant for an evening of quiet conversation, supernal, sustainable food, and an all-in-all splurge. *dm*

Bluehour

Bluehour

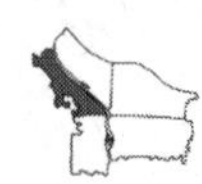

250 NW 13th Avenue at NW Everett Street
226.3394, www.bluehouronline.com
Open: M-F 11:30a-2:30p, 5:30-10p, Sa 5:30-10:30p, Su 10a-2:30p, 5:30-10p
$$$ Ro PW R

This striking establishment is part of what put Portland on the culinary map. Bluehour is located in the Pearl District, a revitalized former warehouse quarter, and next to Weiden+Kennedy, the famously stylish advertising agency that touts Nike as a major client. About as fancy as the city does dining, Bluehour presents its decked out guests with the most taste-bud-delighting entrées. A truffle potato gnocci dish, followed by their frozen banana soufflé are a divine complement to an unbeatable ambiance. They try for locally-sourced meats and organic ingredients, and few diners exit this gem disappointed, despite the dent in their wallets. *dm*

Roux

1700 N Killingsworth Street at Concord Avenue
285.1200
Open: Everyday, 5-10p
$$-$$$ Veg Fr Ro

Tucked up in North Portland, Roux dazzles with a huge dining room and bar, and an indulgent New Orleans inspired menu. I love the upper echelon restaurants appearing with this dressed up Creole food like Roux as well as Screen Door (see **Weekend** chapter) in Southeast; the flavor and weight is debilitating and I'll take its TKO punch any day. If you can't decide on an entrée, or are hung up choosing between the impressive duck or rabbit dishes, put together three sides as your main dish and they'll steal the show. This is the prefect solution for the sampler in all of us. After trying their creamed Brussels sprouts, you'll be able to tell your mother to stop nagging you, 'cause you'll be hooked. A julep is so wonderfully Southern—each sip transports you. Top off the evening with beignets because, well, you've come this far already, you might as well dive into some deep fry too. *dm*

clarklewis

1001 SE Water Avenue at SE Yamhill Street
235.2294, www.ripepdx.com
Open: T-Sa 5p-late
$$$ Ro Fr

Eight years ago, Michael Hebb and Naomi Pomeroy helped create the distinct and fresh Northwest-style cuisine with their underground dinner parties called Ripe Family Supper. When their email invite list reached 15,000 names, the couple decided to open a bistro, which they called clarklewis. The restaurant is located in a candlelit suite in the eastside industrial district, with all the food made from fresh, local ingredients in a beautiful open kitchen. Now, under new ownership, but with the same familiar style, I have been lucky enough to taste the delights of a roasted beet salad with blood oranges, watercress, and fresh and creamy goat cheese, followed by a family-style bowl of mussels in a garlic, fennel and chili vinegar broth. There are always tender meats like duck or lamb and a fine selection of pastas—I have personally enjoyed tagliarini with black trumpet mushrooms, garlic, white wine and parsley. The food on the menu is constantly changing, but the format is always the same; every dish is served small, large or family. Family is for sharing with a group so everything can be tasted. *ws*

Le Pigeon

738 E Burnside Street at NE 7th Avenue
546.8796, www.lepigeon.com
Open: W-Su 5-10p, F-Sa 5-11p, Sa-Su 9a-2p
$$-$$$ Ro

Arrive at opening time, and be seated behind seared foie gras with gingered rhubarb, scallops with duck fat hollandaise, and a modest pork osso bucco. If you get there after the usual rush, you'll be tested to wait as these dishes pass by your jealous nostrils. But I suggest you come to play—you won't be disappointed. Organic and local ingredients have never been so decadent, and yet the atmosphere is reminiscent of sitting on your grandma's wooden counter snacking as she cooks an heirloom recipe. This is Portland's best place to impress your date. *sb*

Lucy's Table

704 NW 21st Avenue at NW Irving Street
226.6126, www.lucystable.com
Open: M-Tu 5-9:30p, W-Th 5-10p, F-Sa 5-10:30p
$$$ Veg Fr Fam R

Lucy's Table is a great choice for exciting food, to surprise the palate. Glance back and forth from the small plate and large plate menu—I like the daily bruschetta sampler to taste a bit of many of the delightful restaurant creations. The meats and seafood are fabulously marinated and dressed in a sauce made from pomegranates and jasmine-infused butter. The atmosphere is simple—a clean canvas upon which to paint a memorable meal. Lucy's Table is very vegetarian friendly, with equally intriguing options for the plant-only eaters of the bunch. *dm*

Phlox

3962 N Mississippi Avenue at N Shaver Street
890.0715, www.phloxpdx.com
Open: Tu-Su 11a-6p

Ladies, get ready for your ultimate night on the town by stopping by Mississippi Avenue to pick up a gorgeous dress at Phlox. For the summer months, choose a flowery wrap-around or floor-length silk dress. Heat up the night with a frilly skirt before hitting the town. The owner hand-picks independent labels and even sells her own handmade line. This boutique is a cornucopia of girlie desire, stocked with the most artful, flattering, and feminine pieces perfect for wearing to one of Portland's many divine dining spots. *sb*

Lovely Hula Hands

4057 N Mississippi Avenue at N Mason Street
445.9910, www.lovelyhulahands.com
Open: Tu-Sa 5-10p
$$-$$$ Veg Fr Ro

The best soup I've ever had—a bacon, sage, sweet potato, and walnut puree—was all it took to distract me from the very intense conversation I was having with my dinner companion. That soup was good to the last drop, as is the restaurant, with its soft pink and brown tapestries and lighting that is just right. It's easy to delight in a complex meal of local fare or an inventive 20's era honey-laced cocktail like The Bees Knees. Lovely Hula Hands' prime location in the heart of Mississippi Avenue leads contented diners to the streets for a night of neighborhood wandering or maybe to take in some after dinner entertainment. *sm*

Bombay Cricket Club

1925 SE Hawthorne Boulevard at SE 19th Avenue
231.0740, www.bombaycricketclubrestaurant.com
Open: M-Th 5-9:30p, F-Sa 5-10:30p, Su 5-9p
$$ Veg Fr Fam R

Closer-in on Hawthorne Boulevard (in Portland speak, 'closer-in' refers to closer to city center or the river), Bombay Cricket Club harkens to one of the vestiges of colonial India, the game of cricket, which has since been adopted by the former "commonwealth" as one of the nation's most popular sports and plays on a television above the entrance. Theme aside, the Indian food here is superb and usually draws a crowd—reservations are a good idea. The curries are all beautiful and the Saag Paneer is a house favorite. To add a lean to the night, the Mango-Rita packs a punch with its Indian spin on the classic Latin beverage. I am also partial to Bombay's naan; add a side of this classic Indian bread to your order. Though there are some pricy items on the menu, this is a fairly relaxed joint, so dress up or don't, depending on your mood. *dm*

Lauro Kitchen

3377 SE Division Street at SE 34th Avenue
239.7000, www.laurokitchen.com
Open: Sun-M 5-9p, Tu-Sat 5-10p
$$$ Fr Fam R

Lauro is one of the famed Portland restaurants and this eatery is able to live up to the notoriety that draws the out-of-towners and food critics while still serving as a neighborhood bistro. Located on quiet Division Street, Lauro is a welcome alternative to some of the more busy downtown restaurants and draws an older crowd with its simple, but flavorful, menu items and its spacious dining room. It is an ideal spot to bring paying parents or relatives. When I was in Majorca, Spain, we pulled off in the midst of an around-island trip for some paella on a cliff side. After that experience, where the view outdid the food, I decided paella was reserved for subordinate seafood. But that was before I had Lauro's version, chock full of first-rate players like clam, shrimp, squid, mussels, and, surprisingly, chorizo. The best paella I've had in Los Estados Unidos! I would recommend sitting at the place settings that overlook the chefs as they concoct your cuisine—it is art in motion. Plus, and this may seem trivial, there is something to be said for a nice big glass of water waiting for you by your plate. *dm*

Buy Me

A unique take on shopping from artichokes to zippers

Helen Bernhard Bakery

Andy Warhol really was onto something when he equated department stores with museums. Indeed, the way to appeal to shoppers is an artful task, and well represents our most modern takes on design and cultural signing. So whether you have a practical purpose, need a little retail therapy, or just want to gaze at the most modern of museums, these spots should fulfill your aims, while also being community and environment-friendly businesses. *sb*

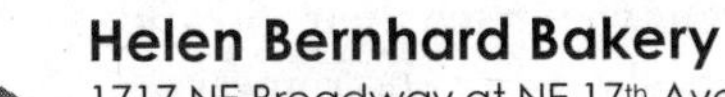

Helen Bernhard Bakery

1717 NE Broadway at NE 17th Avenue
287.1251, www.helenbernhardbakery.com
Open: M-Sa 6a-6p, Su 8a-3p

Helen started baking up mouthwatering cookies and hearty breads in the 1920's, and the neighborhood bakery carries on the same friendly family legacy to this day. Known for their "M and M" cookies, both M's for mouthwatering, the cozy shop is piled high with many varieties, such as psfernussen, Mexican wedding cookies, chocolate nut, and more. Inventive loaves like English muffin cornmeal and cobblestone bread are a close second to their outstanding challah, baked fresh every day of the week. Holiday cookies, candies, and cakes help reel in the celebrations and traditions of each season. Service is warm and samples are plentiful. Come early on Sunday morning, when they set out their day-olds at half price. *sb*

Lived in Lover

3619 SE Division Street at SE 37th Avenue
230.8533, www.livedinlover.com
Open: Th-M 11a-6p

Lived in Lover is another classic Portland vintage extravaganza. It is furniture heavy, but also rounds up heaps of men's and women's clothing—a real blast from the past. *ec*

Pinkham Millinery

515 SW Broadway at SW Washington Street
796.9385, www.pinkhammillinery.com
Open: W-Sa 11a-5:30p, Tu by appointment

Dayna Pinkham's sought after cranial creations push all my desire buttons. Her skills were honed under the tutelage of the European upper crust of milliners, and she's woven a Northwest edge and a modern flair into all the traditional styles. The felt collection will turn any proclaimed non-believer into a bona fide hat person, especially the elegant "cloche turban" and the witty "boney fedora slouch." Custom and bridal hats for special occasions are created with mind-boggling variety and design. Take a second look at all those hatted Hollywooders, and you might well trace their top knot back to this Portland-only shop. Her hats also grace the runways of Seaplane's (see below) delightful local fashion shows. *sb*

Seaplane

827 NW 23rd Avenue at NW Kearny Street
235-2409, www.e-seaplane.com
Open: Everyday, 11a-6p

Seaplane is hands-down the coolest boutique in Portland, perhaps the entire Northwest Coast. Using clothing as a mode of self-expression and artistic whim, you will want to parade the streets for hours in your new outfit from this local designers' smorgasbord. Incredible necklaces are pieced together from found objects; frilly skirts layered from bleached aprons are strung together with seamless nuance. Every piece is a story, a centerpiece, and a flash of beauty. The staff knows the background behind each designer's work, and can fill your ears with inspiring tales that'll make you proud to splurge on any of their fine articles. Near the counter, look for journals made from re-bound old novels—I used mine to take notes while researching this very book, and collected many compliments in the process. *sb*

Flutter

3948 N Mississippi Avenue at N Shaver Street
288.1649, www.flutterclutter.com
Open: M-Sa 11a-6p, Su 11a-4p

A miraculous thing happens when found objects are turned upside-down and painted—they emerge as something new, usable, and desirable. In true homage to Duchamps' *Readymade*, or *Bicycle Wheel on Stool*, Flutter juxtaposes antlers and Buddhas, lace and statue hands all strewn about this fanciful shop in a way that brings them new life. Don't miss the jewelry case, and be sure to look above your head at the inventive light fixtures. *sb*

Steve's Cheese

Located inside Square Deal Wine Shop
2321 NW Thurman Street at NW 23rd Avenue
222.6014, www.stevescheese.biz
Open: W-Sa 11a-8p, Su-Tu 11a-6p

Steve saw his Grandfather's Iowa farm taken over by corporate America, so his love for all things small business and artisan is deep seeded. This incredible cheese case inside one of Portland's best wine stores takes even the fanciest, small batch cheeses off the pedestal and into your mouth. Try the enormous flavors of Northern Italian cheeses, Robiola and Brescianella, or some divine peasant cheeses from nearby Estrella Family Creamery. Even Portland's top chefs get their cheese from Steve—he's the cheese guru, after all. *sb*

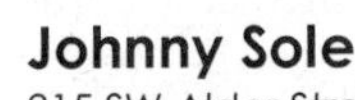

Johnny Sole

815 SW Alder Street at SW Park Avenue
225.1241, www.johnnysole.net
Open: M-Sa 11a-6p, Su 12-5p

Portland's largest independently-owned shoe store is known for its excellent collection of snazzy boots and ultra-modern mens' shoes. Embroidered cowboy boots, gathered leather knee-highs, and suede heels line the multi-level shelves at their two-story downtown store. Find bargains on stylish, high-quality footwear in their sale closet, and a cool hand-printed shirt to match on their upstairs racks. *sb*

Red Light Clothing Exchange

3590 SE Hawthorne Boulevard at SE 36th Avenue
963.8888
Open: M-Sa 11a-8p, Su 11a-7p

When the thought of scouring the Goodwill racks puts a crick in your neck, turn to Red Light for a more easily digestible array of clothing of the vintage variety as well as trendy second-run releases. People watching is a side perk; the Red Light draws hipsters like moths to a flame. If you're low on funds you can hand you're your wearisome duds to the captivatingly accessorized employees for, hopefully, a tidy sum, which is certain to be returned shortly to the store registers after a must-have boot acquisition. *dm*

Redux Reinventions

811 E Burnside Street, Suite 110 at SE 8th Avenue
231.7336, www.reduxpdx.com
Open: W-Su 2-7p

Redux (pronounced re-do or re-ducts—take your pick) is a paradise of design, where everything is made from recycled materials. Surprisingly stunning jewelry fashioned from retired skateboards by PDX designer Maple, messenger bags of old billboard ads from Seattle-based Alchemy Goods, and Resource Revival bicycle chain picture frames direct from Mosier, Oregon, are just some of the crafts that uphold the Redux 'artware reinvention adornment' manifesto. This is an ideal boutique to gather up some gifts for your people back home or to treat yourself to a pair of designer earrings that do a double duty of being both cute and sustainable. *dm*

Stars Antique Malls

SE Milwaukie Avenue at SE Bybee Boulevard intersection
239.0346, www.starsantique.com
Open: M-Sa 11a-6p, Su 12-5p

Antiquing and second-hand shopping need not consist of hunting for finds in a space reminiscent of Great Aunt Rose's attic. The three building that comprise Stars Antique Malls, which run just north and south of the Milwaukie Avenue and Bybee Boulevard intersection, rent space to dealers to arrange their own collection of wares. Visitors will appreciate the Stars' approach to shopping as well as its location in the charming Westmoreland neighborhood, handy in proximity to the equally delightful Sellwood 'hood, both perfect locales for a weekend stroll. *dm*

People's Food Co-op

3029 SE 21st Avenue at SE Brooklyn Street
232.9051, www.peoples.coop
Open: Everyday, 8a-10p

As true neighborhood centers, co-ops bring visitors of unknown cities a sense of belonging. Shoppers can choose to be joint owners of this grocery, and contribute ideas at monthly steering meetings. People's is situated in an energy-efficient building complete with an eco-roof, which is essentially a grassy plot on the roof used to control rainwater runoff, among other nifty community benefits. You'll be happy to find an extensive bulk section and an inviting outdoor patio at the entrance; while you're there, indulge in some dried mango and smile with other happy patrons. If you happen to be in the area between 2-7p on any given Wednesday, People's Farmer's Market sets up shop on this sunny spot. *dm*

Missing Link Toys

3552 SE Hawthorne Boulevard at SE 35th Avenue
235.0032, www.missinglinktoys.com
Open: Everyday, 12-7p

If you are not already acquainted with designer toys or what some refer to as "urban vinyl," step inside Missing Link Toys. As part-owner Shannon Stewart attests, the confused faces are happily aided toward understanding by a staff who can give you the low-down on low-brow art and the designer toy movement overall. Manufactured in short runs and heavily art-driven, these toys are no GI Joe or Barbie, and the prices reflect this. Check out the stuffies by local designer toy producer UNKL, as well as the staple Kid Robot figures and be sophisticatedly sated with the pop culture subversion of these collectible creations. *dm*

The ReBuilding Center

The ReBuilding Center

3625 N Mississippi Avenue at N Beech Street
331.1877, www.rebuildingcenter.org
Open: M-Sa 9a-6p, Su 10a-5p

Stepping through the epic earthen entranceway and into the ReBuilding Center will make you wish that you were renovating a cute bungalow. This lofty open-air facility is not just a place for items seeking a second life in your home; it is part of a network of "Our United Villages" non-profit community resource centers around the country that promote sustainable living, education, and community development. The ReBuilding Center is a warehouse of ready-to-reuse doors, lighting fixtures, lumber, windows and more, stocked up, down, and around such cleverly named aisles as Looking Glass Loop, Appliance Alley, Carpet Square, and Miscellaneous Mile. If purchasing a door would make riding the bus a little awkward, a person can always use some more nails or a new rainfall showerhead like the one I found. *dm*

New Seasons Markets

1954 SE Division Street at SE 20th Avenue (one of several locations)
445.3100, www.newseasonsmarket.com
Open: Everyday, 8a-10p, most locations

Is it odd that a supermarket makes my heart go all a pitter-patter? Stop into any New Seasons Market and you will empathize with me. The combination of a warm and adorable staff is sometimes too friendly when my "non-morning self" enters before 10a. The plethora of organic produce, the short lines at checkout, the surefire opportunity to run into someone you know, and the general community investment of New Seasons is what has pushed the regional chain full-force into the hearts of Portlanders. New Seasons came about when a local Portland natural food grocer was absorbed by a national chain and three employees decided to grow a new market and a new approach. They have a female president to boot. You can grab some snack bars to keep you energized as you explore the city or stop in for lunch—they have a great hot food bar. "The Friendliest Store in Town" is the transition grocer for organics and the answer to an urban eco-friendly dweller's quest for a values-driven business. *dm*

Greenloop

8005 SE 13th Avenue at SE Nehalem Street
236.3999, www.thegreenloop.com
Open: Tu-Sa 10a-6p, Su 12-5p

A recent addition to the neighborhood, Greenloop is a boutique that showcases the pinch of fashion that has gone eco. Greenloop's racks are stocked with designers like Blue Canoe, EcoGanik, and locals Anna Cohen and Sameunderneath, backed up by a well-frequented online business that accompanies the store picks. Not a place for bargain shoppers, it's worth saving up for something extra special, and of course, green. Ensure that the seasons you're gearing up for keep on coming by shopping stylishly at this type of conscientious boutique. *dm/sb*

The Gold Door

1434 SE 37th Avenue at Hawthorne Boulevard
232.6069, www.thegolddoor.com
Open: Everyday, 10a-7p

The Gold Door is a microcosmic amalgamation of the world's artistic treasures. Visitors can browse Portland's largest amber collection, as well as spiritual artifacts from Mexico, Tibet, Brazil and Ethiopia, among many other cultures. Specializing in jewelry and folk art, the store is stocked through direct-travel purchasing. The local owner has carried some of the featured artisans' works for over ten years, occasionally facilitating the art creation himself by personally connecting suppliers with artisans. Conscientious practices extend beyond Gold Door's product selection—they donate to local fundraisers and encourage staff to take time off to travel. Shoppers are sure to catch not only the incense in the air, but also the good vibes that pervade this museum of a store. *dm*

Moxie

2400 E Burnside Street at NE 24th Avenue
296.6943, www.moxiepdx.com
Open: Tu-Sa 11a-7p, Su 12-5p

A boutique that is able to perfectly harmonize local, sustainable and chic, Moxie embraces the urban eco-traveler in its sunny corner shop. For sale are innovative finds made from bed sheets, scarves, vintage clothing, bamboo and even candy wrappers; many designed by fabulous locals. The striking vinyl bags from the wise and hip Queen Bee Creations are made right across the street and can be seen slung on women all around Portland. (My roomie has a tally going for how many bikers she sees sporting a Queen Bee). An alternative to the "been there, done that, bought the t-shirt" travel experience is a Crazy Coconut screen print pillow of the St. Johns or Hawthorne Bridges. Take all of these perks and marry them with adorable dresses and a smattering of vintage shoes and we may have found the perfect boutique. *dm*

Trade Roots

1831 NE Broadway Street at NE 19th Avenue
281.5335, www.traderootsinc.com
Open: M-F 10a-5:30p, Sa 10a-5:30p, Su 10a-4p

What do birch bark boxes from Siberia and Indonesian wood-carvings have to do with one another? Where do Nepalese yak-horn crafts meet with billowing Moroccan skirts? The answer is Trade Roots, a store where all the products come from happy, healthy artisans, who have been paid a living wage for their work. In addition to bringing together unique and affordable gifts, attention is paid to ensure that the environmental impact of the objects is minimal. Trade Roots has taken the care, so you can shop care-free. *sb*

Lady Luck Vintage

1 SE 28th Avenue at E Burnside Street
233.4041, www.ladyluckvintage.com
Open: M-F 12-6p, Sa 11a-6p, Su 12-5p

Lady Luck is a Portlander's top choice for vintage shopping. Such stores are found in great quantity along the eastside streets of the city, but none as totally 60's as Lady Luck. With excellent customer service and idyllic summer dresses o'plenty, there is a reason this locally owned spot is touted as the best. The lady herself has sifted through thrift stores and estate sales to unearth these unique finds just for you. *sb*

Kitchen Kaboodle

1520 NE Broadway at NE 16th Avenue (one of several locations)
288.1500, www.kitchenkaboodle.com
Open: M-F 10a-7p, Sa 10a-6p, Su 11a-6p

Perhaps you are inspired by an amazing meal at Higgins (see **Dress Up** chapter) and want to try imitating and innovating immediately, but note some culinary implements lacking from your inventory. Maybe you just can't help ogling at unattainable stainless steel tools. Whatever your motivation, Kitchen Kaboodle is the kitchen supply store to visit. Another great local chain, the staff is one of the most helpful in town. They never batted an eye as I utilized their expertise down every aisle during my obsession with vegan cupcake baking. *dm*

Broadway Books

Broadway Books

1714 NE Broadway at NE 17th Avenue
284.1726
Open: M-Sa 10a-9p

Portland's Hollywood neighborhood is fed the written word by this comfortable and comedic bookstore. There isn't a shelf in the place without some humorous title or another—the travel guide section is interspersed with Jetlag's hoax guides like *Molvania: A Land Untouched by Modern Dentistry*, and the history section has soft covers with less serious takes on everything from the Spanish Inquisition to modern culture. Get into the well-read scene that is Portland by picking up a new book here. *sb*

Una

2802 SE Ankeny Street at E Burnside Street
235.2326, www.una-myheartisfull.com
Open: Tu-Sa 11:30a-6p, Su 12-6p

There comes a time when you are in need of that dress of dresses. Honor that moment with a voyage to the far-off land of Una, where sheer beauty reigns supreme. Pull together your inspiration, and your pennies, and dive into a gilded sanctuary of soft romance. Una is a small store, but the kind of place that grows larger and larger as you page through the racks, like carefully thumbing through a memorable novel. Dresses and whimsical blouses are carefully chosen from around the globe by a shop owner equipped with fashion's sharp blade and a graphic designer's keen eye. This is a place where that perfect dress is waiting to be discovered, and where you can access a world of small-batch, independent designers. *sb*

Portland Goodwill Outlet Store, aka "The Bins"

1740 SE Ochoco Street at Frontage Avenue, Milwaukie
230.2076
Open: M-Sa 8a-8p, Su 9a-7p

For the ultimate adventure in shopping, head to what Portlanders know as 'The Bins.' It's a factory-sized Goodwill donation center where large bins of clothing, books, shoes, and knick-knacks are carted in by the hour. Wear gloves and pick through the piles to find vintage and designer shirts and sweaters mixed in with broken dolls and old cut-offs. It is a fun excursion where the possibilities are endless—I found a brand new London Fog micro-fiber raincoat and some enviable Levi's. The best part is the price. For up to 20 pounds of clothing and knick-knacks, it is $1.39 and pound. Above 20 pounds is 99 cents and above 50 pounds is 69 cents. That made my coat and jeans a whopping $4.19 all together. Yee haw! *sb*

Oh Baby

1811 NE Broadway Street at NE 19th Avenue
281.7430, www.ohbabyforyou.com
Open: M-Sa 11a-7p, Su 12-5p

Svelte or voluptuous, Oh Baby has something to flatter every body. Whether your style is more conservative, flowery or sultry, the array of undergarments here is sure to up the ante. The friendly staff is well-versed in tracing your personality to help you pick just the right thing—and that goes for guys in search of romantic girlfriend gifts too. When it comes to traversing this seldom-explored universe, the boyfriend or hubby is in good hands. Trust me on this one. *sb*

Furever Pets

1902 NE Broadway at NE 19th Avenue
282.4225
Open: M-F 10a-8p, Sa 10a-7p, Su 10a-6p

Nothing says "I love you" like a huge, Doberman-sized hunk of chicken jerky. At least that is the thinking at Furever Pets, a top-end, all-natural, and locally owned pet-lovers kingdom. I got some organic puppy treats that my little guy loves, and they threw in a whole bag of gifts and give-aways, including his new favorite chew toy that's also good for his teeth! Whether or not your pet philosophy includes kitty Halloween costumes or just the standard doggie bone, you and your best friend's needs will be met here. *sb*

Local 35

3556 SE Hawthorne Boulevard at SE 35th Avenue
963.8200, www.local35.com
Open: M-Sa 11a-7p, Su 11a-6p

A cornerstone to the Hawthorne district, Local 35 brings together area designers and adventurous labels from abroad. Hipster jeans and *au currant* sweaters and button-downs are neatly hung in front of art installations featuring local artists. The hottest styles don't come cheap, but their sale rack is as cool as their front shelf items and more realistic for many of us. Local 35 has a large selection of men's clothes, a huge step towards making any man' s wardrobe more interesting and alive. *sb*

Wham!

617 NW 23rd at NW Hoyt Street
222.4992
Open: M-Th 10a-6p, F-Sa 10a-9p, Su 11a-6p

Wham brings humor to gift giving. Find a plethora of hysterical cards, immature yet lovable chachkes and an epic collection of iconic post cards. A wall of fun miniatures and games is an affordable way to cheer anyone up. Who could keep a straight face when being shot with a rubber chicken gun, or playing toss with a jiggling ball of protruding rubber fingers? *sb*

Hecklewood

2431 NW Thurman Street at NW 24th Avenue
922.1797, www.hecklewood.com
Open: M-F 11a-6p, occasionally open on weekends

A rambunctious group of young and talented graphic designers, screen printers, and self-described music fiends from nowhere USA, found each other and got it together to create one of the top t-shirt stores around. You can't not look cool after donning one of their signature digs. Leopard print and Mondrian fitted tees for women are striking—I like to dress them up with a suit jacket over top. Men will be equally thrilled with the hat and hoodie collection, as well as the edgy printed wallets made of re-used plastic. In addition to the great store, the Hecklewood crew has a rockin' mix tape project online, where you can listen to a new, hand-picked mix tape every couple of weeks. All this and they have graphic prints on the walls that go up monthly, so there is always something new and inspiring to gaze at while you shop. *sb*

Crowds

Major league sports, celebrations, and other exciting sardine cans

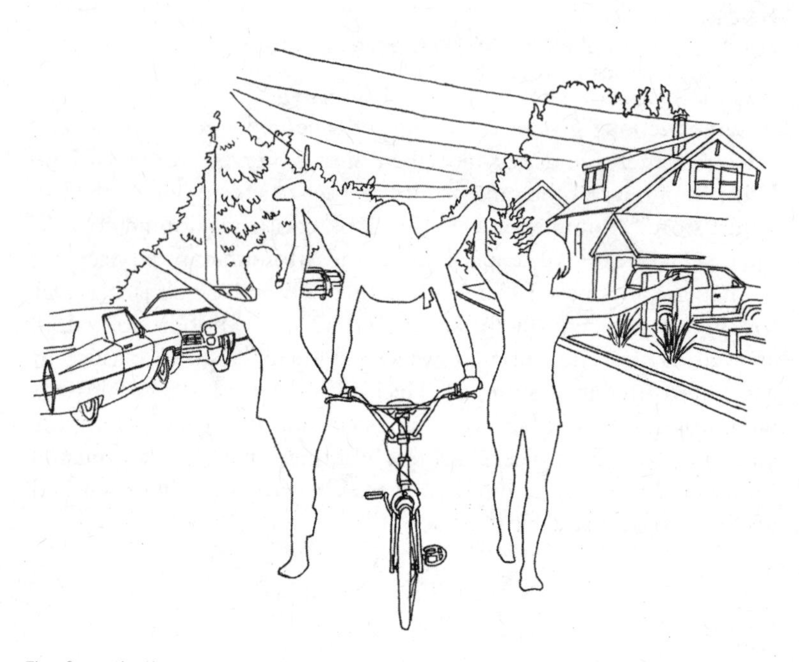

The Sprockettes

Congregating with others for a unified goal of a good time always brings a smile to my face. When my energy is up, mixed with some team spirit or some other excuse, the GR crew gets out and about to watch bike acrobatics or help pack a concert hall. Here's a listing of our favorite crowded places: *sb*

The Sprockettes

www.sprockettes.org (for performance schedule)

What's a bike town without a mini-bike dance troupe? The Sprockettes are more than just a gimicky act. This dazzling all-female group rejects the monoculture of the ideal body type, promoting a positive self-image for people of all shapes and sizes. They are also strong advocates of bicycle riding and community interaction, so grab your ride and go check them out. Like learning to ride a bike, you'll never forget a performance by these strong and talented ladies. *dl*

The Alibi

4024 N Interstate Avenue at N Shaver Street
287.5335
Open: Everyday, 11a-2a

All of us have a singer inside somewhere; it is just a matter of bringing that part out. The Alibi provides the support needed to test out the pipes with a hit rendition of *The Girl from Ipanema* or even an attempt at pop girl rap from the 90's, say *Shoop* for example (don't you dare tell anyone). Come on, you'll probably never see any of these people again anyway. So, order some weak Mai Tai's, take in the smoke, and give yourself a karaoke story to tell. *dm*

Memorial Coliseum

1401 N Wheeler Avenue
www.rosequarter.com

Flower shows, school graduations, ice-skating, and the biggest names in music all grace the stages and corridors of the coliseum. Check the website for what is going on today, and head over for one of the more large-scale events this snug city has to offer. Incidentally, this is also the venue for the yearly Grand Floral Parade, where you'll witness more roses and other flora in one spot than you ever thought possible. *sb*

Portland LumberJax

1401 N Wheeler Avenue, Rose Garden
797-9739 (ticket hotline), www.portlandjax.com

East Coast lacrosse groupies like myself will get a thrill from the serious lacrosse fans in Portland. Finally, this sport has caught on in the west, and the stellar LumberJax fill the season from the end of December to mid-April with nonstop net action. Two-pack tickets are $50 for the front row, $10 for the nose bleeds. *sb*

Trail Blazers

1 Center Court, Rose Garden
797.9619 (Box Office), www.nba.com/blazers

While Portland may not be a city known for its professional sports, it does boast an NBA powerhouse: the Trail Blazers. Put down the latest David Sedaris social critique you're reading and pick up some beer and civic pride at a Trail Blazers game at the Rose Garden. *dm*

PGE Park

1844 SW Morrison Street between SW 18th and 20th Avenues (just off I-405)
553.5555 (Ticket Line), www.pgepark.com

A visitor to PGE Park cannot help but feel a tug at the heartstrings in the face of such nostalgic Americana. Over a century old, this stadium rounds up both Beavers baseball fans and Timbers soccer fans. I go for the soccer where the Timber Army, decked in green and yellow scarves, chant in response to the calls of mascot Timber Jim, a bearded lumberjack fellow who chainsaws a slice off a wooden log for every hometeam goal. Crowds here are rowdy but small in number so don't worry about showing up last minute to heckle the visiting team; just become an honorary member of the hometown crew. *dm*

Roller Derby

2060 N Marine Drive, Portland Expo Center
736.5200, www.rosecityrollers.com
Admission: $15

Around town you might see the signature knuckle logo of The Rose City Rollers stuck to the bumpers of pickup trucks. This collection of roller derby teams gathers hardcore women to duke it out in bouts at the Expo Center. Given the fact that bouts put players on roller skates and require protective gear, they are indeed rowdy, but luckily the gear does minimize injury and beer always follows to mask the pain. Check the website to see when the next throw-down is scheduled. *dm*

Fez Ballroom and Lounge

318 SW 11th Avenue at W Burnside Street
221.7262, www.fezballroom.com
Open: Tu-Sa 9p-2:30a, schedule varies

The Fez is a two-story club with rotating DJ's every night of the week. 80's night brings in a fun and appropriately-dressed crowd. Special events and seasonal parties round out a scheme of theme nights that include everything from House to Hip Hop. Many weeknights are free of cover charge. Fez is the only Portland club with that expansive, cool, European feel. *rrm*

Crystal Ballroom

1332 W Burnside Street at NW 13th Avenue
225.0047, www.mcmenamins.com

The Crystal is the venue where most of your favorite bands below the MTV radar, but heavily rotated on indie radio, will stop when they pass through Portland. A perfect place for acts that the city reared to bring it back for a hometown show, audiences get to rock out on a floor that will certainly throw the unsuspecting for a loop. As the crowd dances and jumps to the rhythm, so does this unique flooring; don't run for the nearest doorway for fear of an earthquake, it's supposed to do that. While the Crystal doesn't have the greatest acoustics, it does showcase some stellar performances. The smaller downstairs venue, Lola's Room, houses an 80's dance party every Friday night, so don the leggings and acid washed jeans and head on over. *dm*

Last Thursday

NE Alberta Street
Last Th night of every month, year round

If you are looking for a great cross-section of Portland's creative Eastside, then don't miss Last Thursday. I love Alberta Street all the other days of the month, but if I've got cash to burn, the sun is shining, and it's the final Thursday of the month, some local artist is going to walk home with my money. This is the night when most of the galleries, shops, and restaurants on Alberta Street open up to the hordes of people flocking to this increasingly crowded stretch of NE Portland. My favorite part, however, is wading through all the street artists hawking their creations. Jewelry, t-shirts, homemade musical instruments, glass paperweights, paintings, drawings, and innumerable sewn items can make for one-stop shopping if you want to bring home real Portland souvenirs. *sm*

City for Free

The ultimate guide to free events, free admission, free talks and more

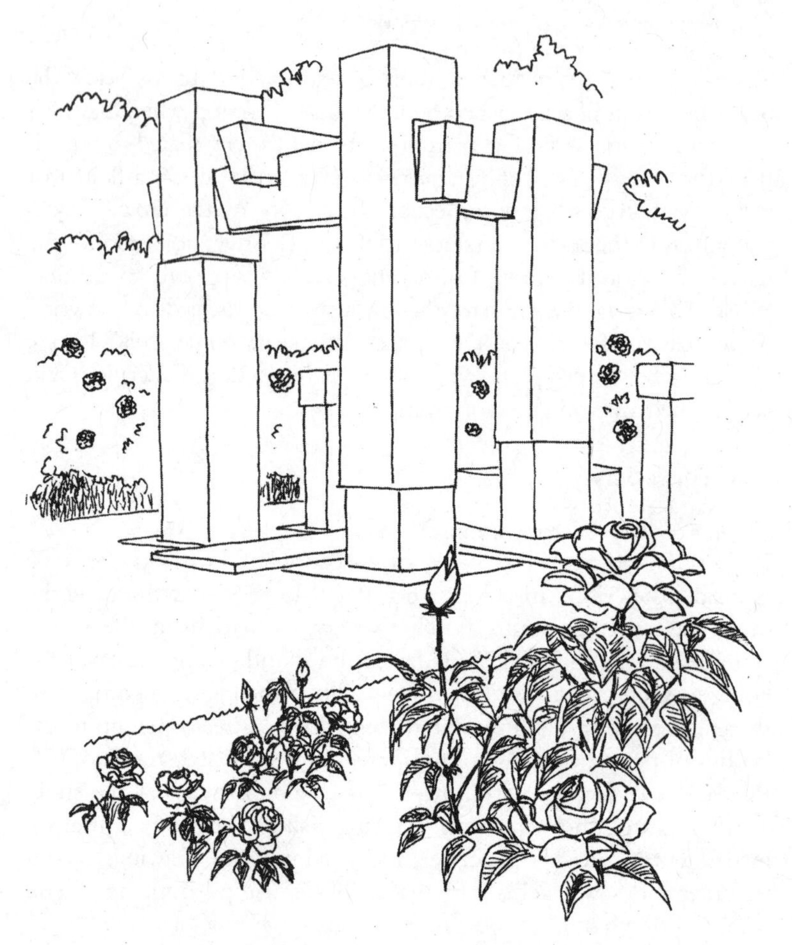

International Rose Test Garden

Just as the saying goes, "the best things in life are free," we've searched high and low to find the best free things in Portland. Maybe this city traded great happy hours for free events and museum days, 'cause we were hard pressed to find an outpouring of money-less activities. But we did find these great events, which are all adventures without digging into your wallet. Don't forget that hiking and enjoying a city walk are also great free fun. *sb*

International Rose Test Garden

400 SW Kingston Avenue in Washington Park
823.3636, www.rosegardenstore.org/thegardens.cfm
Open: Everyday, 7:30a-9p

When the Lewis and Clark Expo of 1905 prompted all locals to plant 50,000 roses around Portland, it became the City of Roses. At the time, the only variety one could come by in that amount was the genteel Madame Caroline Testout, now one of the many highlights on the self-guided tour around the garden, the largest rose garden in the city. Begin at the Rose Garden Shop, and pick up a free brochure that will take you by marvelous fountains, Shakespearian blooms, and over 550 varieties of these most enchanting flowers along a paved pathway overlooking the city. Because of the gentle climate, mild winter and long growing season, roses love Portland, and bloom from May through September. Take a tour with one of the knowledgeable volunteers 10a and 1p on Tuesdays, and at 1p on Saturdays and Sundays. The foliage and views are even worthwhile when the flowers aren't blooming; they provide a nice place to ponder in four and a half acres of solace. *sb*

Free Champagne while you Knit

Knit Purl
1101 SW Alder Sreet at SW 11th Avenue
227.2999, www.knit-purl.com

On Thursdays, from 6-9p, this classy knit shop steps it up by serving complimentary champagne, a weekly bubbly celebration for knitters young and old, novice and expert. Cheers! *dm*

Cupping at Stumptown Annex

3352 SE Belmont Street at SE 34th Avenue
467.4123
Open: Everyday, 11a, 3p

There is so much in life about which to be passionate. For people who love it all, it is difficult to specialize in one passion. That is why it is important to be always diving into subcultures of interest and splashing around in the sea of the connoisseurs' knowledge. Sometimes, the sea is a roast that is bright, acidic, and murky with coffee grounds. A cupping at Stumptown is a crash course on coffee—one of the specialties of this city. Latin and African varieties await the coffee-taster as he steps through smelling the coffee grounds, taking a whiff of the broken pour, and then slurping up a Cup of Excellence Kenyan. The buzz from a tasting is alarming; I'd recommend spitting unless you have a big project due the next day and need fuel for the night. *dm*

Collins Gallery

Central Library, Third Floor
801 SW 10th Avenue at SW Yamhill Street
988.5123, www.multcolib.org/events/collins
Open: M 10a-6p, Tu-W 10a-8p, Th-Sa 10a-6p, Su 12-5p

Full gallery shows featuring everything from modern sculpture to Civil War history are admired by library visitors all year long. Presentations include objects, hung art, installations and film screenings, making this one of the most dynamic non-museum galleries I've toured. Check out a book, then poke your head in Collins to see what's new. *sb*

Story Time at Northwest Library

2300 NW Thurman Street at NW 23rd Avenue
988.5560, www.multcolib.org

After a delicious breakfast at Besaw's (see **Do Lunch** chapter), bring the tikes to the library around the corner for a story-time catering to each age group. Book Babies is Thursdays at 11:15a, Tiny Tots is Thursdays and Fridays at 10:15a, Toddlers is Thursdays at 4p, Preschoolers Fridays at 11:15a and Family Story Time, where kids 0-6 and their caregivers can share in a tale, is Saturdays at 11a. *sb*

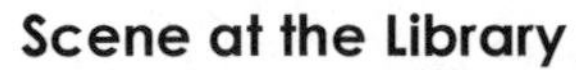

Scene at the Library

Sneak Previews of Portland Theater
Central Library, 801 SW 10th Avenue at SW Yamhill Street, 988.5123
Hollywood Library, 4040 NE Tillamook Street at NE 44th Avenue, 988.5391
www.multcolib.org/events/scene.html

On selected Sundays throughout the year you can catch a glimpse of what Portland's stages have brewing by visiting the library for a free sneak peak. Troupes including Classic Greek Theatre of Portland, Defunkt Theatre, Tabuki Theatre, the Twelve 14 Group, and Artists Repertory Theater perform snippets from their upcoming shows. Check the website for what is in store this Sunday! After you see a preview, you'll know which shows are a must on your ticket wish list. *sb*

Page Turners Book Group

Northwest Library, 2300 NW Thurman Street at NW 23rd Avenue
988.5560
Second Tu of each month, 6:30p

Exchange perspectives on works of fiction new and old. Portland is a city of readers, cluttered with bookish types like myself, which makes for some of the best reading groups in the country. We all love the works of Hemingway, Joyce, Wilde and Fitzgerald, but this group goes beyond simply discussing works by "the dead white guys." *sb*

Hoyt Arboretum

4000 SW Fairview Boulevard in Washington Park
865.8733, www.hoytarboretum.org

It is encouraging to spend time on lands covered with lush growth, including native plants that are considered endangered species. Meander among the green and observe the labeled taxonomy (plant family) as well as geography of the showcased trees in this outdoor museum and laboratory. Some to-go sandwiches are best eaten under the protection of Hoyt's picnic shelter pavilion after or before walking the grounds. Peace is inevitable in this tranquil treasure. *dm*

Portland Art Museum Free Day

1219 SW Park Avenue near SW Main Street
226.2811, www.portlandartmuseum.org

Now and again, every several months, Portland's art institution finds an excuse to host a free day. Unfortunately, there doesn't seem to be a rhyme or reason, no schedule, once in June, once in July, then again for a half day in September. Check their website for updates on when the next gratis art museum trip is in store for you and yours. *sm*

Lone Fir Cemetery

SE 20th Avenue and SE Morrison Street

Certain travel experiences take you to the crux of the culture being explored, such as eating a meal at the home of a local, attending the festivities of a regional holiday and, of course, visiting the burial grounds. Lone Fir captures Portland with its old growth trees and noteworthiness as the final resting place of Asa Lovejoy, a city founder. Head to the grave marker of Elizabeth and James Stephens in the NW corner to catch an example of the zen that has filtered into PDX even way back in 1887, "Sojourning through life awaiting nature's immutable laws to return us back to the elements of the universe of which we were first composed." Even the Slavic city contingent is represented with the faces of the dead photographically embossed on the stones. There is calmness and quirkiness here, and that is what my favorite city is all about. *dm*

Widmer Brothers Brewery Tour

929 N Russell Street at N Mississippi Avenue
281.2437, www.widmer.com
Open: F 3p, Sa 11a, 12p

Where would Portland be without its breweries? Widmer brews up their renowned Hefeweizen and Drop Top Amber right off of Interstate Avenue. Tours happen on Fridays and Saturdays and are free and a perfect prelude to a bite to eat and a brew at Widmer's Gasthaus Pub across the street. *dm*

Free Box

Blackrose Collective and Freecycling Center
4038 N Mississippi Avenue at N Shaver Street
Open: Tu-Sa 12-8p

The idea behind this collective bookstore is a mighty one—to be a thorn in the side of the establishment, pass on information, trade books, and keep up a mixed bag free box. Treasures to one person might be unusable to another, so whether you have some old books, want to peruse some leftist literature, or have too much in your suitcase and need a happy place to unload it, check out this unique Mississippi establishment. Or, you can go when you just want to play with a free stuffed animal. *sb*

Central Library

801 SW 10th Avenue at SW Yamhill Street
988.5123, www.multcolib.org/agcy/cen.html
Open: M 10a-6p, Tu-W 10a-8p, Th-Sa 10a-6p. Su 12-5p

Libraries exist to perpetuate, encourage, and facilitate the pursuit of knowledge but, more importantly, these edifices are refuges for the drifting soul seeking solace. The stacks lure us in silence and solitude and the smell of the pages diffuse a reassuring familiarity. Take a break from the city streets inside Portland's Central Library. Before ascending the grand staircase, take a right into the Children's Library and a peak at the bronze tree, with the lovely adornment of children's book characters. For a more heady turn, the balcony of the government documents room on the second floor houses the agricultural census from 2000 as well as a collection of Khrushchev's letters to Kennedy during the Cuban Missile Crisis. All the possibilities of the world and of our individual lives lie within the covers of these books; a stop in here will inspire a person to go out and pursue their life potential with renewed vigor. *dm*

Powell's Book Events

For info see **Hang Out** chapter

All year long there are author, illustrator, teacher, and creator events for you to join in on, for free. Check Powell's website for an array of different people with unique messages on every thinkable topic. There are only a handful of nights void of some new literary adventure. *sb*

Pioneer Courthouse Square

SW Broadway and SW Alder Street
www.pioneercourthousesquare.com

The posterchild for the quintessential Portland land use battle, this piece of land boasts an enviable chunk of history. Portland's first public school was once located here, as well as the majestic Portland Hotel. In 1951, someone decided that downtown needed another parking lot, but finally, in 1974 the land was secured for public use and transformed into the city's "living room" as the square is called. However, I would more aptly name Pioneer Sqaure, "Portland's Poppin' Patio." Come out any sunny day to crowds of hacky-sackers, cinched up business folks, harried bus drivers, and religious prognosticators. This chaos is a first-class people-watching extravaganza, with brick bleachers to boot (to fund the construction, the city sold bricks etched with people's names—people love seeing their own names chiseled into a brick for eternity!) Buy yourself a taco from the carts, and watch some live bands on Tuesdays and Thursdays at noon in the summertime, outdoor movies on Fridays, and protests galore on the weekends. You won't even miss out on other days: one lunch break at Pioneer Square last summer landed me with a watermelon and a sack of potatoes from a local farm. *ep*

Stay Up Late

Where to find midnight snacks, 24-hour businesses, and casual late night drinking, dining, and dancing

Voodoo Doughnut

Staying up late to dance and dine and relax is something everyone does at least once in a while, so here are the best places around to get in touch with your nocturnal side. *sb*

Voodoo Doughnut

22 SW 3rd Avenue at SW Ankeny Street
241.4704, www.shop.voodoodoughnut.com
Open: Everyday, 24 hours
$ Vn S Fr

After Voodoo works its magic, doughnuts become a thing of beauty, of cultural importance, and of romantic commitment. Yes, romantic commitment. For a mere $157, Voodoo employees (certified to marry couples) will provide a legal tying of the knot, as well as doughnuts and coffee for 10 witnesses. But the reason most come to Voodoo is to satisfy a late night craving for some unconventional doughnuts. Try the ever-popular bacon maple bar—a sugar crystal-covered doughnut with two strips of bacon set in the syrupy glaze. You might gorge on the Memphis Mafia Fritter, stuffed with bananas, and drizzled with melted chocolate and peanut butter, or some equally divine vegan doughnuts. Come in the first Friday of the month at midnight to take the ultimate challenge: how many fried rings you can gobble down. For those more into the speed-eating thing, take the Tex-ass challenge; the current champ had downed one of these plate-sized glazed giants in under 90 seconds, in case you were counting. *sb*

La Casita

607 SE Morrison Street at SE 6th Avenue
234.8894
Open: M-W 11a-11p, Th-Sa 11a-6a, Su 11a-12p
$ Veg Fr S

La Casita's hours fluctuate between late and very late, so any time is the right time to gobble down one of their buck-fifty tacos and free chips and salsa. Nothing goes better with a cool midnight horchata and some Spanish MTV. *ec*

The Hawthorne Theatre

3862 SE Hawthorne Boulevard at SE 39th Avenue
233.7100, www.hawthornetheatre.com
Showtimes vary, most start at 8p

For a real all-nighter of dancing, head to The Hawthorne Theatre. Electronica, DJ's from all corners, and the more hard-core sounds take the stage every night of the week. Party your heart out with fellow Portland music lovers and boogie addicts. Tickets usually won't run you more than ten bucks, and if you're lucky there'll be a free show on the night you decide to invite yourself to the party. *sb*

Ararat

111 NE MLK Jr. Boulevard at Couch Street
235.5526
Open: F-Sa 6p-4a

By day, Ararat bakes up the best challah in town, but by night Russian techno pulses through the restaurant-turned-club making it one of the most fun nights to be had in PDX. An authentic cultural experience, this all-in-one doesn't candy coat the ex-Soviet party scene. People here are serious about getting their groove on, but whether or not vodka is your thing, and there is a lot of it here, it's easy to join in the excitement. *sb*

The Montage

301 SE Morrison Street at SE 3rd Avenue under the Morrison Bridge
234.1324
Open: Tu-Th 11:30a-2p, F 11:30a-2p 6p-2a, Sa 6p-4a
$-$$ Fr PW

New Orleans á la late night, Montage serves up Cajun food to please us all. Their seafood gumbo is delicately balanced, yet bold, and too big to eat in one go. Your server will wax creative when you ask for a to-go container, shaping aluminum foil into swaying swans or fighting swords. The colorful atmosphere is a perfect cap to another epic Portland evening. *ec*

The Roxy

121 SW Stark Street at SW 11th Avenue
223.9160
Open: Tu-Su 8a-Su 3a
$ Fr PW

The Roxy is owned by a famous PDX drag queen (let's not forget Portland has more drag and strip joints than any other U.S. city, so it was bound to pop up somewhere in this book). A boisterous atmosphere, complete with autographed memorabilia hanging from the walls, and breakfast served all day and all night, you have an excellent chance of meeting any number of queer-friendly local celebs. Don't miss the Britney Spears Blueberry Pancakes—they tell me it's her very own recipe. *ec*

Doug Fir Lounge

830 E Burnside Street between SE 8th Avenue
231-9663, www.dougfirlounge.com
Open: Everyday, 7a-2:30a
$$ Vn Fr PW

The Doug Fir will make you feel like a swinger. This log cabin-gone-60's style lounge, restaurant, and live music venue wines and dines guests and then offers them a room in the connected Jupiter Hotel (see **Lodge** chapter), with special after-midnight rates. The Doug Fir is good at what it does. Their meatloaf dinner almost touches your mama's (I like the bacon strips on her's though) and visitors have multiple secluded alcoves to take a drink with a group of friends. There is also an impressive wooden bar built from the reclaimed wood of another project that Doug Fir designer Jeff Kovel worked on at 12th and Alder in Southwest. Downstairs is a fabulous music venue; the low ceiling of the basement and the continued log walls of the upstairs wrap an audience for anything from the jazz workings of the Wood Brothers to the rowdy antics of the local March Fourth Marching Band. At the end of an evening, The Doug Fir takes a Denny's diner and raises it up a notch with a more sophisticated finale and a tastier meal to ease the morning after. *dm*

Holocene

1001 SE Morrison Street at SE 10th Avenue
239.7639, www.holocene.org
Open: W-F 5p-late, Sa-Su 8p-late, hours depend on performance schedule

It's time to go dancing! Holocene will fulfill that relentless boogie itch with its many nights of deejays spinning and people grooving. There are always gay dance parties here and DJ Anjali often makes appearances with her Bhangra and Bollywood mixes, bringing culture from across the planet right to my back door! The space has a large dance floor with incredibly high ceilings to accommodate all that heat. Check out Holocene's schedule; there can also be some great acts that stop by for a show, like Portland's own Horse Feathers. *dm*

Dots Café

2521 SE Clinton Street at SE 25th Avenue
235.0203
Open: Everyday, 12p-2a
$ PW Fr Ro

When you have a hankering for huge hand-cut fries and a staff that is not only attractive but has great taste in music, go slide into a booth at Dots. Against the gold-flecked wallpaper, velvet paintings add just the right oddity to your snazzy Spiked Rikki, a combination of citrus vodka, fresh-squeezed limes, and a splash of 7-Up. Dots has been open for 14 years and has long been a gathering place for people who like an alternative flare to their late night dining. *ec*

Original Hotcake House

1002 SE Powell Boulevard at SE 10th Avenue
Open: Everyday, 24 hours a day
$ Veg Fr S

The Original Hotcake House serves stacks non-stop, 24-hours a day, 7 days a week. Weekend nights there is a small cover charge to pay for a security guard, so go to this classic Portland diner knowing there'll be a true mixed crowd. With Britney Spears, Bobby Brown, and Johnny Cash on the jukebox, you'll be happy to wait in line to order a plate of perfect greasy hash browns, or an omelet as big as your face. Watching the line-cook make your food is almost as entertaining as the guaranteed late-night freaks and post-prom high school students. Thank goodness for that security guard. *rrm*

Le Happy

1011 NW 16th Avenue at NW Lovejoy Street
226.1258, www.lehappy.com
Open: M-Th 5p-1a, F 5p-2:30a, Sa 6p-2:30a
$$ Vn Fr CO

At two in the morning, few things out-do Le Trash Blanc, the bacon and cheddar crepe, Pabst Blue Ribbon combo served with a smile at this trés mignionne café. But all the dishes seem a little more refined at Le Happy, where rosy walls and cheerful baristas live up to the name. For a filling meal, add a half a steak and a salad to your Champignon, Provincal or Curry Crepe. I've always preferred the sweet variety, thinking back to my school days when my mother made crêpes filled with apricot preserves to bring into school for my birthday instead of the usual cupcakes. The confiture is stuffed with the jam of your choice with some fresh whipped cream to top it off. *sb*

Vault Martini

226 NW 12th Avenue at NW Davis Street
224.4909, www.vaultmartini.com
Open: M-W 4p-1a, Th-Sa 4p-2a, Su 1p-10
$$ Veg Ro

Sit at a bar that looks as if it were carved from ice and pour over the 'book' of drinks, including 44 unique takes on the classic martini, shaken or stirred. The Hot and Dirty is made with hot-pepper infused vodka and olive juice; the Giesha is ginger-soaked vodka and saké. Flatbreads, toasty panini, and heaping salads are made with the same care as the drinks. Vault caters to the Ruski in all of us, treating vodka like the czar and surrounding his highness with goddesses of sweetness in the form of fruity drinks, ministers of health taking shape as vegilicious salads, and riches galore of fireplace warmth. *sb*

Hammy's Pizza

2114 SE Clinton Street at 21st Avenue
235.1035, www.hammyspizz.com
Open: Everyday, 11a-2:30a, take out until 4a
$ Vn Fr S

It's going on three in the morning and you've been dancing steady since the sun went down. Or maybe you've been tossing and turning with jet lag or taking care of a friend in need. Whatever your excuse, it is time for a hot pizza pie, a locally brewed root beer, and a salad on the side. Hammy's is there, delivering their handmade pies until 4a every day. This is one restaurant number you'll need on speed dial. For the marathon crowd, start your day with a breakfast pizza, complete with eggs and potatoes to get you going on the right foot. Their vegan, non-dairy pizzas are smattered with nutritional yeast and cashews, so everyone can partake with pizzazz. *ec*

Zach's Shack

4409 SE Hawthorne Boulevard at SE 44th Avenue
233.4616
Open: Everyday, 11a-3a
$ Veg Fr

Zach's Shack is the around-the-corner-quirky hangout in a heartwarming yet humorous television series where all the gang meet up to swap tales from their day while endlessly struggling with that pesky intra-group unrequited love story. But Zach's exists in real life, and finally you have your very own feel-good joint. Highlights of Zach's are its late hours, its ping pong table and old school table top Ms. Pac-Man video game, the owner's quality rock music taste and, oh yeah, they serve up dogs—hot dogs that is. Only straying from the hot dog for fries, mozzarella sticks, chips and jalapeno poppers, Zach's dresses their dogs in everything from cream cheese to sauerkraut and dubs them with props to music legends like Little Feat (Feat Dog), The Beatles (Sgt. Peppers), Bob Dylan (Dylan Dog) and, of course, the Grateful Dead (Grateful Dog). Zach's prides itself on the "snap" of a bite into one of their 100% beef dogs created by its natural casing, so snap into an A Capella Dog for the pure, no topping experience. *dm*

Hollywood Bowl
4030 NE Halsey Street at NE 40th Avenue
288.9237, www.hollywood-bowl.net
Open: M-Th 9a-1p, F-Sa 9a-2p, Su 9a-10p

I didn't bowl with big bowling balls until college. Growing up in Massachusetts, it was candlepin bowling all the way. In this New England specific version of the game, balls do not have finger holes and can even be palmed by the dexterous. It is tricky to knock down the pins with those little guys and the game fully primed me for the real deal, which I especially like to play with dance music, beer, and black lights. Hollywood Bowl has all three Friday and Saturday nights after 10:30p as well as $1.50 lanes Tuesday through Thursday nights after 9:30p. There are also video games and greasy food, plus a pro-shop, sketchy lounge, and the ever-appealing bowling shoes. *dm*

Pamper

Shelters from the hustle and bustle, simple enjoyments, and all things feel-good

Pix Patisserie

Part of the whole pampering process is good, hot, comfort food. The classic is chicken soup. But I find most places load their chicken broth with salt, as a substitute for slow-cooked flavor. This is bad news for the body; instead of pampering you get seriously dehydrated. So, in this chapter I've given special attention to not only the in-the-moment effects, but the after effects as well. Here is a selection of feel-good foods, restful spaces, and of course, spas and salons to refresh, re-energize, and restart your engines. *sb*

Pix Patisserie
3901 N Williams Avenue at Failing Street (other locations)
282.6539, www.pixpatisserie.com
Open: M-Th 7a-12a, F 7a-2a, Sa 8a-2a, Su 9a-12a

I've been called a "different" American; I often live in dreams of European excursions gone by. When I lived in London I attended free classical concerts at least once a week and when in Paris made the trek to Chartres not just for the cathedral but for the best macaroons. I get sappy from time to time, feeling out of sorts in the land of stars and stripes. Enter Pix, a place where any francophile, Europhile, or other phile can be themselves, indulge in quite possibly the best macaroons this side of the pond, and sip mind-numbing Belgian brews while reminiscing of other lands. I could write a whole chapter about Pix, but suffice it to say, this spot makes it possible for me to stay put in the good 'ole U S of A a bit longer for such an authentic experience. Beyond the ever-present macaroons are their stunning desserts, all dressed up and ready for the ball. The Amelié, a suave indulgence of orange crème brulée, chocolate mousse, and toasty hazelnut praline, garnered the Patis France chocolate award, a world competition. Other mousse favorites include the Aphrodite with passionate cherries; another chocolate incarnation, the Royal with cheese, comes with fine French Brie a la Tarantino. There's a smattering of fruitier deserts, French classics, meringues, and even dolled-up cheese cake, but for me the choice is between my perennial aforementioned favorite and the pure chocolate decadence of Shazam and Queen of Sheba, two rather extreme versions of 75% dark chocolate, one with caramel marvel, the second just pure molten goodness.

All this, and I didn't even mention their handmade truffles, of which there are a spectrum of flavors and shapes, or their holiday parties and seasonal specialties. Shake off your sugar buzz with some fine cheese, a single malt or some Chimay, one of many other elegant things to sip on. If you go to one place in Portland, you'll have a really tough choice between Powell's and Pix—it is that good. *sb*

Old Wives' Tales

1300 E Burnside at SE 13th Avenue
238.0470, www.oldwivestalesrestaurant.com
Open: Su-Th 8a-9p, F-Sa 8a-10p

Rumor has it that a well-to-do lawyer with a heart of gold opened the original spot as a soup kitchen for the hungry and strapped. With humanitarian acts still a part of this restaurant's philosophy, everyday customers can relax with classical music and booths in the back, and a friendly play area and high chairs in the front. All this, and one of my favorite menus in Stumptown, where European foods, vegan delights, ethnic cuisine, and an extensive dessert list are all included. In all my travels, I haven't yet found a restaurant so successful at serving such a vast crowd of picky eaters at once. Whatever your food allergy, if you keep kosher, if you have choosy kids, if you have diabetes, or any other possible reason to think twice before chowing down, you'll be able to do so here, and enjoy every minute. Line-caught salmon, prepared with ginger and tamari glaze is perfection together with the inexpensive soup and salad bar. Don't miss the Hungarian Mushroom chowder, an Old Wives' Tales' specialty. Each menu item lists all ingredients, even the unbelievably good dressings at the salad bar. Whether you're allergic to kids or have ten of them, eat red meat or only steamed veggies, your needs will be met in the warmest, most relaxed way at this true Portland treasure. *sb*

Urbane Zen

205 NW 10th Street at NW Davis Street
227.8852, www.urbanezen.com
Open: M-Sa 10a-6p, Su 11a-6p

For the pampering needs of men and women, kids and adults, turn to Urbane Zen, where you'll find cruelty-free, handmade products to sooth every inch of your body. Try a salty foot scrub made with anti-oxident-rich algae, or a nourishing moisturizer for under your new silk PJs. Their eclectic selection, which even includes products especially formulated for athletes, makes this a true find. *sb*

Piece of Cake

8306 SE 17th Street at SE Umatilla Street
234.9445, www.pieceofcakebakery.net
Open: M-Th 9a-8p, F 9a-10:30p, Sa 10a-10:30p

With the message that all shall be happy and indulge, Piece of Cake has something surprisingly moist and delicious for everyone: vegan, wheat-allergic, and all. I'm no vegan, though I try to minimize my wheat intake, and I am careful about the sources of the foods I eat, but I've been known to bug my lovely vegan co-writer and tell her, "Just Eat It!" But here is where you'll find me all over cakes made with no dairy, no sugar, and even cakes created with just spelt flour! That's because some magic takes place at this bakery, voted best cake and best bakery in the city. The vegan black forest with chocolate fudge frosting and marinated cherries tastes about as un-vegan as one can imagine. The less-sweet Irish Oatmeal cake and Carrot cakes are best sellers, and for a breakfast treat I like the vegan pumpkin bread (try it under some cheesy scrambled eggs)! Cakes, pies, brownies, loaves, and even cheesecake are whipped up with dairy, sugar, and wheat in one case, and without any so-called essential ingredients in the other, but frankly you'll be hard pressed to tell the difference. Mingle-on, cake in hand, the vintage cookie tins, cake stands and aprons scattered around this collage-like house cum bakery. After a ravishing, yet exhausting trip to the bins, treat yourself, vegan or no, to a heaping slice of cake. *sb*

Tea Chai Té

734 NW 23rd Street at NW Taylor, upstairs
228.0900, www.tea-chai-te.com
Open: Su-Th 10a-10p, F-Sa 10a-11p

Besides having notable Bobba (tapioca bubble tea), home brewed healthful kombucha, and authentic Japanese Macha, the second floor nook Pearl district location of Tea Chai Té guides the ailing toward ebullience through a lesson in tea. Did you know adding some hibiscus to your black tea could instantly help with constipation or the annoying symptoms of a bladder infection? How about that cloves can reduce nausea, even for hang-overs, or relieve tooth aces? Licorice Root aids in combating depression and fatigue, and those "I didn't get enough sleep last night" sore throats. Browse a wall full of loose-leaf teas in every variety, and mix your own according to your day's needs, then find a cozy spot among the serious writers and studious types that hover here. *sb*

Noble Rot

2724 SE Ankeny Street at SE 7th Avenue
233.1999, www.noblerotpdx.com
Open: M-Sa 5p-12a

I get in moods when the energy is sapped from my body, a sniffle is in full flair, and I need a comforting, hot meal. The trouble is, when I get into that frame of mind, I never want to go out of the house. Noble Rot makes me feel as if I never did, hidden in a fasahionable yet steamy enclave, my belly can settle down with perfectly roasted Brussels sprouts, warm frisée salad, and healthful butternut squash soup. Fish is near-perfect here, though specific varieties change frequently. Last outing, I felt like I was under a friendly aunt's care with baked black cod, and macaroni and cheese. Enjoy a wine flight, where three or four vintages are matched and a few ounces of each are poured, or just snuggle up in a booth with some hot tea to go with your white root and black truffle soup. *sb*

Saint Cupcake

407 NW 17th Avenue at NW Flanders Street (one of two locations)
473.8760, www.saintcupcake.com
Open: Tu-Th 9a-8p, F 9a-10p, Sa 10a-10p, Su 10a-6p

Cupcakes are the new doughnut. They can already be seen in coffee shops during the morning rush, and getting makeovers on gourmet cooking shows. And why shouldn't we celebrate the switch? With far less cholesterol, and gazillions of flavor possibilities, cupcakes shouldn't be reserved for birthday parties alone, and Saint Cupcake agrees. This scrumptious shop serves up an amazing Toasted Coconut Cream confection, topped with their delectable buttercream icing. Stop into the NW store for á la carte options, vegan among them, and to read the tale of the Baker's Daughter, the patron saint of the shop. The SE store offers cupcake combos—you don't get to pick, but you'll be able to find a tasty one—they are cupcakes, after all. It's located in the back of a wonderful gift store, so you can ogle a smart new handbag while you realize that you actually prefer their vegan chocolate cupcake to the dairy version. *dm*

Tour de Crêpes

Tour de Crêpes
2921 NE Alberta Street at NE 29th Street
473.8657, www.tourdecrepes.blogspot.com
Open: W-Th 9a-9p, F-Sa 9 a-10p, Su 9a-6p
Happy Hour: 9-10a, 3-7p

On a blistery day, few things satisfy better than a steamy bowl of French onion soup. Sadly, this favorite is often misunderstood in West Coast versions, but luckily Tour de Crêpes has maintained a delicate slow-cooked flavor. With a crunchy baguette and some stinky Gruyere, Tour de Crêpes does justice to my answer to rainy day fever. But that's not all, this homey spot dollops goat cheese and Kalamatas, or fig onion chutney and prosciutto onto perfectly thin crepes whatever mood change you are in need of. If sweets are your thing, be sure to have them make yours with chocolate crepe batter before piling on toasted coconut, smearing nutella, drizzling grand marnier, and squeezing limejuice. For an extra smile, slurp on a cayenne hot cocoa and look out at the less-lucky passers-by on Alberta Street. *sb*

Wax On

734 E Burnside Street at SE 7th Street
595-4974, www.waxon.com
Open: Everyday, 10a-7p

Girlie-girls beware! Wax On is the best place for princess pampering around, with the highest-quality hot wax, and talented divas to do whatever job necessary. For a modest price, you can prepare for a special night in romance land, or just feel a little more fresh with a long-lasting eye-brow wax. You can even purchase locally-made punky-cute underwear. Whatever your choice, you're certain to feel secretly prettier after a trip to Wax On. *sb*

Root

2526 NE 15th Avenue at NE Brazee Street
288.8972, www.rootwholebody.com
Open: M-F 6a-9p, Sa-Su 9a-6p

Even with all our "time saving" gadgets, it seems our collective stress levels have sky rocketed lately. Preventing stress can be our biggest lifesaver, as more and more studies come out linking stress to disease. If you have a few extra bucks to spend in the name or relaxation and health, you'll find many ways to regain spiritual and physical balance here. Meditatitive yoga classes, expert massage and acupuncture treatments, and a visit to the sauna are all offered here, together with a hot cup of antioxidant-rich tea. *sb/ dm*

Pho Van

3404 SE Hawthorne Boulevard at SE 34th Avenue
230.1474, www.phovanrestaurant.com
Open: Tu-Su 11a-9:30p
$ Veg Fr Ro

Pho Van's Vietnamese food warms my heart and my belly. Fragrant spices pervade every menu item, like the tang of lemon and Vietnamese coriander atop a brimming bowl of Phobrings satisfaction with light, fresh ingredients and scrumptious spices. The high-backed booths, with their floral wood adornment make me feel like I am in my own secluded place, away from the remainder of the establishment. Try the Pho or any of their pork dishes. The Cuon, or hand rolls, are an exciting endeavor, as you dip the rice paper in a special vase of water to wrap up your meal. Pho Van will top off a day of indulgence, or begin a night of relaxation in style without bleeding you dry. *dm*

Barefoot Sage

1844 SE Hawthorne Boulevard at SE 19th Avenue
239-7116, www.thebarefootsage.com
Open: M-Th 10a-8p, F-Sa 10a-9p, Su 12-6p

Gather your foot massage-lovin' friends, or take your sweetie for a little escape at The Barefoot Sage. The billowy sofas, soothing music, fragrant essential oils, and massage therapists work together to create an atmosphere that makes me feel like a princess. It's hard to, but I somehow manage to select from a number of feet treats that include salt baths, hot river rock treatments, scented baths and, of course, massages. After a half hour, or when I'm REALLY feeling like royalty, an hour and a half, I leave filled with tea and chilled-out from my toes on up. *sm*

Bishop's Barbershop

2132 NE Alberta Street at NE 21st Avenue (other locations)
546.4171, www.bishopsbs.com
Open: M-Sa 9a-9p, Su 11a-7p

Going to the salon should never be likened to a trip to the dentist. All the fuss, all the fear, all the questions about your look and where is it going fade away at Bishops, where you are welcomed with complimentary beer and stacks of magazines. They operate on a drop-in only basis, and cater to a huge audience, from punks to classy ladies. Cuts are mostly under 20 bucks, color starts at 40, so take yourself for a true treat at this hip and unique Portland barber shop. Fundraisers for school arts programs and other initiatives, as well as jaw dropping fashion shows keep this place pumping all year long. *sb*

The Meadow

3731 N Mississippi Avenue at N Beech Street
288.4633, www.themeadowflowers.com
Open: Su-Tu 11a-6p, W-Sa 11a-7p

The Meadow is your one stop date supply shop. The focus here is on four products: unique flower arrangements, finishing salt, fine chocolates, and wine. You can't help but feel the potential enchantment that these wares could cast over your sweetheart, or yourself for that matter. Drown in a deliriously delicious chocolate bar of Indian curry powder and coconut, and foray into the mysterious world of finishing salts with a starter set. The Meadow allows your existence to be momentarily wrapped up in romance—oo la la! *dm*

Stay In

The best take-out and take-home activities in town

Sometimes I try to pack too much into a day. By evening, all systems are not go. But taking in the town can be done inside, too. There are many great restaurants that specialize in to-go food, delivery, or places where the seating isn't as comfortable, so you can choose one of these low-energy nights to have an in-hotel or in-home dinner. While you're at it, why not rent a flick, and make a cozy night of it. *sb*

Hot Lips Pizza

SE Hawthorne Boulevard at SE 22nd Avenue (other locations)
234.9999, www.hotlipspizza.com
Open: Su-Th 11a-10p, F-Sa 11a-11p
$ Vn Fr Fam

This family owned, community oriented and sustainable pizzeria encompasses all of the GrassRoutes criteria while delivering the best slices right to your door. It is hard to know where to begin when a restaurant crafts such tasty pizza while being conscientious about their impact on the community and the environment. Each of the Portland locations all compost and are run on green energy. Employees are paid well and cheerfully decorate your pie with locally grown spinach, farm-raised meats, and organic cheeses. Another resolution is to maintain the natural bee population, which is under major stress and disease from all the cell waves and the lack of hives and plants for pollination. Nowhere else can you sprinkle a wide slice of spinach bacon with house-made organic habanero hot sauce, sip soda bottled by the owners themselves and not even have to leave your front and center seat on your buddy's sofa. *sb*

Cha Cha Cha

3433 SE Hawthorne at 34th Avenue (other locations)
236.1100
Open: Everyday, 10a-10p
$ Veg Fr Fam

This local chain, with more than five Stumptown locations, boasts reasonably priced and delicious Mexican food. Cha Cha Cha offers homemade horchata, and a chili relleno-stuffed burrito that will leave you full and with leftovers. You can get any burrito smothered in red or green chili sauce, or try it Christmas style and do both. My favorite location on Hawthorne Boulevard, makes a great pit stop between perusing the shops. *sb*

Movie Madness

4320 SE Belmont Street at SE 43rd Avenue
234.4363, www.moviemadnessvideo.com
Open: Su-Th 10a-11p, F-Sa 10-12a

Movie Madness is a maze of movies. Organized how people actually think, "Hmm, I feel like a Scorsese tonight," this video store arranges by director, actor, as well as genre. Film fanatics will be able to select from a wide array of international features and TV aficionados can schedule weekend long marathons of every season of Arrested Development or the like from the extensive TV series collection. Smattered throughout the store is a museum of movie costumes and props, and you might even get to enjoy a Lionel Richie music video screening as you checkout. *dm*

Video Vérité

3956 N Mississippi Avenue at N Shaver Street
445.9902, www.videoveritepdx.com
Open: Everyday, 12p-11p

For a relaxed evening of quality cinema, Video Vérité is the place to go. Solely a DVD carrier (VHS is so 20th century), this modest video store rests right in the Mississippi Avenue mix, and is primed to accommodate a night of Mississippi Pizza and your favorite cult classic. There are free screenings in the basement a few days a week. Maybe today is one of those days, so stop in and take a load off in the remarkable wooden crab chair and table set at the back of the store before making your way downstairs. *dm*

Belmont Station

4500 SE Stark Street at SE 45th Street
232.8538, www.belmont-station.com
Open: M-F 11a-10p, Sa 10a-10p, Su 12-9p

Belmont Station has moved out from under the shadow of its former neighbor Horse Brass Pub (see **Casual Night Out** chapter), where you could find just as many brews, just not ready for the road. Now they've added a small café, so my beer shopping trips have become a lot more delicious. Belmont Station's latest incarnation maintains a stock of over 700 beer varieties, providing the glint in the eye of every home brewer or home brewer hopeful. Stock up on some suggested local brew or indulge in an import, and revel in the checkout counter items—I love that they have both McVities Digestives and PG tips; all the supplies required for a night's entertainment. *dm*

Monsoon Thai

4236 N Mississippi Avenue at N Skidmore Street
280.7087
Open: M-F 11a-3p, 4:30p-10p, Sa-Su 11:30a-10p
$ Veg Fr Fam

The Mississippi Avenue Monsoon Thai location is attached to a laundromat, but don't be deceived by the modest veneer; this place has pumpkin curry to die for, noodles that explode with flavor, and fresh vegetable dishes to go. The Mississippi locale is artsy Alberta Street, the First Thursday Art Walk destination, and the Mr. Roger's-esque Mississippi Avenue area. If you are staying at the John Palmer House across the street, another jewel in the North Portland crown, Monsoon might end up being a part of your daily explorations. Reasonable prices and a parade of classic Thai dishes are always a crowd pleaser, especially served with a few video rentals. Call in your order ahead of time for fast service. *rrm*

Weekend

Fun activities for Saturdays and Sundays, plus yummy spots for brunch

Tin Shed Garden Café

Weekends have a mood all their own. Laze around, relax with your loved ones, or explore something new. Get out of doors, or while away the hours trying out new desserts or watching bikers speed by. A short weekend getaway is a great time to see this city. Americans don't get nearly as much vacation time as allotted in some other countries, so take advantage of the weekends and kick back. *sb*

Tin Shed Garden Café

1438 NE Alberta Street at NE 14th Place
288.6966, www.tinshedgardencafe.com
Open: M-Tu 7a-3p, W-Sa 7a-11p, Su 7a-10p
$ Vn Fr Fam

If all casual restaurants were like the Tin Shed, the private kitchens of the world would never see a dirty dish. The only thing that would drive people back to their homes might be the hard-to-swallow wait inevitably encountered every morning. Read a paper, drink some coffee, and take a peek at the menu while you anticipate table silence over a serving of Everything Naughty—biscuits and gravy, eggs, meat and the best potato cakes, or Everything Nice—sweet potato French toast, eggs, meat, fruit, and those good 'ole potato cakes. This is a garden café, and their outdoor seating area is unparalleled, even when the heat lamps need to be turned on. The Tin Shed graciously veganizes most of their menu choices and is a crowd pleaser, so bring anyone and everyone you can think of to this cheerful spot. *dm*

Salvador Molly's

3350 SE Morrison Street at 34th Avenue
234.0896, www.salvadormollys.com
Open: Everyday, 5p-late

The face of one of Portland's hardest working caterers, Salvador Molly's is located in the hip SE Belmont area. You will find cocktails you may never have imagined and tamales that will haunt your dreams. Eat here and go hear jazz at the Blue Monk on the same block. *rrm*

Guided Nature Walks

www.tryonfriends.org

Every week there's a new park and a new topic for these informational nature hikes. Take a second look at the world around you, through the foliage, wildlife, and waterways. Check www.tryonfriends.org for this week's adventure with a naturalist. *sb*

ZooBomb

The SW Oak Street at SW 10th Avenue

www.zoobomb.net

Every Sunday night is your chance either to participate or watch from the sidelines as an ever-growing group of wild and crazy cyclists take the brakes off and whiz down one of Portland's steepest hills. Across from Rocco's Pizza on SW Oak Street, the gaggle of bikers, decked out in costumes and helmets, gather round, ride the MAX up to the Zoo (see **Washington Park** chapter) and turn on their bike lights for the ride of their life. Organizers wanted to bring back the fun of childhood to Portland adults. *sb*

Sunday Night Family Supper Club

www.supperpdx.com

Various nights, 7:30p

$25 per person without drinks

The secret might be out about this communal, candlelight dining experience, but the salt cod puree, grain salad and toasty hearth grilled meats are as mouth-watering as ever, whether you're trying something for the first time or are well-versed in culinary knowledge. Come sit at a long wooden table, and be served large dishes that get passed around the table to those you know and those you don't. Take your friend who can never make up his or her mind, and you'll be free of all decisions, except for which local wine to pair with that day's three-course offerings. Chat it up with your table mates and have a good, old-fashioned dinner with other Portland foodies. Check the website for an e-mail contact so you'll get an invite to the next family supper. I'd venture to guess it'll be one of the most memorable and tasty Portland experiences you'll have. *sb*

Russell Street Bar-B-Que

325 NE Russell Street NE MLK Jr. Boulevard
528.8224, www.russellstreetbbq.com
Open: Su-Th 11a-9p, F-Sa 11a-10p
$ Veg Fr

They say the barbecue is all in the sauce. On Russell Street, the barbecue is all in the sauce, the meat, the sides, even the low-emission smokehouse. First choose your meat: pork, sausage, chicken breast, brisket or turkey, all hormone-free, vegetarian fed without antibiotics. They even serve wild grilled salmon and smoked tofu. Sauces are an array of geographic specialties like the tasty thin North Carolina vinegar version, the extra spicy Virginia Killer, or the Classic Virginia, a thick and sweet tomato-based sauce. Look on the counter for more heat—there are bottles of hot sauce from all over with such crazy combinations as tequila lime chipotle and chocolate chili. Every barbecue meal needs dependable sides, and the candied yams and "mess o'greens" fit the bill. Come with a big party so you can sample their whole lineup. *sb*

Burgerville

1122 SE Hawthorne Blvd at SE 11th Avenue (other locations)
230.0479, www.burgerville.com
Open: Everyday, 7a-11p
$ Fr

How can you support your values of sustainability while getting a drive-thru burger and shake? Look no further than Burgerville, where workers have health care, and local chain locations are run on one hundred percent wind power. Seasonal shakes flavors include huckleberries, which are locally harvested before turning the vanilla ice-cream base deep purple. Burgers are made with locally raised country beef, and as an alternative to standard fries, which stand on their own with crispy flavor, you can choose sweet potato fries, or hand-battered onion rings. All this with expeller press canola oil used for all frying: nothing at Burgerville has transfat. So go ahead, break your no fast food rule and head to this American classics. *sb*

Screen Door

2337 E Burnside at NE 24th Avenue
542.0880
Open: Tu-Sa 5:30-10p, Sa-Su 9a-2:30p
$-$$ Fr

My determination is that the Screen Door is actually a huge magnet, drawing me and my foodie friends back repeatedly for soothing southern-esque food and good company throughout. The corner location lets in the softest morning sunlight, warmly coating our satisfied faces with a glow. Screen Door treads in dangerous waters with provolone in their grits and biscuits and gravy that ain't like any I've had south of the Mason Dixon, but are every bit as flavorful and divine. It's an ideal launch spot for a night on the town, whichever direction you head from Screen Door. *sb/ dm*

A Veritable Quandary

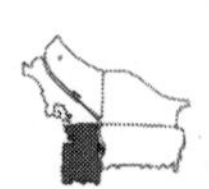

1220 SW 1st Avenue at SW Madison Street
227.7342, www.vqpdx.com
Open: M-F 11:30a-3p, 5-10p, Sa-Su 9:30a-3p, 5-10p
$$-$$$ Veg Ro

On lazy late Sunday afternoons, the jet setter air of Portland's quintessential place of fine dining fades away. A full brunch menu caters to everyone's mood—with hearty quinoa and lentil veggie burgers, brioche French toast, and local Dungeness crab frittatas. Inexpensive and simple kid offerings include grilled cheese and pancakes. With each plate, the utmost care is taken not only to ensure fresh, mostly local and organic ingredients, but that a complementary spectrum of flavors is represented. Sweet vinaigrette-tossed micro greens lighten up heartier dishes. Perfect guacamole and crème fraiche dazzle fluffy scrambled eggs. For weekend brunch, "VQ," as it is lovingly called by locals, has a comfortable family feel and outstanding Northwest fare. And indeed, it is a veritable quandary deciding between the delectable menu choices. *sb*

Papa Haydn wedding cakes

Papa Haydn

5829 SE Milwaukie Avenue at SE Knight Street
291.8350, www.papahaydn.com
Open: M-Th 11:30a-10p, F 11:30a-10p, Sa 11:30a-10p, Su 10a-10p
$$ Veg Ro Fr

On a weekend afternoon, nothing beats the lunch special menu at Papa Haydn for a blissful moment away. Parsnip ravioli, fine sandwiches stuffed with Italian salamis, squash risotto topped with mascarpone, and gorgonzola fondue are stars in their own right, but are nearly overshadowed by Papa's specialty, dessert. You cannot order wrong, but I'll tell you about a few of the plates I've licked clean. Mayan chocolate torte is dusted with spice and rich fair-trade cocoa. The signature Boccone Doce is layers of melty meringue interspersed with fresh fruit and dappled with dark chocolate. Cheesecake flavors are plentiful, and as rich a rendition as I've ever had. A plethora of mousse tortes, pies, and Viennese butter cream-covered cakes on display across the back of this cozy restaurant give you a detailed preview of what you have to look forward to. A second location in the Pearl district has an entirely different feel, but the same cakes.

Amnesia Brewing

832 N Beech Street at N Mississippi Avenue
281.7708
Open: M-Th 2p-11p, F-Su 12p-12a

On a rainy day, get warmed up inside Amnesia with a Desolation IPA and a bar seat with a view of the steel casks. On sunny days, catch some rays on their street-side patio, where there's space for several family reunion parties and bratwurst enough for everyone. The tofu brat is most excellent with a pile of kraut on top, or if spice is your thing, go for the Hot Bier of the Polish. All sausages are made locally with organic or hormone-free meats. Special beers are switched up each season so you can reach for a standard favorite like the Dusty Trail Pale or the Slow Train Porter, or venture into the great unknown with a new flavor. *sb*

Saturday Market

Open-air, on the westside under the Burnside Bridge
222.6072
www.portlandsaturdaymarket.com
Open: Mar-Dec 24th, Sa 10a-5p, Su 11a-4:30p
Fam S Dg

Saturday Market provides optimal grounds for Portlanders, suburbanites, and visitors alike to congregate for what always ends up being hours of shopping, eating and listening to local musicians perform on the cobblestone square. With artisans hawking their wares, local restaurants set up in food stands and all the merriment you could wich for in a marketplace, your next treasure is waiting around the bend. I found a pretty pair of earrings here and my friend Michael a kalimba for the perfect wedding gift. Don't miss the Spoonman's creative ways of re-inventing the purpose of silverware. *dm*

Equinox Restaurant & Bar

830 N Shaver Street at N Albina Avenue
460.3333, www.equinoxrestaurantpdx.com
Open: Tu-Su 5p-late, Sa-Su 9a-2p
$-$$ Veg Fr Ro

Equinox elevates the average brunch to a flavor adventure, hidden away in a simple, yet warm Japanese style lounge, fashioned from recycled building materials. The inventive and unpredictable menu might require a good fifteen minutes of perusing. Anything is possible after partaking of a *Benedict al Killingsworth* with satsuma-harissa béarnaise served over puff pastry, bubbled down with a blackberry mimosa; the stage is set for a marvelous weekend day. *dm*

Blue Moose Café

NE Fremont Street at NE 50th Avenue
548.4475
Open: Everyday, 9a-8p
$ Vn S

This homey, vegetarian café will please all matter of taste buds. In a quiet, peaceful corner of the city, in close proximity to Rose City Park—a favorite walking place—you'll be pleasantly surprised with their delicious soups and satisfying grain and legume dishes. None of the greasy fakemeat products are needed here—even meat eaters like me won't miss a thing. Of all lunch spots in Portland, this is the one I find myself coming back to the most, spending hours with a huge bowl of coconut soup, toast, and scrambled eggs, and a good book. *sb*

Pambiche

2811 NE Glisan at NE 28th Avenue
233.0511, www.pambiche.com
Open: Su-Th 11a-10p, F-Sa 11-12a
$$ Vn Fr S

Pambiche is perhaps the most colorful restaurant in Portland and the food is just as memorable. This cozy place has a few outside tables with heat lamps running at least eight months out of the year. They often sport a line down the block due to the fact that this is the best Cuban food in town and they don't take reservations. The Ensalada de Remolacha (beet salad) is not to be overlooked, the fried yucca is melt-in-your-mouth good, and the wait staff are chatty and full of suggestions. It's hard to pinpoint anything at Pambiche because everything is *that* good. No need to dress-up, but you won't get any sideways stares if you do. *rrm*

Moxie Rx

N Mississippi Avenue and N Shaver Street
285.0701, www.movierx.com
Open: Th-M 9a-4p
$ S Fr

Moxie Rx is the perfect prescription on a sunny weekend lazy day for the low energy blues. Step off the sidewalk and up to this Airstream trailer to place an order for an untouchable egg sandwich and a Moxie Rx—a banana, date and almond butter drink that is sure to rejuvenate. This fresh and retro food stand is just what the doctor ordered. *dm*

St. Honoré Boulangerie

2335 NW Thurman Street at NW 23rd Avenue
445.4342, www.sainthonorebakery.com
Open: Everyday, 7a-8p
$ Veg Fr Fam

French bakeries are irresistible, even on foreign soil. Just ask the Japanese. They have taken the French boulangerie and planted one on every half corner in Kyoto. Portland took one and planted it in the stylish northwest quadrant on the uppermost northside. St. Honoré is a dream of breads, pastries, and panini concocted from the sustainably-harvested "The Shepherd's Grain," and served in a bright and embracing eatery. Pick up one of their signature Miche Banal breads and maybe a croissant or two, then head next door to Food Front Coop for some other vital treats and a languid stroll west to Forest Park. Bon appétit, mes amis! *dm*

Hannah Bea's

3969 NE MLK Jr. Boulevard at NE Shaver Street
282.6334, www.hannahbeas.com
Open: Tu-Sun 8a-4p
$$ Fr Fam

For some finger-lickin' good pound cake, and a soul food brunch worth writing home about, walk past Russell Street to MLK and Hannah Bea's. Fluffy cream cheese scrambled eggs, the way my mother makes them are ready for you to pile on your plate with meatloaf, hot links, or roast beef. Get a side of dirty rice, and get ready for a lingering Sunday meal with friends in a comfortable atmosphere. Most weekends the whole family is working and eating with you, including Grandma Hannah herself. Don't leave without trying the lemon-glazed pound cake, which also makes a good treat to take home for later or to share with a lucky somebody. *sb*

Volunteer

Fun, quick, and easy ways to give back to the city

Volunteering is the best way to meet locals. Unite in a common cause to make a positive impact in some area or another, and you're sure to make fast friends. Portland is a city of eager volunteers, so it follows that there are some interesting opportunities for helpers. Roll up your sleeves! *sb*

PRA

www.praradio.org
222.5278
Send music to: praradio@yahoo.com
Application process, 1-month commitment

PRA, or Portland Radio Authority is the ultimate in free speech wavelengths. Volunteer to be a DJ, or help with community outreach work. You can also send in your songs, record deal or no, and they'll put it in the mix. Fill out a volunteer form under "apply" at their website, or contact them directly when you want to start broadcasting! *sb*

Portland Impact

www.portlandimpact.org/volunteer
988.4996
Hourly, daily, and ongoing opportunities

This wonderful organization does a plethora of good service for low-income elderly and families around Portland. They run several housing complexes, and can always use your help. Give a homebound senior a smile by fixing up his or her yard, or give someone in a shelter a haircut. Help handout donated food or spiff up a room in one of the shelters to make it ready for a new tenant. There are many volunteer opportunities that will get you talking to lots of residents. *sb*

Friends of Trees

www.friendsoftrees.org/events
284.8733
Events year-round, usually weekends, hourly

Get on a sturdy pair of shoes and get ready to have fun with trees and neighbors. Portlanders are seriously tree-savvy, and this group brings together all kinds of people to plant trees and restore wildlife all around the area. Check their events calendar for things to do most weekends of the year. You don't need to register or know anything about how to plant trees, just show up; tools and guidance are provided! This is one of my favorite organizations in Portland, and certainly a fun way to spend a few hours while meeting some great people. *sb*

Parks and Recreation Department

www.portlandonline.com/parks
Hourly, daily and on-going opportunities

One of the most popular ways to volunteer in Portland is with the Parks and Rec department—maybe that's one of the reasons it is so great! Choose to volunteer with kids and community centers, as a youth coach, or just for a day clearing parks of invasive plants. Community-based, and supported by a genuine drive to improve the environment and community life, check the web for the time that's best for you to join in the cause. From the main page go to the conservation drop-down menu to find volunteer options. Search for specific programs like Library Volunteer Program, Community Gardens and Urban Forestry Program on www.portlandonline.com for more. *sb*

Hollywood Theater

www.hollywoodtheatre.org/volunteer.html

Film Action Oregon, the force behind our favorite Hollywood Theater, keeps volunteers happy with free movie passes. Sign up to help with film festival events, or as an usher at the Hollywood Theater. Take a closer look around Portland by delivering newsletters to coffee shops and boutiques around town. *sb*

City Repair

www.cityrepair.org
volunteer@cityrepair.org
Varied opportunities

Citizen activists unite! There are hundreds of events and volunteer-based projects throughout the year that focus on socially integrating neighborhoods and giving a jolt of culture from the grassroots level. The idea has since spread beyond Portland to other cities. Bring back the local, community feel to streets and neighborhoods under threat of isolation. The types of jobs you may find yourself doing is so vast I cannot do it justice here, but go to the website, get involved, and you'll have so much fun, you'll forget that you're working! *sb*

OMSI Volunteering

www.omsi.edu/info/volunteer
239.7814
Varied opportunities

Whether you are greeting school kids or helping with Japanese-inspired summer camp, your time will be well spent at OMSI, whose aim is to make science education fun for all. *sb*

U.S. Fish and Wildlife Service

2600 SE 98th Avenue #100 at SE Division Street
231.6179, 1.800.344.WILD
www.fws.gov
Daily and ongoing volunteer opportunities

Volunteering for the Fish and Wildlife Service can be a real adventure, and a valuable learning experience. They'll teach you to raise fish at a hatchery, band endangered birds at a wildlife sanctuary or train you to lead tours of preserves and parks. There are plenty of ways to lend a hand and events to inspire community action. *sb*

Multiple Sclerosis Society of Portland

297.9544, www.msoregon.org
volunteers@msoregon.org
Mostly short-term opportunities

This caring organization strives to alleviate the stresses and pains of MS through a healing community. Whether you participate in an afternoon social event or engage a patient one-on-one through the Good Neighbor program, your involvement will be greatly appreciated. *sb*

Free Geek

1731 SE 10th Avenue at SE Market Street
www.freegeek.org
Varied opportunities

A computer recycling center and generous tech support resource in Portland, Free Geek will accept your help whether or not you have yet been given your full geek status. Help with recycling and office tasks at their techie thrift store and you can get a recycled computer all your own, or lend your programming, or other turbo-nerd skills for all kinds of good causes, like PRA Radio's website. The people who are a part of this community call themselves geeks, but are some of the coolest people around. Help the recycling efforts and channel the little tech fairy inside of you. *sb*

Other Resources:

www.volunteermatch.org
www.handsonportland.org
www.portlandonline.com
http://volunteer.gov.gov
www.sistersoftheroadfcafe.org
www.loavesandfishesonline.org
www.dosomething.org
www.kpsu.org
www.voar.org
www.scorepdx.org

Lodge

Every place to rest your noggin

If you don't have a friend to stay with in Portland, there are a number of places where you can lay your head. Rooms in eccentrically renovated buildings, sweet B&B accommodations, and boutique hotels are exciting, but pricier options. For the low-budget traveler, motels, hostels, and camping opportunities will fit your needs. Pick a place to stay that is situated in an appealing area where you can dig in your heels and also walk to enticing destinations, so as to cut down on travel time and hit the streets of the city with the locals. *dm*

Featured Stays

John Palmer House

4314 N Mississippi Avenue at N Skimore Street
493.1903, www.johnpalmerhouse.com
Located at the top of the Mississippi Avenue Hill, the John Palmer house is the inner-city bed and breakfast. The house is within walking distance of world-class restaurants, and the rest of Mississippi's bounty. Beautifully re-done, and run by a husband and wife team. If you want an urban retreat, or are interested in old Portland homes, call upthese nice folks up early and secure a room. *rrm*

White Eagle Rock 'N' Roll Hotel

836 N Russell Street
335.8900, www.mcmenamins.com
This is a great way to go budget with a bar and live music downstairs most nights and the signature McMenamin originality to tuck you into bed. *dm*

The Kennedy School

5736 NE 33rd Avenue at NE Killingsworth Street
249.3983, www.mcmenamins.com
WiFi

The McMenamin Brothers, innovators behind pubs, hotels, and movie theaters around the northwest, must have been absolutely tickled by the idea of The Kennedy School. A defunct Portland elementary school morphs into an opportune location for a hotel, pub, restaurant, movie theater, and event hall. Guests walk down the school halls, past student memorabilia hanging on the walls, and into one of the classrooms to sleep beside chalkboards and school chairs. McMenamin's cuisine isn't what I would call manna, but at least it ain't Sloppy Joes. Everyone brings guests from out of town here just for its status as a Portland icon. The kids love to have dinner at the Courtyard Restaurant before prom, so be prepared for crowds and general hubbub. You will finally be able to stick it to your eighth grade teacher for giving you detention the last week of school, by boldly puffing on a stogie with a whisky in your hand right in front of the grownups! *dm*

Jupiter Hotel

800 E Burnside Street
230.9200, www.jupiterhotel.com

Adjacent to the Doug Fir Lounge (see **Stay Up Late** chapter), this Neo-swinger, Ikea-outfitted motel (hotel is a real misnomer here) is filled with locals seeking an inner-city escape and chic out-of-towners. With food, music, and booze next door, styling boutiques across the street and the Burnside Bridge a few blocks down waiting to whisk you over to downtown, the Jupiter is a perfect jumping off point for city wanderings. *dm*

The Georgian House

1828 NE Siskiyou Street
281.2250, www.thegeorgianhouse.com

In the Historic Irvington neighborhood, your friendly hostess Willie Jean will dish up some scrumptious breakfast before sending you on your way for the day. *dm*

B&B's

The Fulton House

7006 SW Virginia Avenue
892.5781, www.thefultonhouse.com

Blue Plum Inn

2026 NE 15th Avenue
288.3484, www.blueplumin.com

MacMaster House

1041 SW Vista Avenue
223.7362,www.macmaster.com

Historic Hotels

These luxurious, upscale hotels are all Portland institutions with a lengthy history to tell. For a time warp in the midst of a constantly evolving city, book a room at any for your visit. *dm*

The Governor Hotel

614 SW 11th Avenue
224.3400, www.governorhotel.com

Benson Hotel

309 SW Broadway
228.2000, www.bensonhotel.com

The Heathman Hotel

1001 SW Broadway
241.4100, www.heathmanhotel.com

Top-End Hotels

The Westin
750 SW Alder Street
294.9000

Portland Marriott Dowtown Waterfront
1401 SW Naito Parkway
226.7600

Hilton Portland & Executive Tower
921 SW 6th Avenue
226.1611

Boutique Hotels

Ace Hotel
1022 SW Stark Street
228.2277, www.acehotel.com

Avalon Hotel & Spa
455 SW Hamilton Court
802.5800, www.avalonhotelandspa.com

Inn at Northrup Station
2025 NW Northrup Street
224.0543, www.northrupstation.com

Hotel Lucia
400 SW Broadway
225.1717, www.hotellucia.com

Airport Hotels

Clarion Hotel
11518 NE Glen Widing Drive
800.206.7892
503.252.2222, www.choicehotels.com

Embassy Suites
7900 NE 82nd Avenue
460.3000, www.embassysuites.hilton.com

Fairfield Inn
11929 NE Airport Way
253.1400, www.marriott.com

Comfort Suites
12010 NE Airport Way
261.9000, www.choicehotels.com

Monarch Hotel & Conference Center
12566 SE 93rd Avenue
652.1515, www.monarchhotel.cc

Mid-Range Hotels

Holiday Inn Express
2333 NW Vaughn Street
484-1100, www.ichotelsgroup.com

Silver Cloud Inn
2426 NW Vaughn Street
800.205.6936
242.2400, www.scinns.com

Budget Lodging

Downtown Value Inn
415 SW Montgomery Street
226.4751, www.downtownvalueinn.com
Rooms: 30
Price Range: $65-75

The Palms Motel
3801 N Interstate Avenue
287.5788, www.palmsmotel.com
Rooms: 46
Price Range: $40-60

Thriftlodge
949 E Burnside Street
234.8411
Rooms: 80
Price Range: $55-70

Hostels

Hawthorne Hostel
3031 SE Hawthorne Boulevard
236.3380, www.portlandhostel.org
Rooms: 33 beds, camping in back
Price Range: $13-51
A portal to the Hawthorne strip, the Hawthorne Hostel provides an instant community, and numerous resources for the newly-relocated and just passing through. I set up my tent in the back when I first moved to Portland (note: an earplug purchase was priceless for a good night's rest) while I mooched off coffee shops and public libraries searching Craigslist for housing. They will take good care of you here and you might even catch a fire dance in the yard. *dm*

Northwest Portland International Hostel & Guesthouse

425 NW 18th Avenue
241.2783, www.northwestportlandhostel.com
Rooms: 19
Price Range: $21-72

With rooms ranging from private, dorm, guesthouse and group lodging, this hostel puts visitors right in the midst of the Northwest action. *dm*

Camping

Fir Grove RV Park

5541 NE 72nd Avenue
252.9993, www.traveloregon.com, search "fir grove"
15 tent sites

Jantzen Beach RV Park

1503 N Hayden Island Drive
289.7626, www.jantzenbeachrv.com

Huge park with plenty of spaces and amenities, including two heated pools. *sb*

<u>Nearby Camping:</u>

Oxbow State Park

3010 SE Oxbow Parkway, Gresham
663.4708, www.metro-region.org
Rooms: 67 campsites
Rates: $15, $4 parking fee

People think it's strange that I camped here by myself when I first decided to relocate to the Rose City. It is a calming place to call home after a tiring day attempting to find housing and potential employment. Located on the Sandy River, Oxbow is just outside the city, down Division Street in Gresham or, to more quickly arrive, off exit 17 on I-84. *dm*

Columbia River RV Park

10649 NE 13th Avenue, Vancouver, WA
285.1515, www.columbiariverfronrvpark.com

76 campsites for tents and RVs needing electrical plug-ins.

Milo McIvor State Park

24101 S Entrance Road off of Springwater Road and Highway 224, 4 miles west of Estacada, 45 minutes from Portland
www.oregonstateparks.org/park_142.php

There's plenty of fun, nature-oriented activities in the immediate vicinity of this state park campground. *sb*

Champoeg State Park

8239 Champoeg Roud NE, St. Paul, off US 99, 7 miles east of Newberg
633.8170

With 48 electrical plug-ins, 6 walk-in tents, and a log cabin museum, camping here is "hooked up." *sb*

Nearby

Highlights from around the area

Bridge of the Gods

Portland is surrounded by picturesque towns, the perennial beauty of the Columbia River Gorge, the Pacific Coast, and several lush valleys of vineyards. Take the time to explore outside the city limits—you won't be let down. *sb*

Columbia River Gorge and The Bridge of the Gods

Running parallel to I-84 East

If a group is ready and a vehicle handy, pack it in and head for a drive down I-84, past the box stores and into the Gorge. Sigh… the Gorge. With the windy Columbia River on one side, speckled with world-class windsurfers and banked by Washington State, and the rising peaks of the Cascade Mountain Range framing the ride, the impressiveness of this place will silence even the most rowdy bunch. The landscape is spectacular, especially when cast in the extreme lights of dawn and dusk. If a more meandering route is desired, hop off the interstate and onto the Historic Columbia Highway, which parallels I-84 and showcases waterfalls and overlooks. The Gorge leads to outdoor adventure like a hike up Angel's Rest, or possibly a stop by the homey town of Hood River, a good place from which to jump to sports like kayaking, windsurfing, or snowboarding on Mt. Hood. You'll be heartbroken when it comes time to leave this dreamy setting. *dm*

Sake Tasting and Factory Tour at SakeOne

820 Elm Street at 9th Avenue, Forest Grove
800.550.SAKE
Open: Everyday, 11a-6p

The first American-owned Sake factory offers tastings everyday of their special sakes. Momokawa is a refined junmai (no added alcohol), ginjo (made with rice polished to roughly 60% of its original size). For a little extra you can sample the luxurious imported diginjo (polished to 40%), not what you'd even use in a saketini. If you visit in the spring, you'll be in for an extra treat when the sakura (cherry blossoms) are in full bloom around the tasting room. The traditional Shinto Kura festival celebrates these flowers, and the barrel opening of the first sake of the year. *sb*

Waucoma Bookstore

212 Oak Street at 2nd Street, Hood River
541.386.5353
Open: M-Sa 10a-6p

As one of the community centers of Hood River, Waucoma Bookstore is a meeting place for locals, who come to enjoy one of the "Staff's Pick" books, or one featuring the Gorge and surrounding area. A well-picked selection of employee favorites and a wide section of photographic hardbacks make this a great place to stop while you are enthralled with this riverside town. *sb*

McMenamin Pub Course at Edgefield

2126 SW Halsey Street at NE 244th Avenue, Troutdale
669-8610, www.mcmenamins.com
Call for Tee times
Admission: Front $9, Back $8, Full Course $17

When I brought my dad to Edgefield, we made a day of it. We started meandering around the garden, passed the distillery, grabbing a brew in the Little Red Shed (so freakin' cool), then catching a jam band act on the grass, before heading into the manor (once a homeless shelter for poor farmers) for some chow at Lucky Staehly's Pool Hall. I sometimes forget that people from the "outside world," beyond Portland that is, are often struck by a uniqueness of some of our attractions—but learn to love them immediately if not sooner. Go astonish yourself with all that Edgefield has to offer, located only about 20 minutes from downtown Portland in Troutdale, down I-84. I would recommend delighting in a round of golf on the Pub Course for a real respite from city living. The landscape is beautiful—Edgefield even houses a winery—and can be fully absorbed during a game on fairways modeled after Burningbush, a fantasy course constructed to work on the short game, with holes only 40-80 yards in length. *dm*

White Salmon Glassworks

105 E Jewett Boulevard at N Main Avenue, White Salmon, WA
509.493.8400, www.whitesalmonglass.com
Open: W-Sa 10a-6p, Su 10a-3p, free demonstrations F 9p

Watch the artists in action—the furnaces and glass blowing set ups are located right in the gallery, which is loaded with magnificent colorful pieces. Some objects are made to hang on the wall awaiting your gaze, others are utilitarian like vases and salad bowls. All are unique and made on site in this small town overlooking the river. *sb*

Tamastslikt Cultural Institute

72789 Highway 331 at Tamastslikt Road, Pendleton
541.966.9748, www.tmastslikt.com
Open: M-Sa 9a-5p, Café M-F 10a-4p

The name Tamastlikt is an honorary term respecting the Umatilla tribes, which are presented here in their own voice. The center rewrites the history of westward expansion without prejudice, and encompasses a true depiction of Indian life. The building itself is made in the traditional fashion, a beautiful monument to the native culture of the Northwest. *sb*

Sauvie Island

Sauvie Island Bridge off I-30 West
www.sauvieisland.org

For those times when you need complete country in the city, Sauvie Island offers 12,000 acres of island oasis dotted with organic farms, lavender fields, and bike trails. Gather up a picnic at one of the many farm stands and u-pick fields, and cycle to one of the beaches for a dip in the river and a bit of sunny relaxation. Bird reserves on the island provide a home for sandhill cranes, blue heron, tundra swans, and during the winter months, bald eagles. As a beautiful respite from city adventures, Sauvie is a locals' favorite and a splendid place to take a leisurely bike ride. *sb*

Argyle

691 Highway 99W at SW 7th Street, Dundee
538.8520, www.argylewinery.com
Open: Everyday, 11a-5p

One of the reasons Willamette Valley pinot is so widely admired is because of the magic the climate plays on its grapes. Argyle's pinots are among the most admired, garnering a spot on the prestigious Wine Spectator Top 100 List years in a row. Enjoy the sustainable tasting room where you can taste Nuthouse and Reserve Pinots, or if white is your thing, their small-batch Chardonnay is no push-over. Tour the beautiful estate on your journey out to Dundee. There are a number of other tasting rooms and vineyards around the valleys of Portland, for a full list and more info, go to www.oregonwine.org. *sb*

Hood River First Fridays

541.490.0022, www.downtownhoodriver.com
May-October, 5p

In downtown Hood River, the lights stay on a little later the first Friday of each month, when art and entertainment flow out into the streets. Several local galleries host openings on this same night, and cafés and pubs keep longer hours. Each month there are special events and performances, depending on the season, so two trips are never the same. *sb*

Hood River County Historical Museum

300 East Port Marina Drive at Hood River Bridge, Hood River
541.386.6772, www.co.hood-river.or.us/museum
Hours: M-Sa 11a-4p, Su 12-4p

On your way between a hike and a bite to eat, stop at the Historical Museum to check out artifacts from ethnic cultures, Native American livelihood, and pioneers journeys through indoor and outdoor displays. Look into the deep dark past of the timber industry, and what measures are being taken today to preserve forest land and replant trees for sustainability. Admission is free, but donations are greatly appreciated. *sb*

The Eagle Creek Trail

Exit 41 off I-84 East

Milford Sound is a most amazing place. It is lush, dissected by waterfalls, and located halfway around the world in New Zealand. I never thought I would see something so verdant and breathtaking again. After hiking Eagle Creek, I discovered a Milford Sound experience right here in the Northwest. I cannot say enough about this hike. The trail runs by the creek and is a mild grade into the woods, rather than up a steep mountain, so many different hiking levels are accommodated. Waterfall after waterfall and mossy rock faces escort awestruck hikers on what always seems to lead to a spiritual awakening. Pack in a tent and arrive early and maybe an open campsite can be claimed at the seven-and-a-half mile-in camp. Those up for a longer jaunt can trek up to Wahtum Lake, 13.3 miles up. Park at the trailhead with a day pass permit for $5. Silence, perhaps a camera, and the necessary food and water will take your crew or just you on an unforgettable walk in the woods. *dm*

Columbia Gorge Interpretive Center Museum

990 Rock Creek Drive at SW Atwell Road, Stevenson, WA
800.991.2338, www.columbiagorge.org
Open: Everyday, 10a-5p
Admission: $4-6

Fifteen thousand years of history are revealed at this trail's end museum. Look at the area's unique geology through their permanent exhibits, as well as Native American tribal history, Lewis and Clark's journey, a steam engine, and the world's largest rosary collection. *sb*

Clatsop State Forest

Highway 202, Astoria
325.5451, www.oregon.gov/odf
Camping Fees: Vehicles $10/night, Hike-in $5/night

When William Clark pitched his tent here on his historic journey with Merriwether Lewis, he wrote in his journal, "Today I behold the grandest and most pleasing prospects which my eyes ever surveyed." With three unique campgrounds, one near the Northrup Creek Stables, and a lake trail complete with wooden bridges, this park is a leafy oasis. The charms of nature are abundant in a park where old growth and new reforestation practices co-mingle. At Astoria Demonstration Forest, you can follow a self-guided tour to see all the steps to recreate a forest habitat. *sb*

Evergreen Aviation Museum

500 NE Captain Michael King Smith Way, McMinnville
434.4180, www.sprucegoose.org
Open: Everyday, 9a-5p
Admission: $11-13

What is that huge glass structure and, wait a minute, is that an enormous plane inside? Evergreen Aviation Museum will make an airplane enthusiast of every land lover. One look at the infamous wooden boat of a plane, The Spruce Goose, Howard Hugh's pet millions-of-dollars project, necessitates another familiarization with Bernoulli's Principle of Flight to affirm that it really touched the clouds. An executive of Evergreen Aviation and former US Air Force pilot founded this museum, so there are lots of weird pro-military paraphernalia and propaganda in the gift shop, which, along with the wide array of historical planes on display, make this a true Americana experience. *dm*

6th Street Bistro

509 Cascade Avenue at 6th Street, Hood River
541.386.5737, www.sixthstreetbistro.com
Open: Everyday, 11:30a-5p, 5-10p (10:30p on weekends and holidays)

This casual bistro serves the best hamburger on the river, and every Tuesday evening, two eat for one, or four eat for two. Still unclear? It is true. Come in on a Tuesday night and two hamburgers with fries and the works are the price of one meal. Come with an even number of friends, and if there are eight or more of you, call first to reserve a table. There's a great list of local beers to go along with this classy yet relaxed Gorge restaurant. *sb*

Wet Planet

White Salmon, WA
800.306.1673, www.wetplanetwhitewater.com

Whitewater rafting and kayaking the Columbia River Gorge are some of the most memorable experiences you'll have venturing outside of central Portland. Cross one of the bridges, like the Bridge of the Gods, into Washington, and wind along the river and up into White Salmon, a cute rural community. Wet Planet has a private rolling pool, so you can practice your Eskimo Rolls before you get on river with a guide. These guys lead trips on four nearby rivers: Tieton River, White Salmon River, Klickitat River, and Wind River. If you want to spend the night just pack your tent and sleeping bag and they'll provide the campsite. *sb*

Multnomah Falls

Exit 28 off I-84 East

Waterfalls are countless in these haunts. Multnomah Falls is one of the most accessible of these, and is good if you are short on time, energy, or accompanied by a non-hiker, as it can literally be seen from the highway. Take a minute to pull off and follow the throngs to check out the impressively large cataract close up. If the numbers bother you, hiking up a bit further will thin out the crowd and leads to a stream by which to write a journal entry or just take a breather. *dm*

Astoria & Cannon Beach

I-30 W and US-26 W to US-101 S respectively
www.oldoregon.com, www.cannonbeach.org

Portland is not an overwhelming metropolis, but there are still those times when I still need to be out on my own. Astoria is notable to many as the backdrop of the classic 1980's epic, The Goonies ("hey, you guys!"). It currently draws many a weekend visitor and cruise ships, situated beautifully at the junction of the Columbia River and the Pacific Ocean. Making your way up to the Astoria Column will lend a birds' eye view of the area if the wind doesn't blow you away. Take the winding 101 down the coast to Cannon Beach for another picturesque coastal town that boasts one more Goonies' landmark, Haystack Rock. Here you'll find Ecola State park, suitable for a light hike to a small camping area with views of the offshore lighthouse. Surfers come to ride the waves at this beach and the time might just be right for you to zip up the wet suit and dive in. *dm*

Breitenbush Hot Springs

Located off NF-46
854.3320, www.breitenbush.com
Reservations: M-Sa 9a-4p

Less than two hours away, Breitenbush is an escape from metropolitan life and a chance to commune with nature. A place of healing, choose from yoga, meditation, massage, or one of their weekly workshops to complement soaks in the natural hot springs (clothing optional). Lodging styles are seasonal, with the possibility of camping during the warmer months, and all rates includes three full organic vegetarian meals. Portlanders head to Breitenbush to spend time in the fantastical world of, "What if I just quit my job and lived off the land." Breitenbush gives us a taste of that world, even if we don't make that move to the country. *dm*

Oregon Coast Aquarium

2820 SE Ferry Slip Road at SE 29th Street, Newport
541.867.FISH, www.aquarium.org
Open: Summer 9a-6p, Winter 10a-5p
Admission: $7.75-13.25

If you're headed to the coast, the Oregon Coast Aquarium is an essential stop on your route. The old home of Keiko the Orca Whale (Free Willy), this aquarium has a certain charm that you don't often find. The aquarium houses more variety of species than most aquariums of its size. Some of the highlights include: the hands-on tide pools, where you can grab and poke all that you want, as well as the "passages of the deep," a giant glass tunnel walk-through, where you can feel like you're standing right next to all of the scariest and most intriguing creatures of the ocean. It's also worth it to try to catch a glimpse of the ever-elusive octopus. But by far the most fascinating entertainers are the sea otters. They can easily take up hours of your time with their simple routine of eating, playing, scratching, and then sleeping, all while floating on their backs. And, when they rub their cheeks, it makes your heart melt. The nice thing about the Oregon Coast Aquarium is that the animals' surroundings flow very naturally and organically. And since you're already in Newport to see the aquarium, why not stop by the Rogue Brewery after to enjoy some of Oregon's best brew. It will be a nice way to cap off your day of sea life. *ks*

Index

0-9

A

B

C

G

H

I

J

K

L

M

N

O

P

Q

R

S

T

Bios

Serena Bartlett

Having lived and traveled in over 20 countries, Serena has devised many philosophies for seeing the world and its myriad cultures. With a degree from Long Island University's Friend's World Program, she is passionate about social justice, environmental sustainability and community. Her first guidebook, Oakland: The Soul of the City Next Door, has pioneered a unique form of travel—dubbed urban eco-travel—that combines sustainability with a local's perspective. She currently resides in Oakland with her loving partner and their toy poodle, Dutsi Bap.

Diana Morgan

From Japan to Central America and back to her native United States, Diana has delved into her diverse interests wherever she has set foot. Sustainable and ethical philosophies are central to her literary, bilingual journeys. She graduated from Long Island University and Friends World College and has since been a part of several practical initiatives towards environmental longevity. She lives in Portland and volunteers with kids in her free time.

Daniel Ling

Born and raised in Oakland, Daniel's style of freehand line drawing continues to evolve with each new GrassRoutes guide, and he is known to reinterpret his illustrations into colorful paintings on wood. Daniel studied anthropology at UC Berkeley, where he learned to see beyond the superficial by putting aside all preconceived notions. He is an archaeological illustrator and freelance graphic designer.

Dutsi Bap

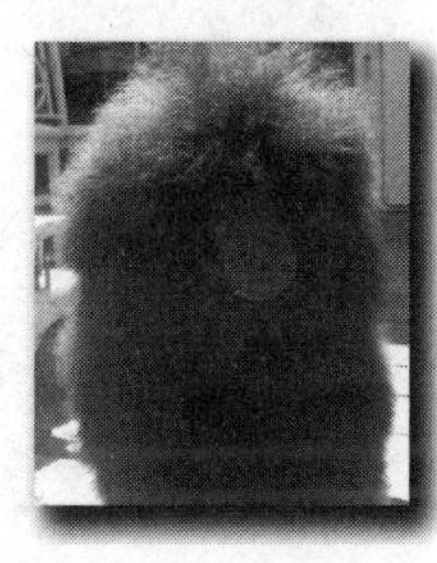

Our cheerleader, research assistant and referee, Dutsi's morale and support are crucial to the GrassRoutes team. When he's not on the road testing out new locations, he visits local nursing homes to spread joy and fluffiness. He earned his Therapy Dog certificate and believes that the meaning of life is to eat roast chicken, run in the park and take long naps on the feet of writers.